...book you are about to re........latest bestseller from the St. Martin's True Crime Library, the imprint *The New York Times* calls "the leader in true crime!" Each month, we offer you a fascinating account of the latest, most sensational crime that has captured the national attention. St. Martin's is the publisher of Tina Dirmann's VANISHED AT SEA, the story of a former child actor who posed as a yacht buyer in order to lure an older couple out to sea, then robbed them and threw them overboard to their deaths. John Glatt's riveting and horrifying SECRETS IN THE CELLAR shines a light on the man who shocked the world when it was revealed that he had kept his daughter locked in his hidden basement for 24 years. In the Edgar-nominated WRITTEN IN BLOOD, Diane Fanning looks at Michael Petersen, a Marine-turned-novelist found guilty of beating his wife to death and pushing her down the stairs of their home—only to reveal another similar death from his past. In the book you now hold, LOVE HURTS, Keith Elliot Greenberg sorts out a shocking multiple murder in Texas.

St. Martin's True Crime Library gives you the stories behind the headlines. Our authors take you right to the scene of the crime and into the minds of the most notorious murderers to show you what really makes them tick. St. Martin's True Crime Library paperbacks are better than the most terrifying thriller, because it's all true! The next time you want a crackling good read, make sure it's got the St. Martin's True Crime Library logo on the spine—you'll be up all night!

Charles E. Spicer, Jr.
Executive Editor, St. Martin's True Crime Library

TITLES BY KEITH ELLIOT GREENBERG

Perfect Beauty

Love Hurts

FROM THE TRUE CRIME LIBRARY OF
ST. MARTIN'S PAPERBACKS

LOVE HURTS

KEITH ELLIOT
GREENBERG

St. Martin's Paperbacks

LOVE HURTS

Copyright © 2011 by Keith Elliot Greenberg.

Cover photos: Sky / clouds © Kevin Russ / iStockphoto; grass © Shaun Lowe / iStockphoto; house / trees © Lauri Wiberg / iStockphoto; second image of house © Auke Holwerda / iStockphoto; pendant © Mikhail Kovtonyok / iStockphoto; photo of girl by Nicole Hill / Getty Images.

For information address St. Martin's Press, 175 Fifth Avenue, New York, NY 10010.

EAN: 978-0-312-94360-8

Printed in the United States of America

St. Martin's Paperbacks edition / January 2011

St. Martin's Paperbacks are published by St. Martin's Press, 175 Fifth Avenue, New York, NY 10010.

10 9 8 7 6 5 4 3 2

ACKNOWLEDGMENTS

When I first visited Emory, Texas, I found a town in pain, and a population eager to offer opinions. Some were informed, others pure speculation. As an outsider, I tried to absorb everything, and depict the community honestly and respectfully. I hope I've accomplished this goal.

Even from across a courtroom, it's impossible not to feel awed by the sight of Terry Caffey standing upright, a survivor who lives by his beliefs and has chosen to channel his suffering into something greater. Despite all the talk about spirituality and the hereafter, Terry's message resonates in this world. Some find it interesting that he's opted to enter the secular realm of the public school to speak to young people. But Terry's goal isn't just saving souls, it's saving lives. I am positive that Terry's words have already rescued a few teens, and maybe a couple of adults, from destructive choices.

The nature of his crimes notwithstanding, I appreciate Charlie Wilkinson's decision to spend time with me while incarcerated.

I don't know if I could have written this book without the assistance of Ron and Stacy Ann Ferguson. Initially, I viewed them as interesting personalities, able to step back from the swirling bazaar of the courtroom, and maintain their humor, compassion and integrity. Now, I consider them friends.

I am also deeply indebted to Texas Ranger John Vance.

As with prior projects, Jessica Chong and Tom Fitzgerald provided prompt and competent assistance. At St. Martin's Paperbacks, my editors, Yaniv Soha and Charles Spicer, helped make this experience a positive one.

In many ways, this story should remind us never to take anything for granted. And so, I'll use this forum to tell my family—my wife, Jennifer Berton Greenberg, and my kids, Dylan and Summer—that I'm grateful that we all have each other.

CHAPTER 1

"Don't leave me, Mom."

The ambulance bumped along gravel roads and dry creeks, twisting past blackjack oak, walnut and redbud trees, the swirling sirens piercing the quiet of the dark Texas night. In the rear, as EMTs carefully treated Terry Glynn Caffey, the forty-one-year-old home health care aide and aspiring preacher looked up at his neighbor, Helen Gaston, begging her to help him live another day.

Terry had always viewed Helen and her husband, Tommy, as parental figures—referring to them as Ma and Pa—and, now, a crisis had forced the older couple to step into the role. With his shock of white hair, sparkling eyes and face creased by years of life experience, Tommy was a rugged but caring man partial to cowboy hats and flannel shirts. Molded into the archway to his homestead were the three words that best expressed his life philosophy: DEDICATED TO GOD. His wife had a matronly, proud countenance, not because she felt more righteous than her neighbors, but—some would argue—because she legitimately was.

Tommy and Helen had rescued Terry when he'd stumbled through their door, after crawling some three hundred yards through a wooded field from his burning home. Blood poured from five separate bullet wounds. One of the slugs had entered

Terry's face, breaking his nose before crashing through an ear. Another narrowly missed his brain. Terry's arm, back and shoulder were punctured in the assault. Yet, like the Biblical character Job—to whom Terry would regularly be compared in the coming months—he remained alive, empowered by his faith and the goodness he felt radiating from Helen.

The barrage had come in the dead of night—Terry estimated the time at about three AM—as he slept in the ground-floor master bedroom beside his thirty-eight-year-old wife, Penny. She was the source, friends said, of the musical ability the couple's three children inherited and regularly exhibited during worship at the Miracle Faith Baptist Church.

Penny screamed, and, as Terry lifted an arm to protect her, the couple was peppered with more bullets. One literally shot Terry out of the bed.

From another part of the house, there was the sound of one of the children shouting out in pain and bewilderment.

In the scattered homes nearby, few heard the commotion. Those who did stirred in their beds, mistaking the gunshots for thunder, before rolling back to sleep.

Terry blacked out. When he came to, Penny's throat was slashed, and flames engulfed the upstairs area where the kids slept: Tyler, eight, Matthew—or Bubba—thirteen, and Erin, the petite, pretty, sixteen-year-old blonde who'd recently enrolled at Rains High School in nearby Emory. Somehow, Terry managed to get to his feet. He felt nothing on the right side of his body. Desperate to help his children, he thought about rushing into the main part of the house. But the fire was impossible to infiltrate.

He decided to save himself, wiggling through the bathroom window. "The hardest thing I ever did that cool winter night," he later wrote in an excerpt published by his ministry, "was to . . . leave my family inside an inferno, knowing that I would never see them again this side of heaven."

Outside, Terry's eyes darted. He dropped to his hands and knees, uncertain if his attackers were following. Tommy and Helen's home seemed an eternity away, but he started there, knowing that once he reached the couple's doorstep, he'd be safe. It was a lengthy journey, aggravated by the loss of blood. At times, he'd manage to stand and walk a few paces, then crumple to the ground. Terry staggered into trees and fell over logs. He was light-headed, weak and distraught over the fate of his family. At one stage, he claimed, he asked God to take his life. Still, Terry kept going.

"God," he said, according to *Walking in the Light of the Living*, a CD produced for his ministry, "just give me the strength to stand up and get over there and tell who did this. Somebody needs to know who murdered my family. . . . Then, you can take my life."

The long, draining expedition continued. Terry slipped into a creek, gulping water and nearly drowning. His feet pushed forward and fingernails dug into sediment, as Terry clawed his way out. From a distance, he spotted a flicker of light in the Gastons' window. He'd later compare that sparkle to the brightness of his Creator, leading him away from the wickedness he'd suffered.

"For thou hast delivered my soul from death," he quoted Psalms 56:13. "Wilt thou not deliver my feet from falling, that I may walk before God in the light of the living?"

An astounded Tommy Gaston discovered his friend on the welcome mat, struggling to prop himself into a sitting position, dirt and grass mixed with the blood caked onto his skin.

"Terry?"

"I need help."

"Where's Penny? Where are the kids?"

"They're all dead."

The exchange broke Tommy's heart. His nephew Joey Weatherford, the editorial cartoonist at the Greenville *Herald Banner*, later noted the bond that his uncle enjoyed with Terry. Tommy "thought the world of Terry," Weatherford said. "He thought he was a really sweet guy."

Like Terry, Tommy was "in the world, but not of the world," focusing on church-centered activities while earning a living as a propane truck driver. Penny Caffey, the pianist at Miracle Faith Baptist Church, played in Tommy's gospel band, the Gaston Singers, performing at local churches and recording independently produced albums.

"Everybody kind of knows everybody at the little churches out here," said Weatherford. "We might go to different churches, but we'll say, 'Hey, come over and sing at our church.' And everybody will go. It's kind of a friendly thing, going to see your neighbor or your friend."

The pattern has led to an enriched musical atmosphere in the region. In 2005 *Kerosene,* the debut album by country singer Miranda Lambert—the daughter of a husband-and-wife private investigator team from the town of Lindale—went platinum. Three singles on her next album, *Crazy Ex-Girlfriend*, released in 2007, yielded three Top 40 hits on *Billboard*'s country charts.

Yet, when Penny and her children played in church, their role model was never some nationally known entertainer, but their neighbor, Tommy Gaston. The admiration was not based solely on Tommy's musical abilities, but the qualities he exhibited day to day. As a result, when Terry was in the throes of his worst tragedy, he found the presence of Tommy and Helen familiar and soothing.

The Caffey and Gaston properties were set deep in the woods, in places where children could romp in nature, isolated from the decadent variables available in large cities and, to a lesser extent, small towns. This was the country. By day, horses and cattle lazed on the grass of nearby homes, beside large bales of hay. At night, stars twinkled from the heavens, and it was easy to stand, enveloped in blackness below pine tree canopies, and feel a connection to the higher power invoked in Bible study and the hymns the Caffeys sang so passionately in church. Yet now, as police cruisers blared off U.S. 69, the secluded nature of these homesteads could have been an obstacle to emergency medical personnel, were it not for the flames guiding them to the Caffey homestead.

Moments after their arrival, the oxygen tanks in the van Terry used to deliver medical supplies to home health care patients exploded, igniting the scene even further.

As night gave way to dawn, the long blood trail investigators discovered winding across some twenty acres of woodland told the story of Terry's agonizing flight from the crime scene. Remarkably—or miraculously, as his friends would later opine—even after traversing the length of three football fields, Terry was conscious, providing small details in a barely audible tone.

He estimated that his laborious escape had taken nearly an hour, and he quickly concluded that the killers did not finish him off because they thought he was dead.

Rains County sheriff's deputy Charles Dickerson found Terry on the floor of the Gastons' living room, clad in a soggy t-shirt and pajama bottoms. His feet were bare, save for one sock.

"I'm not going to make it," he said.

"It's okay," Dickerson replied reassuringly. "Help is on the way."

In the months to come, Helen would suffer recurring nightmares, recalling the ghastly sight of her neighbor, hovering between life and death. At the other end of the blood trail, back at the Caffey home, Helen knew that the findings would be worse. But she didn't want to lose Terry, as well. So, for the forty-mile ride to East Texas Medical Center in Tyler, she provided the prayers and reassuring words he needed to stay alive.

Back on the Caffey property, officials arrived from a number of agencies. Agents from the federal Bureau of Alcohol, Tobacco and Firearms (ATF) conferred with the Texas Rangers, and determined that a sifting operation was necessary to retrieve the spent shell casings from firearms used in the attack. A canine named Nina was deployed to detect the remains of any flammable liquids used to set the fire. Members of the Emory volunteer fire department who'd earlier responded to the emergency call at the Gaston residence noted that only a portion of the Caffeys' southwest wall remained standing. Inside, the pier beams and first-level floor were intact—nothing else. Firefighters fanned out along the grounds, extinguishing flames. But every so often, they'd be required to double back and snuff out the hot spots that re-kindled after their arrival.

The items salvaged from the home reflected the story of the Caffey family, as well as the account of the assault: stan-dard household appliances taken for granted during their day-to-day routines, the piano where Penny refined her skills and passed them on to her children, a clock—previously lo-cated on a wall above the kitchen refrigerator—stopped dead at 3:55 AM.

Penny's body was found in the doorway between the master bedroom and utility room, with three .22-caliber rim-fire shell casings below her body. Police noted that two were in relatively good condition—most likely because the corpse protected them from the blaze. Bubba, the seventh-grader, was located in the living room, in front of where the couch had been positioned. Nearby was the guitar stand that he gen-erally kept in his room.

Police theorized that both Bubba and the stand had crashed through the second floor after the home was set on fire.

Back in the master bedroom area, the charred corpse of the fourth-grader, Tyler, was discovered on top of the rem-nants of his parents' bedsprings. In between were several coat hangers, as well as sections of unburned clothing be-longing to his sister, Erin.

Police concluded that, during the attack, Tyler had ended up in Erin's closet. When the second floor collapsed, Tyler's body plummeted onto the first level.

Of all the Caffeys, only Erin could not be accounted for at the crime scene. This was bewildering, since Terry and Erin had spoken earlier in the night. In recent months, there'd been a great deal of tension between Erin and her parents. The girl could be strong-willed, defiant, even, some alleged, calculating, when she wanted her way. But not so calculating, friends of the family presumed, to play a role in anything this vicious.

* * *

In an area where incidents of this type were rare, and residents tended to know one another through church and family ties, the effect on the emergency workers was immediate. One firefighter, upon seeing the bodies of the Caffey boys extracted from the home, fell to his knees in despair.

Rains County sheriff David Taylor told the press that authorities could not determine whether the victims died from gunshot wounds or the fire: "The bodies have been so badly burned."

Texas Ranger John Vance had been in law enforcement for two decades, working as a highway patrol sergeant and Walker County sheriff's deputy prior to joining the Rangers division. "I've seen a lot," he said. "But—because of the brutality here, and the fact that the children were targeted as victims—this was as upsetting as anything I ever encountered."

As members of the community woke up, word slowly spread about the disaster at the Caffey house. The moment he heard the news, Carl Johnson, a family friend, drove to the scene, hoping to assist in some way, remembering the imagery of the family performing in church and the paternal feelings he'd always had for Terry.

"I just love them to death," he told KLTV News. "It was just like losing one of my kids when I found out about it, Erin, Bubba, Tyler, I knew every one of them since they were just kids."

Private investigator Jerry Carlisle, the former police chief in the small town of Point, learned about the crime from a congregant at his church. "We have a phone system," he explained, "where if anything happens to anybody, or somebody needs prayer, we all call each other. Well, I got the call, and I went out there. And I talked to a friend of mine who was guarding the entrance to the property. He was an old law enforcement man, and he was almost in tears. And this was several hours after it happened."

Sometime in the morning, Erin Caffey was located at a home not far from the crime scene, and rushed by ambulance to

Hopkins County Memorial Hospital in Sulphur Springs. The girl appeared distressed and extremely confused. Police and relatives wondered if she'd been drugged and kidnapped by the assailants.

Penny's mother, Virginia Daily, met Erin in the hospital. "I went in and I told her that her mother and brothers were dead," Virginia told *The Dallas Morning News*. "She broke down. I saw grief and terror in her eyes."

As hospital personnel attended to Erin in the trauma room, Shanna Sanders, the youthful chief of police for the Rains Independent School District, interviewed the student, alongside Sheriff's Deputy Serena Booth. Erin replied to most of their questions in a mumbly, little girl voice, telling a tale about being trapped in a smoky room inhabited by two males with swords.

According to Erin, they commanded her to "get down and stay down, face down."

"What were they wearing?" Sanders asked in an understanding tone.

"They were wearing all black."

"All black. Where were you at when you first saw them?"

"I was in this house that was, like, full of smoke."

"You were in a house full of smoke. Was it your house?"

Erin shook her head.

"You don't think it was? Were you in a bedroom or a living room?"

"There was a couch."

"A couch . . . You were by yourself and when they told you to get down, did you get down?"

"Uh-hum," Erin responded affirmatively.

"Right. And then, what happened?"

"And then, they left. And I tried to call my friend Charlie, and he wouldn't answer his phone."

"You tried to call your friend, Charlie, and he wouldn't answer. Okay."

"And that's the last thing I really remember until this morning, I guess, when the cops woke me up. I can't even remember where I was or what happened."

Sanders asked if she recognized the males' voices. "Do you know who it was?"

"No."

"Did you do anything last night?" Sanders continued. "Any drugs or alcohol?"

"No."

As they spoke, an unfamiliar sound suddenly permeated the trauma room, a persistent beeping noise that momentarily added to Erin's disorientation.

"They're just checking your heart, I guess," Sanders explained. "Are you okay?"

"Uh-hum."

"Yeah," Sanders added enthusiastically. "You're a tough little girl."

The reassurance appeared to do little to allay Erin's paranoia. "They're coming back," she blurted.

"Huh?"

"I just know they're coming after me."

Despite Erin's apparent fears, Virginia Daily said her granddaughter seemed comforted by the fact that Terry had survived, albeit in critical condition at the East Texas Medical Center, and asked to visit with him. A police escort was arranged to take Erin and her grandmother on the sixty-mile trip to Tyler.

Accompanied by his sister, Mary Horn, Terry had been rushed into surgery to remove the bullets from his back and head. As he recovered, drifting in and out of consciousness, he asked for his daughter.

"An hour went by," he told *The Dallas Morning News*, "then two or three hours went by. I was like, 'Where's Erin? Where's Erin?'"

The news that she was healthy and en route to Tyler renewed his commitment to live.

In a parched voice, speaking barely above a whisper, Terry theorized about Erin's fate. "They told me my daughter's safe," he told a detective. "They found her wandering around. I don't know if she escaped" the house.

He recalled "being conscious through some of what was

going on." And he remembered another salient fact: he'd been shot by two young men. Terry couldn't identify the first one. But—he couldn't be more certain—the second was nineteen-year-old Charlie James Wilkinson.

Charlie. The same Charlie his daughter said she'd tried to phone after the mysterious kidnappers left with the swords. The clean-cut but luckless teen who Erin had been dating for close to four months. The Charlie who initially attached himself to the Caffey family, only to become aggrieved and angry when Terry urged him to back off.

His lawyers, friends, even some members of law enforcement, would describe Charlie Wilkinson as a lonely but likeable kid desperate for love and acceptance—the reason, it was theorized, that Erin appeared to control him with such ease. Some fellow Rains High School students claimed his greatest crime appeared to be wearing his cowboy hat in class. But when police tracked him down in the hours after the murder and arson at the Caffey home, he did nothing to help his cause.

"I ain't got no conscience," he said. "I'm a psycho maniac."

CHAPTER 2

Before the massacre on the Caffey property early on March 1, 2008, the police who came into contact with the family were usually off-duty, and interacting with the handsome clan at social or church functions. Neighbors and friends noted little tension within the family beyond the typical clashes that occur in a home with three active children. The Caffeys were strict, and Erin, Bubba and Tyler appeared to be polite and well-disciplined. Nobody in the family had a criminal history. Neither the cops nor Child Protective Services had ever been compelled to visit the quiet 1800 block on County Road 2370 in the tiny town of Alba, three miles from State Highway 69.

In fact, the only record of dissension in the household is a report filed with police two months before the murder. The complainant stated that Erin felt endangered by Penny.

The accuser was Erin's boyfriend at the time, Charlie Wilkinson.

At Miracle Faith Baptist, Terry—a small-featured man who wore his hair in a military-style crew cut—and his wife worked with young members of the congregation, coaching them on Scripture and life lessons. When their children were younger, the couple were the church's youth pastors, teaching classes, organizing activities for the teens and, once a year, supervising Miracle Faith's Bible camp.

"It's basically just a retreat," said Todd McGahee, the church's pastor. "They have a good time during the day and a church service every night. Generally, you're teaching the youth the Bible by putting it on a level teenagers can understand. Of course, you're talking about sex and drugs and alcohol, and just the peer pressure of being a teenager. The Bible tells you about all that, how to deal with temptation. And if you're the youth pastor, it's your job to help the kids grow up and be spiritually mature by the time they leave the house, and start making decisions about their own lives."

Every Sunday, Penny stirred the faithful with her renditions of gospel standards:

Over the sunset mountains
Heaven awaits for me

At the foot of the Caffey driveway, a split cedar log carved and varnished by neighbor Tommy Gaston was nailed to a tree, proclaiming Terry's view of the world and the way he intended to raise his family. Under THE CAFFEYS, there was a quote from Joshua 24:15: "But as for me and my house, we will serve the Lord."

"These were people who didn't have to say anything," close friend Diane Dunlap told the *Tyler Morning Telegraph*, "you knew they were Christian people."

The Caffeys were Missionary Baptists, as opposed to members of the Southern Baptist Convention, the largest Protestant denomination in the United States with forty-two thousand churches and 16 million adherents. Because the Southern Baptists appeal to such a wide range of followers, Missionary Baptists complain that the organization is too willing to compromise. The issue over female ordination exemplifies this controversy. Although the Southern Baptist Convention decreed in 2000 that women could not become pastors who lead congregations, certain factions argue that females should still be ordained. By contrast, Missionary Baptists would never entertain the notion.

"Women play a magnificent role in the church," explained a church friend of the Caffey family. "The church wouldn't exist without them. But the Bible says that women shall never teach over men. Because the Southern Baptists are bigger, their organization is more liberal in its thinking. We're smaller and, consequently, more conservative."

A decade before the tragedy, Todd McGahee had been studying to become an Assemblies of God preacher when, at age twenty-three, he switched denominations. "The Assemblies of God believes that you can lose your salvation, and I don't believe that personally," he said, referring to the special status one apparently attains after becoming "born again." "Once you're saved, I believe the Holy Spirit fills you, and you can't ever lose that. Once you get saved, you're a new creation."

Miracle Faith holds its services in a modest building, located along Highway 276 in Emory. Like many preachers at smaller churches, McGahee has had to find alternative ways to subsidize his income and, from the time he entered the Assemblies of God ministry, he'd been working construction. The experience likely served him well. When a newcomer enters his church, McGahee is in the doorway, clad in pressed jeans and black cowboy boots, interspersing his Scriptural references with real world terminology. Unquestionably, the preacher is charismatic, but not like a televangelist or theologian unable to function beyond the seminary walls. Rather, McGahee's appeal is rooted in his ability to project man-to-man honesty with a handshake and a look in the eye.

"Whether you're dealing with the youth or dealing with adults, we make sure that everyone is saved in the church. You can't take it for granted that, just because somebody's raised in the church or comes from a godly family, that person is saved. You preach about salvation a lot."

And residents of Rains County tend to contemplate the topic. While driving through Emory, a female voice suddenly comes over the airwaves on a local AM station singing, "Let's Take Jesus to the White House." In the song, Jesus Christ is elected president of the United States. He nominates a Baptist minister for chief justice of the Supreme Court. Roe vs. Wade is overturned and prayer reintroduced in public schools.

The less-than-tolerant ideology in some churches, combined with the overall insular nature of the region, entitles some residents to judge others with impunity. "The facts don't matter to people in these small towns," complained one local woman. "It's what it looks like. That's what matters."

It's a sentiment uttered by virtually everyone in East Texas—from high school students to hotel clerks to even those occupying high positions in their respective places of worship.

Although they'd known each other for less than a year, McGahee represented much of what Terry Caffey admired. At the time of the crime, Terry was about to be ordained as a minister and had preached several sermons in McGahee's church—never realizing that the challenges of losing his wife and two sons would test his faith not only in God, but in himself.

Religion was interwoven into every aspect of Terry Caffey's life. He'd met his wife at a revival meeting at a Garland church. It was one of the few times the then twenty-four-year-old Terry allowed his attention to drift from his prayers.

As always, twenty-one-year-old Penny Lynn Daily was behind the piano, enrapturing the worshippers. Like her daughter, Erin, would be, Penny was a pretty blonde with a friendly smile, as well as an inquisitive face that gave even casual acquaintances the impression that she was deeply interested in whatever they happened to be uttering. To Terry, the fact that she'd even entertained the notion of conversing with him was something divine. "Basically, she had me at 'hello,'" he told *The Dallas Morning News*. "I was captivated."

The couple began dating, and the relationship moved

quickly. Within eight months, they were married. Erin was born a year later, in 1991.

From the moment he brought her home and rocked her in his arms, Terry intimately understood the unconditional love a parent feels for a child: "I just began thanking God for her. And I remember thinking, 'No matter how big you get, you'll always be Daddy's little girl.'"

Through the joys of childhood and the turbulence of adolescence, he never forgot the pledge. "I made a promise that I would stand by her," he said. "I didn't say, 'I'll stand by you if you're a good girl,' or 'I'll stand by you if you do what I say.' I told her I'd stand by her."

The family expanded. Bubba, formally named Matthew Ryan, was born in 1994, and Tyler Paul five years later. In keeping with their church's traditions, the couple did not baptize the children, believing that an individual needed to comprehend celestial topics and formally accept Jesus as a savior before the ceremony could take place.

"Bubba was a good guitar player," Pastor McGahee remembered. "And he played *Amazing Grace* a lot on the harmonica. His sister would sing, and his mother was our elite piano player. But she also had a very good voice."

Even to those with a lesser sense of piety, the spectacle of the Caffeys rocking the rafters of a small country church roused the spirit:

> I just feel like something good is about to happen
> And, brother, it could be this very day.

Outside of church, Bubba was a true Christian soldier, preaching the word—or "witnessing"—to the both the curious and the cynical.

He counted Isaiah 40:31 among his favorite Bible passages: "But those who hope in the Lord will renew their strength. They will soar on wings like eagles; they will run and not grow weary, they will walk and not be faint."

He included this verse on a "Me Sheet" he compiled for school, listing his interests and talents. His goal: "to have fun and learn." His greatest achievement: "I learned to play five different instruments." His preferred pastime: fishing. His favorite song: "Sweet Home Alabama" by Lynyrd Skynyrd.

Under "One Very Important Thing to Me," Bubba wrote "Jesus." When he was "upset or mad," he lifted his mood by playing guitar and talking to God.

So far, he professed, his young life had been "great, success."

Rains High School student Vanessa Hendricks knew Bubba through a mutual friend, a boy named Kevin who'd met the eldest Caffey brother at school: "Kevin told me about this new kid, Matthew, who had an older sister in the high school, that he was a good guy. Matthew really looked up to Kevin. I guess the Caffeys didn't have many friends, since they'd been homeschooled for a long time, and Kevin was one of his first friends. Matthew even wrote a paper about how he looked up to Kevin, how Kevin had been really nice to him, and made it easier to transition.

"Kevin thought that, you know, Matthew was the best guy in the world, that he was very nice, that he was really cool."

McGahee described Bubba as "a really, really sweet boy. I have a son the same age, so Matthew's been over to our house, and my boy's been over to their house." The pastor thought enough of Bubba to bring him along to the family timeshare on Lake Palestine, where visitors fish for largemouth and spotted bass, crappie and sunfish.

"I just remember him being a very polite young man, not causing a bit of trouble," McGahee said. "He was the same way in church, polite, and very interested in music, and basically pleasing people."

Tyler exhibited similar traits, but because of his age, he clung close to his parents, still uninhibited about hugging and kissing his mother in public. "We also had a boy around Tyler's age," McGahee recounted. "Tyler was a very shy little boy. I'm sure at home, he acted differently. But he was just getting warmed up to me when this happened."

One of Tommy Gaston's fondest memories of the youngest boy next door was the time Tyler received a red wagon for Christmas. It was the perfect gift for a kid who loved playing outside. "He'd get out there in the dirt," Tommy told the *Times* of London. "And the dirtier he got, the more fun he had. All he wanted for Christmas that year was his little red wagon."

To Jerry Carlisle, the former police chief in the town of Point, the child was a work in progress. "Tyler hadn't come out of his shell yet," said Carlisle. "He had a really good voice, even at his age. He could really sing. Just like his mother, he had a natural-born, God-given talent. Matthew, of course, was always ready to sing and play his harmonica. And this little Erin, she could sing like a cherub. I don't remember ever seeing Erin play an instrument, but she could sing. Since she was eleven or twelve years old, she was singing every Sunday in church."

Erin's soft church solos were especially moving, affecting not just the congregants, but the teenager herself. When Erin sang, she dug deep into her soul—arms splayed into the air, as she stood beside Penny's piano—expressing herself with such devotion that she'd start to cry. From time to time, Erin had to stop in the middle of a song to compose herself before continuing.

"The tears would just flow," said Helen Gaston.

Terry was so touched that he'd tell his daughter that he hoped she'd sing at his funeral.

Like her brothers, Erin could be coy, as well as caring and affectionate to her parents and siblings.

Diana Wolfe, a family friend, told the Associated Press about taking Erin shopping on several occasions: "I . . . had a great time with her. She wouldn't look at the high-cost items on the rack; she would look at the lower-cost items. She was just a good kid."

The anecdote illustrates the respect Erin had for her family's limitations. Even in their remote patch of Texas, Terry and Penny never naively assumed that God would pay their bills. The family cars were always used. And they were unashamed to point out that much of the children's respective wardrobes came from garage sales.

Very little free time was devoted to secular endeavors. In addition to Sunday church services and Wednesday night Bible study, Penny and her children practiced their gospel renditions at home. On Saturdays, Penny cooked a meal to bring to church the next morning. There was also "family Bible time," during which the family discussed fine points of Scripture. Terry clearly enjoyed these exchanges, envisioning himself as a preacher directing an entire congregation. Penny playfully teased her husband, suggesting he used her as a test audience for his sermons.

Given Terry's goals—and Penny's knowledge of the subject matter—it was a productive process. "Before you're ordained, there are questions you are asked," McGahee said. "In our church, you don't have to have a formal education, but you need a basic understanding of the Scriptures. Some churches will license a preacher first, on kind of a temporary basis, then ordain him later on."

Even in the workplace, Terry and Penny applied their Christian values. Terry's home health care job enabled him to assist the housebound. Penny was a driver for Meals on Wheels, delivering food to the elderly and disabled. There were more lucrative trades, but the couple derived joy from extending a hand to people modern society forgot or overlooked.

The Caffeys had lived in the area about three years, after residing in the small towns of Point and Celeste. According to Erin, Terry wanted to live in closer proximity to his job. At a certain point, she said, he'd hoped to become a youth minister at a church in Celeste. When he didn't, the family moved near Miracle Faith.

Vanessa Hendricks's mother, Debbie, runs a roadside vegetable stand on her front lawn, next to Miracle Faith's property, offering potatoes, summer squash, green beans, turnips, cucumbers and pinto beans. In addition, she sells corn that she grows in the garden beside her enlarged mobile home. Unlike many in the community, Debbie is a bona fide Yankee, from a rural section of Connecticut. She was raising two children in San Diego, working in property casualty insurance, when she was laid off six years before the murders.

"I already had a sister down here, so I knew the area," she said. "I thought it really reflected a lot of the same values we had when I was young—family, a strong sense of community, neighbor helping neighbor. Also, most people are God-fearing folks, and their emphasis is really about the kids. My kids are native San Diegans. They grew up around gangs and violence, and they'd never seen a simpler life. I'm also Native American—Mohican—on my father's side, so I was really yearning for getting back to basics.

"They're very big on athletics for kids here—football, baseball, soccer, basketball. They have a wonderful theater department at the high school. The churches, especially the Baptist churches, are very youth-driven. So my kids go to a lot of church-sponsored events: horseback riding, bonfires, swimming, fishing."

Residents often recreate along nearby Lake Fork, created and deliberately stocked with 732,514 Florida black bass between 1979 and 1987. With 315 miles of shoreline, the lake has lived up to its goal of enriching the region as a celebrated fishing retreat for both locals and tourists.

"Lake Fork really helped put us on the map," said Joey Weatherford, the editorial cartoonist for the Greenville *Herald Banner*, "because it's become the bass fishing capitol of Texas. People come a long ways to fish here, from Japan and everywhere.

"We all like our bass. But, of course, everybody here also likes catfish—and fried chicken."

The Caffeys moved onto a dusty strip of property where three families shared more than a hundred acres with opossum, pocket gophers and cottontails. The town of Alba, eighty miles east of Dallas, had been settled in 1841 by a gunsmith named Joseph Simpkins on the land straddling present day Rains and Wood counties. The area was so inaccessible that a ninety-mile oxcart trip to Shreveport, Louisiana, could take weeks. In 1881, the tiny town expanded slightly, when the Missouri-Kansas-Texas Railroad began running through the community. If Alba had a boom period, it began in the early twentieth century when lignite coal was discovered. By the 1920s, there were 2,000 people in Alba, many working in the mines producing 20,000 tons of coal each month. But the Great Depression hit the area hard and, in 1940, the mines shut down.

At the time of the 2000 census, 420 people lived in Alba, more than ninety-eight percent of them white.

"There's racism here, but I don't think it's intentional," said high school student Vanessa Hendricks. "There are probably less than ten black kids in the whole school. They usually group together. But they're friends with everyone else, too. You hear racist jokes, but they're usually said out of ignorance. If kids met more black people, they'd think differently."

Outside T.J.'s Café, patrons are assured of "Good Ol' Country Cooking." Inside, customers eat their chicken-fried steak beneath a photo of John Wayne. Horseshoes adorn the walls. A pair of laminated cowboy boots sits on a shelf near a picture of Clint Eastwood, while a decorative sign warns NO DANCING ON TABLE WITH SPURS ON. Another pronounces COWGIRL KITCHEN, TAKE IT OR LEAVE IT.

On a hot Saturday afternoon, the sun beats down on the blacktop in a town square that is devoid of humanity, save for the couple running the hardware store. The First State Bank shares a building with the Alba-Golden Credit Union. A small fan blows in front of an open garage door. Two wrought-iron chairs rest beside a waterless fountain. A number of one-story, Western-style buildings have FOR SALE signs in the windows.

Sid King is among the few Alba residents who've truly been out in the world. A close confidant of Roy Orbison, the well-coiffed singer/songwriter once headlined a *Louisiana Hayride* show at Shreveport's Municipal Auditorium, after Johnny Cash and Johnny Horton—of "The Battle of New

Orleans" fame—warmed up the crowd. Beginning in 1948, the *Hayride* radio show was a launching ground for such acts as Hank Williams, Elvis Presley, George Jones and Faron Young, modeled after "barn dance" programs like the Grand Ole Opry. "Sensational" Sid King's apex occurred in 1956 when he released the hit "Oobie Doobie" with his band, the Five Strings. In 1981, Sid and his friend Orbison were nominated for the Texas Music Awards, along with Pat Boone. At the time of the murders, he was performing with his most recent band, the Barnstompers. But day to day, he cut hair in his barbershop in Alba and recorded music in the back.

"I've always done rockabilly, which makes me a little different than a lot of people around here," he noted. "Most of the people here like country and bluegrass. And then, as you probably know, a lot prefer gospel."

When Alba residents go into "town," the destination is usually Emory, population 1,241. There are three stoplights, one supermarket and seventeen churches, including Miracle Faith. Both the foreign-born and college-educated populations are below the state average. The number of homeowners identifying themselves as gay or lesbian is zero.

On Route 19, it's not uncommon to see residents on horseback. At Rains High School, teachers inform students of reports that cows have meandered into the road, urging everyone to show caution on the drive home.

"It's easy to get bored," pointed out a woman sitting with friends and family in a fast food restaurant near Miracle Faith Baptist Church. "Teenagers drive from Sonic to Dairy Queen, on a strip that's about a mile long, and go cow-tipping."

When asked if the alleged pastime—involving sneaking up on a cow, asleep while standing on all four feet, and tipping it over—actually occurs, the woman delivered a noncommittal smile.

"There are a lot of good things, too. The place is so small that it forces kids to behave. If you start any trouble, everybody knows about it."

She was asked what constituted trouble in Emory.

She grinned at a friend. "Cow-tipping."

Much of the action in town seems to center around the Emory Livestock Auction. The building is open on Tuesday and Saturday—with some visitors driving as far as a hundred miles—when the parking lot overflows with pickup trucks and attached campers. There, men in Dallas Cowboy t-shirts, baseball caps and cowboy boots climb a long set of stairs to a bridge crossing through the building, stopping to look down on dozens of pens holding up to twenty-five hundred cows, bulls, ponies, goats, even llamas.

No one wants his name on the record.

"Emory's quiet," observed a regular, above the baying of the beasts, "very, very quiet. This is the noisiest place in town."

At Miracle Faith Baptist Church, congregants must agree to a number of "covenants," including abstention from alcohol. The prohibition is rooted in Biblical passages like Galatians 5:19–21, equating intoxication, with heresy, sorcery, fornication and idolatry, among other evils, and warning, "Those who practice such things will not inherit the kingdom of God."

Although it's not uncommon to smell beer or harder liquor on the breath of the random cowboy, it's virtually impossible to stroll into a convenience store in Rains County and purchase a six-pack. To satisfy the demand created by this prohibition, bootleggers do a brisk business, selling moonshine, among other spirits.

When police raid the illegal stills, though, many in the community roll their eyes. "There's a perception," said one courthouse worker, "that they're hypocrites asking you to do one thing, and taking care of themselves at the same time."

This lack of trust was aggravated a short time after the Caffey murders, following media accounts of a Rains County sheriff's deputy flipping his personal vehicle on Farm-To-Market Road 779, just outside Emory. What made the newspaper reports stand out was the assertion that the officer was riding with a group of teenagers—including a girl just one year older than Erin. Authorities said that, inside the Chevy truck, the group had open containers of alcohol, as well as a torn evidence envelope of marijuana from a case the lawman had worked. Even more shocking was the allegation that one of the passengers was the actual defendant in the case.

The deputy "drifted into oncoming traffic, and one of the passengers actually grabbed the wheel and yanked it back," said Trooper Joe Hogue of the Texas Department of Public Safety. "That's how the truck flipped over." In the crash, the deputy and the seventeen-year-old girl were ejected from the truck.

While the deputy was fired and authorities contemplated bringing a variety of charges, ultimately the case was dropped. Still, a spokesman for the Rains County Sheriff's Department said, "Things like this make us all look bad."

CHAPTER 3

Despite her wholesome good looks and ability to awaken the hearts of worshippers with her stunning voice, Erin Caffey struggled with academics. At age sixteen, her reading skills were equivalent to that of a sixth-grader, while math computation and application, vocabulary, language mechanics and reading comprehension hovered between the fifth- and sixth-grade levels. Because of Erin's problems in school, her parents had taken her to a community clinic in 2002. There, she was diagnosed with Attention Deficit Hyperactivity Disorder (ADHD), inattentive type, and prescribed Adderall, a psycho-stimulant known to increase concentration, alertness and cognitive performance.

Much of the burden of keeping Erin engaged in her schoolwork fell on Penny. Three years before the murders, shortly after the family moved to Alba, the Caffeys made the decision to homeschool their children. It's an option many fundamentalist families exercise, with varying results. The motivation may be a loss of confidence in public education—with its emphasis on evolution, sex education, even diversity—or belief that parents should take a more active role in raising their children. Certainly, Terry and Penny hoped that the one-on-one attention would help their struggling daughter advance in her studies.

What made the choice seem abrupt to outsiders was the
fact that the kids were already in public school; Erin was an
eighth-grader at Rains Junior High, while Bubba and Tyler
attended Rains Elementary. Then, one month into the school
year, they were pulled out. Much would later be made of
Terry's contention that another female had developed a crush
on Erin, and kissed her in the hallway.

It seemed that, to the Caffeys at least, Emory—its livestock auction and church culture notwithstanding—was bub-
bling with secular permissiveness.

"I guess you'd call it culture shock," Terry told *The Dallas Morning News*. "Emory has a lot of bisexual kids. It's
like it was almost cool to be bisexual. One of the first things
that happened was some girl wanted to be Erin's little girlfriend. And I was like, 'That ain't happening.'"

A psychological report would later assert that Terry
wanted to homeschool his daughter "to keep her away from
the negative influences at her school. . . . Erin was prone to
thrill-seeking. . . . When the family removed Erin from the
public schools, the father noted many girls proclaimed themselves to be 'lesbian.' . . . Psychological data indicates Erin
likely has issues in this area."

Terrry would later contend that he'd been misunderstood:
"I just spoke of one incident while my daughter was attending school there. Many people think that is the reason why
we homeschooled. That is not the case. Erin was having a
learning disability, and I have high respect for the school
and the citizens [of] Rains County."

Regardless of Erin's feelings about same-sex relationships, the psychological report maintained, "The history
implies she desired to be sexual before her homeschooling ever began. All of these attributes derive from a strong
developing Borderline Personality core"—the potential to
experience sudden eruptions of anxiety, depression or anger, resulting in substance abuse, self-injury or impulsive
aggression—"Erin appears to have had for years, possibly
preceded by attachment issues and even early sexual abuse."

If Erin endured sexual abuse, nobody knew about it.

There was absolutely no suggestion or evidence that any family member was involved.

Those who saw them regularly generally noted that the kids were extremely well-mannered, if also a bit introverted. "None of the kids were real outgoing," said Pastor McGahee. "Part of that is probably being homeschooled. . . . Part of it is personality. [They were] kind of shy."

Miracle Faith congregant Chad Darby claimed that Erin "was just starting to interact with people her age. She was kind of sheltered, to tell you the truth."

And, like teenagers everywhere, she was trying to navigate through emotions she couldn't fully comprehend, while struggling to reconcile her own desires with the values of her parents. During her three years of homeschooling, Erin argued with Penny often, demanding to bust loose from the homestead and socialize with her peers.

Chelsea Wright, a friend of Erin's later interviewed by investigators, recalled, "I'd been to her house all the time. Her family was very nice and caring, but Erin always seemed mad at her mother."

When someone administered discipline, though, it was usually Terry who withheld Erin's cell phone or car privileges.

A main source of contention was dating. "Penny and I talked," remembered Sarah Meece, the youth leader at Miracle Faith Baptist Church, "because her and Erin were on totally different sides on this. Penny didn't want her going out at all. Erin felt like she was old enough . . . to do it."

The one place where Erin *could* go and receive the adulation of the opposite sex was church. When young men approached, Erin seemed interested, smiling at their sometimes clumsy remarks, her bluish-gray eyes flashing. "They all seemed like nice boys," said McGahee, "but they were all teenage boys. They had one thing on their minds.

". . . It seemed to me that Erin was very naïve, being homeschooled. I don't think she really realized what all these boys were after. She was eating up all the attention. . . .

We'd have a pew full of boys" all competing with one another for Erin's attention.

The pastor once joked that he needed five or six reproductions of the Caffey daughter to fill up his sanctuary.

Her popularity did not go unnoticed by the females in the church. "I don't mean this ugly," Sarah Meece told investigators, "but Erin a lot of times changed boyfriends like the rest of us changed our clothes. . . . You never knew who she was going out with. She had lots of little boys—young boys, young men—around her. So we never knew. We never knew."

Her opportunities expanded when she took a job at Sonic in July 2007—cruising to work in her old Chevy pickup in the afternoons, then returning to Alba for Penny to homeschool her at night. A co-worker told *Texas Monthly* that the chance to intermingle with the public seemed novel to Erin: "It was like she was seeing the world for the first time."

Erin was a carhop at the hamburger palace, attracting a host of young men who made sure to park in whichever section the alluring blonde was working. Of all the carhops, Erin was the only one who served her customers on skates, impressing the boys with her sense of daring. For Halloween in 2007, she dressed as a carhop from the 1950s in a pink and white poodle skirt made at home, a pink scarf tied around her neck.

Had James Dean pulled up on his Indian 500 motorcycle, it seemed like Erin would have mounted the seat behind him and blown out of town.

Terry and Penny might have been traditional, but they weren't naïve. The couple was aware of Erin's flirtatious habits, and made no secret of their disapproval. "She was wanting to date all these little thugs who wouldn't work," Terry told a reporter, "and these little bums and troublemakers. She was drawn to them. It was aggravating."

At one church fellowship meeting, Terry learned, Erin openly made out with a boy she considered her boyfriend, at a picnic table. As the other kids watched, Erin's beau slowly slipped his hand up her skirt.

The Caffeys, with their clear sense of right and wrong, knew that this was no way for a Christian girl to act. And Terry wasn't reticent about expressing his expectations for his children. He'd been a youth minister, and he delivered the same message at school and church: Sex was a sacred act for the marriage bed. Erin had shamed the family with her spectacle, and Terry demanded that she and the boy break up.

When police later asked Meece if she believed that Erin was sexually active, the youth leader responded, "As an adult and a parent, I just sort of had a feeling, you know, maybe she is. You know? I just sort of had a feeling. But I don't know, and that doesn't mean she was."

What Meece did know is that the moment Erin entered a room, everyone's concentration shifted in her direction: "You just didn't know how she was going to come to church. Most of the time, you didn't know if she was going to have shoes on. It was like a big joke . . . 'I wonder what Erin's going to be wearing to church today?' Or 'I wonder how blonde her hair is going to be this week.' It was just a big joke with us."

At least once, Meece took it upon herself to correct Erin on her appearance. "She started wearing her pants really tight," the youth leader contended. "She was wearing them so tight and low, I was like, 'Erin, you have got to pull those britches up and get a shirt to cover up.' . . . I was like, 'Wow.' I mean, that's unbelievable. I cannot believe that they were that tight and that low. And she had been told—her parents told her all the time—not to go out in public like that."

Toward the end of the summer of 2007, Erin met Charlie Wilkinson.

Charlie and his friend Tanis Condit had pulled into the Sonic parking lot, watching the attractive blonde tend to other customers. Charlie noticed as she glided back into the restaurant at one point, then looked over at Tanis.

"You see that girl over there," Charlie predicted. "I'm gonna marry that girl."

Before Erin took their order, Charlie scrounged up a pen, and scribbled his phone number on a piece of paper. When she appeared at the window, Charlie smiled at the carhop with his light-blue eyes. Then he handed the information to Erin with his money.

"Call me," he told her.

For several days, Charlie waited for a call that never came. "She lost my number," he recalled. "That's what she told me. But I met her anyway because I'd dated her step-cousin."

Once the couple managed to talk face to face, and Erin responded positively to the sandy-haired young man's mixture of bravado and self-effacing humor, he vowed to never let her go.

Charlie was seventeen at the time, and when he wasn't taking rides from friends, he rumbled around Emory in a battered 1991 Ford Explorer that was in such chronic condition, he sometimes had to beg strangers to help him push-start the vehicle. His general attire—Wranglers, cowboy boots, a large belt buckle and black Western hat just a little too big for his head—was fairly typical for Rains County. Yet Charlie viewed himself as an outsider. "I always was the nerd," he'd later write a friend. "Guess that's what happens when you join band instead of athletics. Plus, growing up, I never got an option to play sports. Otherwise, I would probably of been a prep."

Although Charlie was good-looking—when viewed from a certain angle, one could imagine some Renaissance sculptor chiseling out his cheekbones and lips to depict an apostle or boyish king—there was a sadness to his demeanor that other kids exploited. "Some guys would really tease him and pick at him until he would get angry," a former classmate told *Texas Monthly*. Charlie generally avoided fistfights, satisfying his tormentors by slamming his hand on his desk or stamping out of the classroom.

Charlie enjoyed describing himself as a "country boy." His MySpace profile featured the young man in a baseball cap and t-shirt under the nickname he'd bestowed on himself, "Hillbilly," in capital letters. His password: "Jack-Daniels," the whiskey distilled in a Tennessee town that—at

the time of the brand's trademark, at least—boasted a population of 361.

Old friend Phillip Lewelling would tell detectives that
Charlie's celebration of his small-town heritage was not an
act; everything Wilkinson ever wanted could be found in
the pastoral settings of East Texas. "I grew up with Charles,"
Lewelling said. "We met back in 1996 when I was in first
grade. We rode the school bus together. We used to go mudding," also known as mug bogging, an activity that involves
racing vehicles through mud pits and, along with truck and
tractor pulls, occasionally draws crowds to county fairs.
"We took a rifle and shotgun to go hog hunting."

In January 2007, Lewelling pulled his truck up in front of
Charlie's home, and Wilkinson excitedly greeted him with a
new object in hand.

"Look at my pistol," Charlie said.

It was a .22. Charlie told his friend that he intended to use
the gun to kill coyotes, a nocturnal animal that frequently
roams Rains County, along with gray fox and beaver.

Charlie's mother and father separated when he was ten years
old, and left it up to the child to decide whom would be the
custodial parent. "I was a little boy," Charlie said. "Every
boy wants to be with his dad. For the most part, the divorce
was better for me, so I wouldn't have to hear them arguing."

But attorney Ron Ferguson later maintained that the acri-
monious nature of the split deeply demoralized the boy.
Ferguson said, "There were . . . a lot of custody fights, trying
to control Charlie, one parent trying to keep him from the
other parent. And I believe that has a devastating effect on
children."

Eventually, Charlie's mother moved to Del Rio, across
the Rio Grande from Ciudad Acuña in Mexico, more than
480 miles from Emory. Charlie only saw her once or twice a
year while he was living with his father, along with a stepmother, half-sister, stepbrother and stepsister.

"I looked into if there was any physical abuse," Ferguson
recounted. "Charlie said his father never abused him." But

he did talk about another relative outside of the immediate family. "I said, 'Charlie, were you sexually abused?' And he was very quick to say, 'No, no!" My next question was, '[Were] you physically abused?' He kind of indicated that [the relative] had been abusive in some way."

Teresa Myers, mother of one of Charlie's good friends, recalled that Charlie and his father, Bobby, were close: "If Charlie were over here in the evenings, it wasn't uncommon for him to say, 'Dad's expecting me home. I need to call and let Dad know where I'm going to be.' I always found it quite impressive that Charlie would make an effort to make sure his dad knew exactly where he was, and what he was doing."

Bobby Lee Wilkinson had worked in a paper plant, but neighbors in Emory describe him earning money by doing woodworking in private homes, crafting interiors designed with raw cedar. Charlie sometimes accompanied his father on these assignments, impressing homeowners with a strong work ethic. "Charlie will never forget me," laughed one resident. "He and his dad were installing a fireplace in my home, and the poor kid got stung by a scorpion."

Another local reminisced about Charlie earning a few dollars by working on the golf course, moving carts around, while politely addressing the golfers: "He talked to everyone."

The teen's deportment was hardly a surprise to Stacy Ferguson, the investigator/mitigator for her husband Ron's law firm. "I found Charlie to be very friendly," she said. "He was searching in many places to be accepted and loved, to feel like he was part of a solid family. The months prior to the murders, he visited different churches, trying to find the right church-family where he could feel at home."

Yet, the teen was never embraced in a way that gratified him. "He told me that, before Erin he'd been with one other girl," Stacy said. "She broke up with him, and it broke his heart."

To many of his peers, Charlie's quest for warmth and gratification was too obvious—and a little disturbing.

"Charlie Wilkinson had a crush on my friend," Vanessa Hendricks claimed, "and, like, he was really weird. He would drive by her house and stuff like that, and I thought that was really creepy. I was like, 'Oh my God, this guy's a stalker.'"

Charlie doesn't deny feeling needy. "My dad says our family comes from a long line of people with lost puppy dog syndrome," he said. "We want to be taken in. We want to help others. We like to help the underdog at any cost, without thinking about the circumstances."

From the day he began dating Erin, everyone around Charlie Wilkinson could tell that he'd fallen hard. "He seemed very infatuated with her," said Teresa Myers. "I felt like he was in love with her. And, you know, of course, I'm a mom, and I'm like, 'Dude, okay, come on now.' Same thing I tell my son. 'Yeah, you're in love for this moment, but realize it's going to change, and life is going to take you down many paths.'"

Still, because Charlie seemed so anxious to fill a gulf created by the deficiency of a day-to-day mother figure, Teresa viewed Charlie's fascination with Erin Caffey with concern, and even a touch of pity.

Like Debbie Hendricks, the woman who runs the vegetable stand next to Miracle Faith Baptist Church, Teresa could step back and analyze the social dynamics of East Texas because she'd been raised somewhere else. A self-described Air Force brat, Teresa was born in Florida and graduated from high school in Irving, the sprawling suburb that was once the home of Texas Stadium, where the NFL's Dallas Cowboys played from 1971 to 2008. After working in banking operations, she and her husband, Bill, a maintenance supervisor, decided to move their two children to Emory for a frequently-cited reason: "Life is slower here."

She first met Charlie when Wilkinson and Teresa's son, Justin, became involved in a Future Farmers of America (FFA) project together at Rains High School. Justin was several years younger than Charlie, but the age difference was not a deterrent to either of them. "It's odd," Teresa noted, "but, over here, seniors don't only hang out with seniors. It's one big school, so everyone kind of ends up together. It's not unusual to find seniors and freshmen as friends. My son's very social anyway; he knows everybody. It's doesn't matter what age group they are, or their clique."

While Charlie generally placed himself on the sidelines, Justin maneuvered easily between the jocks, cowboys, preps—also known as the socialites—and goth kids. Justin may have been the younger of the two, but Charlie was impressed by the boy's social dexterity.

For their FFA project, Charlie and Justin decided to construct a log hauler. Teresa remembers Charlie's father, Bobby, becoming immersed in the planning, even paying for some of the materials.

"Justin and Charlie, they had to literally design and build this project from the ground up, then take it to the FFA fair in San Antonio," Teresa said. "It was statewide, and they took it very seriously. We have one of those houses where the boys love to come over, and just kind of hang out and cut loose. Charlie was one of those kids. He was over here a lot. He was a likeable kid, a trustworthy kid. He followed our rules, because he was older than our child. Justin couldn't do the things Charlie did—drive, go to certain types of parties. He was fifteen years old and, by then, Charlie was going on eighteen. He dipped tobacco, and we didn't want Justin dipping tobacco. And, of course, we didn't want him drinking.

"We sat down with Charlie, and said, 'Look, we know that you're older, and we're trusting you to follow our rules.' And Charlie respected us. He was the first one to pick up the phone and say, 'Look, I've got Justin, and we're running late. But we're on the way.' "

At one point, Teresa and her husband compared Charlie to their son's other friends. Most kids minded their manners in the Myers home, although a choice few rankled the couple more than others. "These were the kids I'd have to tell, 'Look, you're just not welcome here anymore,' " Teresa said. "I hated doing that, but Charlie was never one of those kids. Everything was 'yes, ma'am,' 'no, sir.' If we ever had a disagreement, he listened to what we had to say and—if it was necessary—asked us to forgive him."

"Justin looked up to him a lot. Charlie was very good about giving advice. If Justin was in the middle of a down time, or something was bugging him, Charlie was usually the person he'd call. Justin could talk to Charlie about girls, or if Mom and Dad were driving him crazy. He'd always lean toward Charlie. And Charlie always seemed to give him good advice. He was like a big brother to Justin, basically."

Conversely, if Teresa was having difficulty conveying a certain point of view to Justin, she'd appeal to Charlie to communicate the message.

"All right, I'll talk to him about it," Charlie would pledge. "Don't worry, Mom."

Charlie jubilantly told Teresa stories about going to church with his father and siblings, conjuring up some of the theological discussions that followed. "He could sit down and tell you his deepest thoughts about God," Teresa said. "He said he knows that God is always with him, and will always take care of him. He was very secure in his thoughts about that. It was really weird to me because I was just then really getting into the whole church thing. So here I was, at forty-four years old, talking to a kid who was so in tune with this. It was really amazing."

At times, Teresa noticed that Charlie could become quiet and draw into himself. But she attributed it to his depth: "He was very complex. You could tell that he always had something on his mind. He had to get to know you before he opened up. But he was a kid who just had a heart of gold. When you were his friend, he always had your back. He was a true friend."

Charlie concedes that there was a side to the persona that he didn't let people like the Myers family see. "I think I had a drinking problem," he said. "I always had a bottle of Ezra Brooks [Kentucky bourbon] under my mattress, and a case of beer under my bed."

By the time he was a senior, his teachers reported, Charlie

would occasionally fall asleep in class. Was this the result of alcoholism, indifference to his studies or the fatigue of an unstructured lifestyle? Apparently, officials in the Rains County school system never took the time to hone in on an answer. As it was, no one—especially Charlie—expected the young man to continue his education immediately after high school.

That didn't mean that Charlie didn't have goals. Indeed, he had a better sense of the future than some students bound for Texas A&M or Baylor. Between his junior and senior years, he'd attended a boot camp in Fort Sill, Oklahoma, as part of a Texas National Guard program for high school students. And one weekend a month, he trained with his unit in Greenville, Texas. The moment he received his diploma, Charlie was going into the military.

"I had a ten-year plan," he said. "Graduate high school, beginning of ten-year plan. Join the Army. I'd already been accepted. I'd finish my Army training and come back home. If they didn't ship me off, I'd get the certificates I needed in diesel mechanics to get a good job. Then, I'd go to junior college for business training. I'd go to a bank. If I had credit—I'm sure I would have worked my credit up with little loans here and there—I'd open my own shop. That was the ten-year plan."

Charlie spoke to his friend, Justin, about the strategy, as well as the boy's parents. Teresa Myers admired Charlie's focus, even if she expressed concern over the teen's fixation with his new girlfriend. "He was pretty crazy about her," Teresa said. "So I always said, 'Remember, Charlie, you have this plan. You're going into the Army. You're in school now, but remember, in six months, you're leaving, and she's not going to be yours when you come back. She's a young girl who'll still be in high school and, believe me, she's going to move on. Let's think about this rationally. If you think she's going to wait for you forever, that's not going to happen.'

"And he always said, 'I know. I know.'"

Charlie and Erin were becoming inseparable. At night, he said, he'd stop by the Caffey home, politely greet Terry and Penny, and chat with them about work and people they knew in common. Then, he'd hang out with Erin and her brothers. On those occasions when the family built an after-dinner bonfire, Charlie helped out—but usually made sure that Erin was standing close by.

"You know them family pictures that they print in movies and stuff?" he told *Texas Monthly*. "The old-timey ones with the white fence? When I was at their house, that's what the family was like. They were perfect."

At nine PM, Terry would tell his daughter that it was time for Charlie to leave. Once again, Charlie claimed, he'd address the Caffeys with courtesy as he said goodbye, then rush home to wait for Erin's phone call. They'd generally talk until her ten PM curfew.

The next afternoon, when Erin took her half-hour break at Sonic, Charlie would be waiting to join her.

"He was totally in love with her, and considered her his soulmate," said Charlie's friend Dion Kipp, Jr. "Charlie talked about Erin twenty-four seven. . . . When Erin and Charlie first started dating, Charlie said that her parents liked him, and had no problem with them being together."

What Charlie didn't realize was that Erin's father had a poor impression of him. The first time they'd met, Terry walked through the door to find his armchair occupied by Charlie, feet dangling off the side. The young man neither stood up to properly introduce himself, nor offered a handshake. Those who knew Charlie would explain the incident by pointing out that Erin's suitor came from a more casual background, and didn't understand the Caffeys' strict sense of protocol.

"Do you always sit like that?" Terry inquired.

"Yeah."

"Well, not in my chair you don't. Stand up and greet me when I come into the room."

Charlie thought little of the exchange; in his mind, Terry was just laying out the rules of his home, just as Teresa Myers and her husband had done. But, to Terry, the damage was done.

"I don't like that boy," Terry complained to Penny. "If he can't show me any respect, how does he treat our daughter?"

Only later would Charlie realize the extent to which Terry disapproved of the relationship. "Mr. Caffey said that he saw a difference in the way Erin acted when we started dating," Charlie said. "She'd disagree with her parents more. I think she was doing that even before she met me. She was getting in that rebellious stage.

"My perception of her was that she'd been the perfect, church-going little angel—as long as her parents had complete control of her. The kids did everything their parents wanted. When she got a job and started dating me, she wanted more freedom. She was breaking away from them."

In a *Dallas Morning News* web chat, Terry would disagree with Wilkinson's analysis. "She had lived with us in our home for nearly seventeen years, and no one knew her like her family did," Terry argued. "Our problem with her did not arise until she started dating Charlie. That is when we noticed a change in her."

As a pastor, Todd McGahee had heard congregants confide about every type of quandary, and understood exactly what the Caffeys were experiencing: "I pretty much saw Penny and Terry just trying to keep that happy medium between allowing their daughter to have a little bit of free run, but then not enough. And I could see . . . she was thinking that they may have been keeping her under control too much. . . . But, you know, that's just typical raising kids stuff."

Both friends and church members knew that Erin was not beyond lying to her parents. In fact, she'd admitted as much to Miracle Faith Baptist youth leader Sarah Meece. "Like she told her parents she was going to meet up with her friends to go shopping," Sarah remembered. "They told the girls' parents they were going shopping, and then, she told me that she didn't know why her parents were mad at her because they'd . . . come to find out that she'd gone and met Charlie."

At one point, Penny's mother Virginia Daily later testified, the atmosphere had become so heated at home that Erin chose to stay with her grandmother for a short period.

Compared to some of the other problems he heard from church members, McGahee did not fret over the friction in the Caffey house. "I have two teenagers myself," he pointed out, "so that's to be expected. I don't think anyone thought it was any more serious than what you'd find in any household with teenagers."

As for Charlie, he claimed that he wanted the Caffeys to work out their differences with Erin, and view him as the standup guy he perceived himself to be. He liked the family, after all, and he loved their daughter. Why couldn't they simply be happy that Erin was with such a pure-hearted young man?

"To this day, I don't know why they didn't like me," he said. "I don't know what I did. I don't know if it was something someone told them I had done in the past, or something I'd just done and didn't notice."

CHAPTER 4

Around Thanksgiving 2007, Charlie began coming to Miracle Faith Baptist Church with Erin, holding hands with her in the pew when she wasn't performing solos beside her mother. "I had several conversations with him," Pastor McGahee said, "and he told me that he was planning on joining the Army. When he first started coming, he wore fatigues all the time. He was kind of arrogant in the way that seventeen- or eighteen-year-old boys can be—like maybe he thought a little too much of himself—but he seemed like a polite young man. He shook your hand and made eye contact."

McGahee had no reason ever not to be cordial to Charlie, even though he knew that Terry and Penny Caffey disapproved of their daughter's boyfriend. "They told me he was a bit older," the preacher said, "and I knew that Terry didn't like that. And Terry told me that Charlie had been disrespectful to him. I never saw that in church, but Terry said that . . . he came over when they asked him not to, and he didn't respect their wishes."

Youth leader Sarah Meece tended to share the Caffeys' view of Erin's new love interest. "He didn't belong in our church," she told investigators. "He wasn't a member of our church. He was only there for Erin. Only for her."

Charlie never acted as if Erin *hadn't* been the one who

drew him to her church. But he was offended by the notion that his sole purpose in attending Miracle Faith was affixing himself to his girlfriend. "Of course, I came there because I wanted to be with her," he said. "I think a lot of boyfriends go to their girlfriend's church when they start dating. But I also went to the church because I liked the preacher. I liked the way he talked, I liked listening to what he had to say."

Not only did Charlie turn up at Miracle Faith on Sunday, he also appeared on Wednesday nights when Erin attended youth group. "He would sit with the group and everything, but he generally looked at me out of the corner of his eye, to see where I was at," Sarah said. "He didn't like other people being around Erin. If she was talking with the other girls, he'd look at them like, 'Stay away. She's mine.' He always had kind of an attitude. And that why I felt, 'I don't know about this guy.'"

Away from church, Charlie confided to his friend's mother, Teresa Myers, about the antagonism he was beginning to feel from the Caffeys' church crowd.

"Her dad hates me," Charlie despaired.

"I don't think her dad hates you," Teresa answered reassuringly. "It's that her dad doesn't understand what's going on with y'all."

As a parent, Teresa could empathize with the Caffeys. Charlie seemed obsessed and possessive, and there was nothing positive about that. But Charlie's friends believed that Erin could be just as controlling of her boyfriend, and arguably more manipulative.

As Justin Myers and Charlie continued working on their log hauler project, for instance, Wilkinson's dedication began to wane. "He'd say, 'I'm coming over to work on it,'" maintained Teresa, "and then, he would never show up. And then, we would hear that he was at the lake with Erin or something, and we were like, 'What's up with that?'

"Charlie would tell us, 'Well, you know, it's complicated.'

"It just seemed like Erin had a problem if Charlie was around anyone else but her. She just didn't like his friends, didn't want them to spend time with him. And that's kind of weird. It's funny because in this society, we know there's something wrong with a boyfriend who has that kind of jealous influence over his girlfriend. But a girl like Erin, she was just as bad. Or maybe worse."

The kid who'd animatedly spoken about his ten-year plan a few months earlier now seemed worn down by the demands of his relationship. "At a certain point, Charlie kind of withdrew, and I just started worrying about him," said Teresa. "There was tension with Charlie and some of his friends, and I realized the issue always seemed to be Erin. Erin didn't want Charlie hanging out with Michael Dickinson. I mean, Michael Dickinson and Charlie were like brothers. They lived in the same house! Those two would start fighting, and it always stemmed from something that Erin had created.

"There was a time when Erin accused my son of getting in a car and physically attacking her. Well, for one thing, that's not my son at all. He never had interest in her like that. But she told Charlie. And what was Charlie going to do? I mean, this was his girlfriend.

"So Charlie came over here and started asking questions. He was very confused. And I'm like, 'Charlie, come on now. You know Justin. Justin would never do that to you.' And we talked and went through it, and Charlie and Justin talked and went through it."

Convinced that Erin was a pathological liar, Teresa overstepped her boundaries, and suggested something Charlie didn't want to hear.

"There's all this drama created around Erin," she told Wilkinson.

Charlie stared hard at his friend's mother. But he did nothing to prevent her from continuing.

"Look what Erin's doing, Charlie. She's trying to pull you away from your friends. You guys are all fighting. You and Erin are fighting, and you're on again, off again. There's always some disaster y'all are in the middle of."

Teresa was worried that, sooner or later, Erin would

announce that she was pregnant. At that stage, Charlie would be stuck in Emory. Any effort to go through the Army, study business and open a machine shop would be dashed. Charlie would be grinding away, another unskilled laborer in a less than privileged slice of the Lone Star State, scrambling to support his teenage girlfriend and their baby.

"Dude, you need to walk away," Teresa declared with certainty. "She is going to ruin all your plans. She is going to create trouble in your life."

Charlie bristled, but refrained from protesting.

"I'm telling you the truth," Teresa persisted. "I think she's playing you. So just think about what I'm saying. I've told you this before—you're graduating in a few months. And she's not going to be here waiting for you. So be careful. Please be careful."

Charlie walked over to Teresa and hugged her around the neck. When he pulled his face away, he appeared visibly touched that this surrogate mother had taken so deep an interest in his welfare.

"I appreciate you talking to me," he said. "And I'll think about it."

Teresa stroked Charlie's arm. "Okay," she replied. "You know I love you, and I'm always here. Anytime you want to talk to me, I'm always here."

"I know," Charlie said. And he paused for a moment to try to make sense of his swirling thoughts.

"A lot of people warned me," Charlie said later on. "I really don't know how it got this far because, personally, I didn't notice it. But my friends, they started noticing. They told me she was being controlling, and trying to get me to break away from them. But I didn't want to see it."

Just before Christmas, Erin expressed her desire to go back to public school. Despite the clashes at home, the Caffeys agreed; like Charlie, Erin was considering a career in the military, and her parents were proud and supportive. Bubba and Tyler had already started school in the fall after Bubba told his parents that he wanted to see his friends day to day, and the experience had been a positive one, so far. Also, the Caffeys needed money and, if the responsibilities of educating the kids were shifting elsewhere, Penny would be free to earn it.

"Penny was trying to be schoolteacher, mom, everything," Sarah Meece told investigators. "It was too much. . . . It's just very overwhelming . . . trying to teach them and deal with everything."

Pastor McGahee remembered Bubba's satisfaction about finally being around boys his age, and the way the other children seemed to accept him. Tyler "never had to get up at seven-thirty to go to school," McGahee said, "and they had a hard time getting him to school, but I think he enjoyed it when he got there."

In fact, he recollected, the Caffeys had planned to send Erin to Rains High School for a while. But because of her academic limitations, the parents tried tutoring her at home for a few months to train her for the challenging curriculum. "She was a little below speed," McGahee said. "They didn't want to put her in . . . being way . . . below the other kids."

The preparation only worked to a certain extent. Although Erin was old enough to be a junior, when the school tested her, officials decided to place her in the ninth grade. She'd also tell investigators that she was registered into a special education program.

Charlie was a senior, and he and Erin ate lunch together every day. In the hallway, the couple held hands and sometimes cut out of the building to make out in Erin's pickup. The Caffeys were struggling to be open-minded about their strong-willed daughter's wishes, and permitted Erin and Charlie to go out to dinner on occasion—with the provision that Erin would have to be in the house by 9:30 PM. Frequently, they skipped the restaurant and went to a friend's house, where they could disappear into a bedroom. It was there, Charlie said, that they had sex for the first time shortly after Christmas.

For a brief period, a peaceful co-existence appeared to settle in the Caffey home. On the surface, Erin was following her parents' guidelines. Charlie accompanied his girlfriend to church, and seemed sincere in his commitment to the Caffeys' form of Christianity. Either way, he'd be leaving for the military soon, and—Terry and Penny hoped—Erin's interest in him would fade.

But Charlie was so possessed with Erin that he wanted to do something to solidify the relationship, and presented her with a gift that would remind her of the Army recruit after he pulled out of town. One night, as they drove down a country road, Charlie stopped and parked. He and Erin got out, and Charlie knelt in front of her, holding a ring between his fingers.

"My grandpa proposed to my grandma with it," Charlie explained. "And my dad proposed to my mom with it. I called it a 'promise ring.'" In other words, even though Charlie was officially not asking Erin to marry him, he viewed their relationship with a certain degree of permanence. Erin happily slipped on the ring.

"Charlie told me that, once he had his own business, he saw himself married to Erin with several children," said Stacy Ferguson, the investigator/mitigator for her husband, Ron, Charlie's attorney. "He described in detail his picture of the perfect family down to having a cute little home with a picket fence, playground equipment and toys in the backyard for the children. He wanted Erin to be the perfect wife and mother, a full-time homemaker waiting for him every day with dinner cooked. He said he pictured driving home from work, and seeing Erin playing with the children in the yard when he pulled up.

"He just wanted a solid family life—for once."

Once again, he fantasized about being part of a unit very much like the Caffeys, except in *his* household, Charlie played the role of Terry, watching proudly in the pew as Erin and the children sang their gospel hymns. But Terry was disturbed by the concept. After all, Erin still *was* a child—a ninth grader who deserved to have a full high school experience without an over-assertive boyfriend pulling her into adulthood.

"The problems with Erin's parents really started when I gave her that ring," Charlie said. "Until that point, it wasn't too bad."

Several days passed before Penny spotted the ring on her daughter's finger at church. She immediately informed Terry, who went searching for Charlie. The teen was playing basketball with some kids outside the fellowship hall, and Terry motioned him over.

Charlie either didn't understand or didn't care about Terry's trepidation. As Erin's father made his point—a little girl shouldn't be parading through school and church with the equivalent of a wedding ring—Charlie shrugged.

"This is totally inappropriate," Terry pronounced. "You're promising yourself to my daughter. Do you realize that she's sixteen years old?"

No longer was Terry willing to mask his disdain for the young man. The Caffeys "didn't like the boy, and were trying to break them up," neighbor Carl Johnson told the Associated Press. "They told me at church they didn't have any use for him."

Erin was told to get rid of the ring—and dispose of her boyfriend.

A short time later, Charlie and his friend Phillip Lewelling pulled into the Sonic parking lot. Erin served each of them soft drinks, but said little. Phillip turned to Charlie in confusion.

"I asked Charlie what was wrong with her," Phillip said. "He told me her parents made them split up. He asked me what to do, and I told him to keep me out of it."

Lewelling's instinct was to advise his friend to forget about Erin. But he assumed—correctly—that the couple would soon reconcile. Once they got back together, Charlie was the type of guy who'd remember the negative comments others had made about Erin. So Phillip was careful not to disparage her.

Phillip excused himself, and went to the bathroom. Along the way, he ran into Erin and paid her for the beverages. "I asked her what was wrong," Phillip said. "She told me the same thing that Charlie told me, that her parents made them split up."

Charlie was wounded and confused. "I always showed her father respect," he asserted after the crime. "I showed him respect even when he didn't to me."

Contemplating his options, Charlie considered persuading Erin to run away with him. She was sure to agree, he reasoned to friends, because she loved him and didn't like her parents. But because of her age, he feared that they might break the law. To clarify the legality of his plan, Charlie visited Kurt Fischer, the chief deputy for the Rains County Sheriff's Department. "I'd been to his house," Charlie said. "I played pool at his house. I went fishing with his sons. I even stopped by there every now and then, just to talk to him. I asked him about Erin. I wanted to know how old she'd have to be to leave her house."

According to Charlie, Fischer affirmed that Erin was a minor, and he shouldn't consider doing anything reckless. Charlie graciously thanked the lawman for his guidance.

Around the same period, Erin discussed her predicament with Rebecca McGahee, the preacher's wife. The two prayed together, and Rebecca repeated what others in the church had told her about Charlie: He seemed unusually possessive. Plus, she was unnerved by Charlie's appearance—the close-cropped hair and camouflage pants. Sure, he was joining the Army. A lot of young men in the community did the same thing after high school. But Rebecca didn't like how Charlie appeared to adopt the whole soldier-of-fortune façade. It hinted of violence and general evil.

She suggested that Erin consider the way her parents felt.

"I know," the girl answered. "I'm confused. I want to please my parents, but I like him."

On January 18, 2008, Charlie and Justin Myers were working on their FFA project when Erin called, hysterical. "The next thing I know, my son's late coming home," Teresa

Myers said, "and I'm furious because I find out he's at the police station with Charlie."

At the Rains County Sheriff's Office, Wilkinson announced that he wished to file a report. "Erin was telling Charlie things that made him think that she was in danger in the house," said Teresa. "And that's why he ended up doing what he did. Because he really, in his mind, believed that he was saving her from real danger."

Deputy Eddie Sisk handed Charlie a document, and he ended up filling out this handwritten statement: "Erin Caffey called me at about 1720 hours. She sounded sad and crying. She stated to me that her mom had hit her, and she had . . . bruised her face. Erin said that she couldn't stay on long because she was worried her mom would hit her again. She called again at 1740 and she confirmed that her mom did hit her. I missed another call at 1758. She left a message on my phone saying that I shouldn't call back because she was afraid her mom would hit her again. I called and talked to her aunt Mary. Mary said that if they need to get her out of harm's way Mary and her husband would take her in until all of this is settled."

Terry later insisted that Erin was never hit by either of her parents.

Deputy Sisk noted that Charlie seemed "very concerned and upset." "Wilkinson stated that he knew Erin and her mother were having problems at home, and the problems were due to Erin seeing him," the officer wrote in his report. "Wilkinson showed signs of anger towards Erin's mother, and does not seem to like her at all. I could sense this during the long conversation I had with him while he provided a written statement."

"Have you seen Erin?" Sisk asked.

"No."

"Well, stay away from her house for a while. If you come by, it'll only cause more problems for Erin."

Charlie said that he wasn't sure what type of injuries Erin had sustained, and promised to call the authorities when he had more information. "Wilkinson contacted me later this date," Sisk wrote, "and advised me that Erin had remedied the problem and I did not need to go out to Erin's house."

When Charlie and Justin returned to the Myers home, Teresa was livid. "You went down and filed a police report, not knowing what the hell really happened?" she questioned Charlie.

"Well, Erin said . . ."

"You could really ruin her parents' reputation. And you don't know what happened! You can't always assume the person giving you the information is giving you the *correct* information."

Terry appeared to be unaware of the fact that Charlie had attempted to call the cops on Penny. And, as before, the Caffeys were trying to work out some type of compromise with their daughter. Charlie was still permitted in their home, but with more restrictions than ever. The boy could visit once a week, but Erin was not allowed to leave the house with him.

One night in February, Penny heard giggling upstairs in Erin's room. She opened the door to find her daughter on her cell—past her phone curfew—talking to Charlie. The Caffeys immediately banned Wilkinson from their house, and confiscated Erin's cell phone and car keys. In the morning, they dropped her off at school. When she was finished with her classes at the end of the day, they were waiting to pick her up.

"They made her quit her job," Charlie said. "They'd take her to school late, made her leave early, all to keep her away from me. She was stuck in the house. They were constantly watching everything she did. The only time we could talk was in school. But I also had my friends pick her up and take her out so we could meet."

At times, Charlie laughed about his talent at circumventing the restrictions. But he never felt victorious. "The fact that Erin's parents would not let them date openly really upset Charlie, and he told me that it bothered him that her parents did not accept him," said his friend Dion Kipp Jr.

Erin felt suffocated. "She told my sister-in-law . . . when she turned seventeen, she was leaving," Terry would tell police. "She didn't like our strict rules. She was going to move in with him, and I said, 'No, you're not going to shack up with someone.'"

By now, either Erin or her parents had revealed the specifics of their conflict to the other members of Miracle Faith Baptist Church. But even those unaware of the strain within the family would have sensed that something was amiss. Both Erin and Penny appeared preoccupied. Penny opted not to go on a women's retreat, claiming that family issues required her to be at home. At a Valentine's Day dinner organized by the youth group, Erin was so inattentive that she neglected to fill the water glasses.

Terry wanted to purge Charlie from any involvement in the family, and the Caffeys started building a case against him. Since they didn't have the Internet at home, Penny—at the urging of her sister—went to the library and looked up Charlie's MySpace page. Because of some modifications done to the account, she did not need a password to gain access. Upon studying the page, it became clear that Wilkinson did not match the depiction Erin had conveyed to her parents.

"She claimed that he was a good Christian boy," Terry said. "He didn't drink. He didn't do anything. . . . He was using bad language, like the F word, cussing."

Erin's cousin, and good friend, Courtney Daily described the firestorm that followed: "He was talking on the Internet . . . that they were going to go and get Erin messed up and wasted and all this stuff. . . . So then her parents found out, and . . . they were just like, 'Well, I don't think you should see Charlie anymore.'"

The Caffeys had Bible study that night, but Terry—tired from work and emotionally drained after his father's recent funeral—had chosen to stay home. "Do you want to talk to her now," Penny asked her husband, "or wait until after church?"

"I'll talk to her now," Terry answered, and walked up to his daughter in the living room. He told her about the

MySpace page, then stipulated, "Either you break up with Charlie, or we're going to do it."

Erin burst into tears, and turned her back to her father.

"It's over," Terry stated. "You're breaking up with him today. I mean, it's over now."

Given their recent history, Terry was ready for a fight, and he had all his points lined up. But Erin did not defy her parents. In fact, she maintained, she'd been thinking of ending the relationship for some time. She just wasn't sure how to cut Charlie loose.

Everyone knew that Erin would see Charlie that evening, when he showed up at youth group. Erin vowed that she'd break up with him at church.

Charlie knew that something was wrong as soon as he arrived. In youth group, Erin went out of her way to sit on the opposite side of the classroom, telling people that she didn't want to be anywhere near her boyfriend. "Erin wouldn't talk to me because her mother was there," he said. "I could tell that [Penny] was watching us."

A rumor spread around the building that Erin was considering dating another boy whose mother was a member of the church, a quiet, bespectacled kid who bore little resemblance—in appearance or attitude—to Charlie Wilkinson.

Sarah Meece remembered Charlie being "pissed off . . . all night long. He even got mad at me because he would not put all four feet of the chair on the floor. . . . He literally fell over, and I told him, 'If you can't keep all four feet [on the ground], you'll have to stand up.'"

Charlie leaped out of his seat and gave Sarah a military salute.

"I said, 'If you want to stand like that, I don't care,'" she said. "I just kept teaching, trying to ignore him . . . because he was very angry at Erin. That's what it came off to us, that he was very angry at Erin."

To Pastor McGahee, whom Charlie liked a lot more than Sarah Meece, the teen seemed to be in a good mood. "He told me he was having a job interview," the preacher said. "He was going to get a job . . . working nights, and he told me he probably wouldn't be here on Wednesdays anymore. . . . He never really seemed upset."

There were few secrets in this incestuous corner of East Texas. At this point, many of the kids in the youth group—and even some of the adults—were gossiping about Erin's plans to break up with her boyfriend. But when McGahee later detailed the night to investigators, the pastor wondered if Erin was truly serious. The girl had been known to tell a tale or two before. And, as anyone who'd witnessed her dramatic solos in church could authenticate, she was adroit at working a crowd. Could all the chatter about a split been an elaborate performance staged to pacify Terry and Penny?

Sarah Meece wasn't sure. "It was really warm. We had really unseasonably warm weather, and we have a big swing set and basketball goal, and all of our kids were outside playing. And all of the sudden, I just hear somebody taking like half the pavement with them. And I immediately go outside and try to find my daughter because she has a real bad habit of bouncing balls in between cars and stuff."

She saw Charlie grinding his truck out of the church parking lot. "I thought he was angry and pulled out," Sarah said.

But McGahee claimed that there was an explanation for the noisy demonstration. After church, Charlie had re-entered the building and told the pastor and some male congregants that the truck wouldn't kick over. McGahee and the men went outside to help Wilkinson push-start the vehicle. "We had pushed him in reverse," the preacher said. "He was trying to get the tires back before it dies. I don't think he was speeding. . . . He always spun the tires and, you know . . . and that's what everybody heard."

As the pastor drove home with his family a short time later, he spotted Wilkinson again, this time near the Caffey home. "He was in front of me," McGahee said. "He turned, going sixty. . . . I thought he was going to turn over. And my kids told me then, 'Well, he's probably mad because he and

Erin broke up. That's why he's driving like that.' But talking to him, he didn't seem upset. . . . He didn't act like they had broke up. I don't know if the whole thing was just a show between them. I don't know."

If Erin was also pretending, she had much of the church convinced. "She told me she was breaking up with him, and that she was scared," said Sarah. "And honestly, I believed her. But Erin . . . was known to sometimes tell one side one thing . . . Her mother and I both said to her, 'If you're going to break up with him, do it where there's people around, and do it here.' And she refused. She said, 'No,' and she just walked out. . . . I even called Terry just to make sure that they got home okay."

The night had ended much as it had begun, with the Caffeys ordering an end to the courtship, and Erin promising to acquiesce. Because she'd missed the opportunity to break up in church, she'd have to do it the next day in school.

"Her parents finally got her to break up with me," Charlie said. "She gave me back the ring, and my dog tags. She gave them back in school. She said, "Here's your stuff. I can't have it. My mom's going to take it away. We can't be together because of them.' We had a heated conversation, and I ended up talking her into taking the stuff back."

Penny's mother, Virginia Daily, said that, even then, Charlie was exerting control over Erin: "She gave him back the dog tags, and told him that she needed to break up, that they were through. . . . And he put the dog tags back, slipped them back into her backpack. . . . Erin said that she did not take them back—he had slipped them into her backpack."

That night, Dion Kipp Jr. went over Charlie's house, hanging out with Wilkinson, his father, stepmother and siblings, as well another close friend, Michael Dickinson. According to Michael, he had moved in with Charlie and his family after the Dickinson parents were busted for drugs. "I don't want to be around that stuff," Michael later explained to police.

"I stayed overnight, and hung out with Michael and Charlie in Charlie's room," Dion said. "Throughout that evening,

Charlie seemed depressed and gloomy. He talked about wanting to get Erin pregnant."

According to Charlie's reckoning, a baby would link him to Erin for life. Plus, once they discovered that their teenage daughter was pregnant, he assumed, Terry and Penny would banish Erin from their house.

Charlie later told police that Erin had an even better idea. "Let's just kill them," he said she suggested.

CHAPTER 5

Charlie claimed that this was not the first time Erin had broached the subject of murdering her parents. About a month earlier, "we were talking about how we didn't get to see each other that much," he said. "We were trying to decide when I would get to see her. And I think the way she said it was, 'I think the only way we can stay together would be if my family was dead.'

"At first, I thought she was joking. But we kept getting pushed farther and farther apart. It keeps escalating, and she talks about it more. And I said, 'You can run away.'"

Because of the pressure from the Caffeys, Charlie had taken this option seriously enough to research it, locating a room available in a friend's house for fifty dollars a month. "I told Erin, 'I got everything worked out,'" he said. "'I'll pay for your clothes, food. You won't have to worry about nothing. When you turn eighteen, you just come out of hiding.' That sounded good to me.

"She said, 'No, they'll search me down and find me.' That's how the conversation went for about a week. She said, 'They're always going to look for me. We can't be together unless they're gone.'"

Erin also allegedly told Charlie that her parents were thinking of relocating her to Arkansas. Charlie said that he'd driven to Arkansas before, and didn't view the move as an obstacle. When he came home on leave from the Army, he'd go directly to Arkansas instead of Emory.

"I tried to explain that to her," he said. "I tried talking her out of [the murder]. But she told me, 'They're still not going to let us see each other. This is what has to be done. This is what we have to do to be together.'"

As time passed, and Charlie demurred from taking this drastic step, one of his friends contended, Erin broke up with him for "not loving" her enough: "Charlie stated the following day, while at school, Erin was all over some other guy. He was very jealous seeing Erin with another guy. . . . They reunited because Charlie agreed to do as he was asked, to protect her, to love her."

In Charlie's depiction of events, he's an emotionally frail teen being worn down over time. But other associates argue that Charlie and Erin were plotting to kill her parents as early as Thanksgiving—some three months before the incident.

Lisa Velasquez, an acquaintance of Charlie's from their childhood days at Emory Baptist Church, told police about running into him on November 18, 2007, at a countywide Thanksgiving service: "During becoming reacquainted with him, he told me that he had a girlfriend that he intended to marry, only that her family did not like him. He said that he guessed he would kill them. I began saying how the Lord opens doors and windows . . . and told him that I would be praying for the situation. But I did not realize that he was seriously considering this action at the time."

Nonetheless, Lisa said that Charlie seemed so bitter that she was uncomfortable speaking to him. When her father passed by, she told him, "Look, it's Charlie." Wilkinson greeted the man, and Lisa used the opportunity to get away from the Army recruit.

During the same period, Erin apparently confided to Rose Brannon, a friend from church, "I think I am going to hire someone to kill my parents." Shortly after Christmas break, Rose told police, Charlie came up to her in the school cafeteria, and introduced the topic as well.

"Charlie Wilkinson . . . told me, 'I think I am going to hire someone to kill Erin's parents,'" Rose said.

Apparently, the couple was less than discreet over who was listening, as they weighed their decision. Two weeks before the crime, Kyle Answorth, a junior at Rains High School, was sitting at an outside table during lunch, when he spotted Erin and Charlie walking by, speaking loudly.

"My parents don't want us to be together," Kyle told police he heard Erin say, "and the only way we can still see each other is if we killed them."

Kyle didn't report the scheme to the authorities because he didn't believe that a conspiracy was truly taking place—especially when, immediately after Erin uttered her comment, the couple began laughing.

Courtney Daily—Erin's cousin and Charlie's friend—had also heard this kind of talk directly from Charlie. "I said, 'What's wrong with you and Erin? Why are y'all fighting?' . . . Because Erin was mad at him all the time, and told me that he was being a butthead . . . and he said that it was her parents . . . and he said that he just wished that they would die, and that he wanted to get somebody to either, I guess, hurt them, or do something to them.

". . . I never thought that he would do something like this. And me and Charlie were like always close. We were like brother and sister. . . . And I told him, I was like, 'How would that solve anything?'

"And he said, 'I don't think I would go off that deep [and] do something like that.'"

That was enough to pacify Courtney, and assuage the fears of others who'd caught wind of the plot. Emory residents tell a story about being in a store, and hearing a group of kids talking about an approaching murder. But because so many teens fantasize about eliminating dictatorial authority figures, the words sounded hollow.

Originally, Charlie insisted, he never intended to harm the Caffeys himself. "I had one guy, whose name I won't say, who said he'd done this kind of thing before, and had gotten away with it," Wilkinson claimed.

In Charlie's mind, the hit man would hunt down Terry and Penny, and take them out. But Wilkinson said that he had an overriding concern. What if Bubba and Tyler were around? Charlie was adamant that he never wanted the children to be harmed.

Erin came up with a satisfactory resolution, Charlie said, by arranging for the boys to stay with Penny's mother on the night the hit man was supposed to strike.

"He would do it for us. He wanted me to be in a public place, where people could see me, so no one could accuse me of anything. But then, Erin's grandpa died, and she called it off."

The sudden death of Terry's father, Clarence "Sonny" Caffey, of a heart attack on February 21, 2008, momentarily pulled the family together. Terry and his father were not particularly close, but no one would have detected this when the Caffeys gathered at Grace Baptist Church in Garland with Terry's two sisters and various other relatives. As always, Penny played "Amazing Grace" on piano, while Bubba and even Terry joined her on harmonica. Only Erin appeared to be off her game, her robust voice uncharacteristically flat. For the first and only time, a less talented cousin overshadowed the pretty teenager. Observed Rebecca McGahee to *Texas Monthly*, "Erin's anointing had lifted. She couldn't sing a lick."

Obviously, the thought of three members of the family dying viciously a week or so later was inconceivable. But Pastor McGahee shared his wife's sense that something was wrong with Erin: "She was very distant at the funeral and after the funeral. And I figured it was because she was close to her granddad. But then, later on, I understood that [the Caffey children] really didn't know their granddad that well."

The girl who used to sweep into youth group, blabbering about her private life now had become "tight-lipped," according to Sarah Meece, "didn't have a lot to say to anybody. . . . I'd be like, 'Are you okay? Is everything okay?' And she'd be like, 'Yeah,' and she would just kind of walk off. . . . She quit kind of being free-spirited . . . with the hair and the clothes and the earrings."

Police would later ask Sarah to elaborate further on the ways that Erin had changed. "She wasn't happy," the youth leader replied.

Analysts who viewed a sample of Erin's handwriting from that period noted that her letters were "very small and still legible. Such writing is a form of attempting to control when you feel helpless, and is referred to as emotional constriction. It relates . . . that Erin likely wanted to simply get away from events starting to spiral around her. In the context of offenses, it at least implies Erin was having second thoughts."

Nevertheless, when the purported hit man didn't work out, Charlie said that Erin encouraged him to go to other sources for assistance. "There's a lot of people who knew about it," he contended. "I ain't giving no names. It could get them in trouble."

What Charlie needed most was a partner who wouldn't back out of the conspiracy and possessed the temperament to pull the trigger. He found him in twenty-year-old Charles Allen Waid, a moody father of two whose older brother often let Wilkinson and other friends crash at his place. Erin had told Charlie that the Caffeys kept $2,000 in a lockbox in the house. Once the parents were dead, Charlie promised, his accomplice could leave with the cash.

Waid was just a year older than Charlie, dark-haired and goateed, but his face was a weary one. He considered his friend's offer, then consented to the arrangement. After all, he had children to support.

Opinions about Waid vary. "He was really friendly," said Rains High School student Vanessa Hendricks. "He just seemed like a nice guy."

But other acquaintances, as well as police, characterize Waid as a young man with a perennial chip on his shoulder. "I met Charles through Charlie," said Wilkinson's friend Dion Kipp Jr. "I did not care for Charles because he always acted like he was some tough guy. . . . We got in several fights over stupid things because he was always trying to prove how tough he was."

According to his academic records, Waid's early years were buoyant ones. A kindergarten report card trumpets, "Charles is doing good," and "I enjoy having Charles in my class." In subsequent years, teachers portrayed him as an average student with above-average writing skills and excellent conduct. By fourth grade, though, he was beginning to slip. That year, his Iowa Test performance was equivalent to that of a student in the eighth month of second grade. In fifth grade, he was functioning at the level of a boy in the seventh month of third grade. By sixth grade, he'd been diagnosed with dyslexia, and his score had fallen to that of a pupil in his first month of third grade.

At the bottom of the Iowa Test that year, his parents received this message: "Charles' national percentile rank of 4 on verbal ability means that, compared with other sixth grade students nationally, Charles scored higher than 4 percent. Charles appears to be well below average in verbal ability."

The educational system became an adversary for Waid, agitating and frustrating him. He looked elsewhere for acceptance and—like Charlie Wilkinson—could be sincere and thoughtful to those he cared about. Said his ex-wife Diane to *TheDailyBS* website after the crime, "Charles was never violent. He had a temper, but never did he hit me or my kids. He was a great guy. That is why I married him. He treated me well, and my children wonderful."

Diane had first dated Charles's brother when she was fifteen after meeting the boy at the Round Up Roller Rink in Grand Saline. The relationship lasted six weeks. But during that time, Diane met Charles at Riverside Mission Church. As with Wilkinson, Waid had a deep belief in God, but couldn't find a community he regarded as a "church family."

"He was very religious," Diane said, "but just didn't attend church like he should have."

Initially, Diane was uninterested in the boy. "He was chubby, annoying and acted like a puppy dog to his brother,"

she said. But a few years later, in 2006, the pair reacquainted themselves at a Lake Holbrook barbecue, where a
pregnant Diane and some friends had repaired after a night
at the Grand Saline Rodeo. Some two months later, Waid
proposed to Diane in front of her parents. On September 23,
2006, they married in her family's backyard. Charles wore
a black cowboy hat and what Diane described as a "Garth
Brooks–type outfit."

Life began moving faster. In October, Diane gave birth to
a boy named Logan. Charles adopted the child as his own.

Despite his youth, Waid seemed committed to sustain-
ing the family. He worked at Wal-Mart, then Basic, an oil-
drilling concern, then a company providing construction
and maintenance services to track and transit systems. However, when Diane learned that she was pregnant again—this
time with a daughter they'd name Haylee—she claimed,
"Charles wasn't ecstatic to learn he was a father. He showed
this by continuing to hang out with Charlie Wilkinson, drinking with him on the weekends."

There was something about Wilkinson that troubled Diane. "Charlie, when he drank, I saw him once get mad and
try to fight another guy," she told KLTV News. She worried
that Wilkinson might blow a circuit one day and beat someone badly enough to end up in prison.

"I didn't want Charles to have anything to do with Charlie," she stated.

Diane also had problems with Waid's mother, claiming
that the woman disliked her daughter-in-law and provoked the
young couple to fight. By the end of 2007, Charles and Diane
had separated. "We argued about everything and couldn't
agree on nothing," she told *TheDailyBS*. "So we decided as a
couple it was best that our kids grew up without Mommy and
Daddy fighting. So we split."

Waid alternated residences. Sometimes, he stayed with his
parents, sometimes with his brother, Matthew, next door, and
sometimes with his new girlfriend, a big-boned, eighteen-year-
old Rains High School student named Bobbi Gale Johnson.

Wide-faced and blonde, Johnson came from a colorful

family. Her grandfather was known in Emory as "Monkey Man" for riding around town on a motorcycle while a simian did tricks on the handlebars.

"He went to our church," one neighbor recounted, "a very nice guy."

Until she met Waid, Bobbi tended to blend with the scenery a bit more. "I'm not a complicated person," she wrote on her YouTube page. "I like to hang out with my best friends and that's pretty much it."

Her hobbies, she mentioned, were football, music ("rock, rap, all that crap") and boys.

Almost to a person, acquaintances described Bobbi as a likeable girl serious about her studies and willing to work hard at her after-school job at Dairy Queen. Retired teacher Susie Collins taught Bobbi in a freshman teen leadership class. "She was a highly motivated student," Collins told the *Tyler Morning Telegraph*, "and was intelligent, articulate and seemed to have a very strong sense of right and wrong—a strong value system."

"I knew Bobbi since the sixth grade," said Vanessa Hendricks. "We sang 'The Star Spangled Banner' together at a pep rally in junior high. We weren't close friends, but we were kind of acquaintance friends. We were both into theater. She was in *Oklahoma!* with me at Rains High School, and *Joseph and the Technicolor Dreamcoat*."

Vanessa's mother, Debbie, recalled interacting with Bobbi backstage during theater performances, characterizing the exchanges as pleasant ones: "I'd say she had above-average intellect, and certainly participated in a lot of activities, after-school activities. She wasn't idle. But I did get the impression that she was insecure about who she was. Like a lot of adolescents, there was some awkwardness. She was a larger girl, and taller than the average boy."

Vanessa concurred with her mother's evaluation. "She definitely had low self-esteem. I mean, people liked her. But she was a big girl just trying to put it all together."

One MySpace entry, from September 2007, illustrates the degree to which Bobbi could marinate in gloom: "i thought i was a good person and that i was fun to be around . . . but obviously im not . . . and one day i hope these ppl grow hearts as big as mine and realize that they were assholes to me."

She titled the passage, "YOU KNOW WHAT F**K YALL . . . F**K THIS . . !!"

In December 2007, her spirits lifted considerably when she started dating Charles Waid. He became a regular at the Dairy Queen, flirting with Bobbi over the counter. Although Diane was still technically married to Waid, friends told her that Bobbi could be a positive influence on him.

"From what I had been told, Bobbi was a great person," Diane said, "someone who overextended herself to do things for other people. I think sometimes Charles took advantage of that."

Breanna Bright worked with Bobbi at Dairy Queen, and noticed that the girl's routine was changing. "We slowly stopped hanging out," Breanna said, "as she became closer with Charles."

Yet few of her old associates initially found this alarming. "Bobbi *did* seem to change a lot," said Vanessa. "It seemed like everything was going better for her. She met Charles, and kind of got happier. She was going to be graduating soon, she was planning to go to college, and it just looked like she had everything going for her."

Bobbi indulged Waid in one of his favorite pastimes, hunting, even buying him a gun for that purpose shortly before his birthday in February 2008.

On Bobbi's MySpace page, her hair was pulled back and her lips slightly puckered. White hoop earrings dangled beside a semi-tilted chin as she gazed into the webcam. Above the photo, in bold black letters, she'd written, "I LOVE CHARLES ALLEN WAID!!!!!!"

She described herself as a nonsmoking "Christian" who didn't mind a drink, and wanted to have children one day. Her heroes: God, the members of the military willing to sacrifice their lives for the United States and her theater director. "Now that is a man of characteristics," she wrote. "He

gives great advise [sic] and when you take it everything
turns out right."

In the section about literary choices, she revealed that—
on a fantasy level, at least—she craved a type of exhilaration
not often found in her bucolic environs, a place she termed
"the middle of nowhere, Texas":

"This may sound a bit wiered [sic] but I like vampire
books because of the fact that there [sic] never boring, something crazy always happens in them, also I like Stephen Kings
books because he is a wiered guy and he make [sic] them
odd."

Her life philosophy: "oh well shit happens!!!!"

In other words, Bobbi had reached a phase in which she
wanted to take risks, leaving fate to dictate the outcome.

She knew that Waid had barriers that hemmed him in
and threatened to choke him—according to Diane, he'd been
taken to court for child support and ordered to pay her $69.00
a week, plus medical insurance. And, while Diane had no ill
will toward Bobbi personally, Charlie's wife believed that
his fixation with his girlfriend had diverted him from his
kids. "He started to date this other girl," Diane told KLTV,
"and everything was more important to him than having anything to do with his children."

But Bobbi was completely devoted to Waid, and ready to
follow him wherever he wished to go.

Suddenly, Bobbi was skipping school and slacking off at
work. "She called in [sick] to work all the time," Breanna
Bright told investigators. "She was late, and always wanting
to leave early." In February, she was fired from Dairy Queen
for excessive absences.

A few days later, she was hanging out in the theater room
at Rains High School—a place where the drama kids lounged
on couches and practiced their lines on a miniature stage—
when she burst into tears.

"She was really freaking out," Vanessa said. "Everybody
was like, 'What's wrong?' And she wouldn't tell us.

"We just assumed it was her job. She worked at Dairy

Queen for, like, *ever*. Now, she didn't know how she was going to pay for college or anything like that."

Vanessa later found out that Bobbi had gone over a mutual friend's house, and began crying there, as well, over her termination, money and college.

Within days, though, Bobbi had a new job, washing dishes at the Oak Ridge restaurant on Lake Fork. Vanessa and the other kids who knew her felt reassured that Bobbi had made some quick alterations to improve her circumstances. The very fact that she cared so much about college was evidence that she was ambitious, and not one to throw her life away.

Certainly, no one expected to learn that Bobbi Gale Johnson had become enmeshed in a murder plot.

CHAPTER 6

Although Charlie was apparently uncomfortable with the likelihood of Erin's younger brothers getting hurt, Erin allegedly had no such misgivings. According to one law enforcement source, she told Charlie, "You'll have to kill the older one because he'll talk. And go ahead and kill the younger one because he's a brat and I don't like him anyway."

There may have been a touch of philanthropy connected to her logic. With their parents gone, Erin did not want the boys placed in foster care, according to Waid and Bobbi. The pair also told *Texas Monthly* that Erin disliked her brothers because they picked on her.

Charlie's attorney said that his client claimed that Erin felt closest to her father, and regarded Penny and the boys as mean. The mutinous teen may have suspected that Penny loved her dutiful sons more than she did her daughter.

One insider claimed that Erin had particular disdain for her youngest brother, Tyler—police said that Charlie told them she only spoke to Bubba, and avoided conversation with the fourth-grader.

While planning the murder, "Erin said she wanted them all gone," alleged Charlie. "And Charles (Waid) told me that there could be no witnesses."

Wilkinson and Waid contemplated various ways to make Erin's family disappear. Among the proposals: planting a story that Terry and Penny had taken the boys to Arkansas, the state where they'd threatened to relocate Erin, and never returned. If enough people accepted this explanation, Charlie and his accomplice assumed that no one would notice that the pair had actually dumped the bodies in the Sabine River, a 555-mile waterway running through the pine forests of Texas, as well as Louisiana's bayou country. Charlie and Waid made an exploratory trek to the Sabine—referred to as the "evil old river" and "mansion of the snake" in Jack Kerouac's 1955 novel *On the Road*—only to discover that the water was too low and not flowing to their liking.

Anyone who ran across Charlie and Erin at Rains High School on Friday, February 29, 2008, realized that something unusual was transpiring. Phillip Lewelling and Charlie were chatting about going mudding the next weekend when Erin suddenly materialized. She appeared happy. With a big smile, she hugged Phillip, then her boyfriend. As Phillip continued the conversation, Erin lingered next to Charlie. Her body language indicated that she wanted Lewelling to make himself scarce.

Erin and Charlie made eye contact, and he nodded and turned to Phillip. "Uh, I have to talk about something with Erin, man."

"Do you want me to leave?"

"Yeah, would you do that, please?"

Erin smiled gratefully at Phillip as he departed, believing the conversation that would ensue involved nothing more momentous than basic boyfriend-girlfriend stuff.

Chelsea Wright had met Erin in seventh grade, and remembered Terry and Penny as youth leaders at church. In fact, she knew the entire family, and had even babysat for Bubba and Tyler when the boys were younger. She enjoyed Erin's company, but was even more fond of Charlie and Bobbi Johnson.

"I had kind of liked Charlie," she told detectives. "He

was really sweet and funny. Bobbi was . . . a good student and friend."

Just before second period, Chelsea was greeting friends in the hallway when she noticed Erin and Charlie involved in deep dialogue. Although their voices were subdued, Chelsea could tell that the couple was arguing.

It was the routine everyone had heard before.

"Well, your parents don't like me anyways," Charlie uttered.

"Well, you know I love you," Erin responded.

It wasn't the first time Chelsea had seen the pair engaged in this type of drama. She gave the scene little thought; she never did. Then, at lunchtime, she saw the couple again, standing by the doors leading toward the Rains High School exit.

"They were . . . yelling at each other," Chelsea said. "I couldn't hear them, but you could tell they were mad. I walked off because they were always breaking up and getting back together. So I thought nothing of it."

Jamie Chamberlin, a junior who considered Charlie a friend but fell out with Erin after leaving the Caffeys' church, happened upon the exact same incident. "I walked in from outside," Jamie told police, "and I heard Erin say, 'I hate you.' "

Dion Kipp Jr. had recently lent Charlie a pair of sneakers. Sometime after school, Dion phoned Charlie and asked him to bring over the shoes. At about six PM, Charlie and his friend Michael Dickinson appeared at Dion's door.

"Charlie gave me my sneakers, and we visited for about fifteen or twenty minutes," Dion told investigators. "He still seemed gloomy and down, and I just assumed it was because of the same thing that always got him depressed, the fact that Erin's parents wouldn't let them be together."

Tommy and Helen Gaston dropped in at the Caffey home around dinnertime, and found Erin in exceptional spirits.

She lifted a Magic Marker and playfully drew on her mother. Penny pretended to be outraged, but was clearly amused. When Erin directed the pen at Tommy, he warned, "Don't do that, gal, or I'll get you."

Tommy laughed. Erin laughed, too.

But always, the specter of Charlie hung over everything.

Terry arrived home from work at nine PM, after the Gastons had left. He'd instructed Erin to break up with Charlie on Wednesday, and he wasn't sure that she'd followed through. The day before, while going through Erin's backpack, Penny had found Charlie's dog tags. When Penny informed Terry, he wanted to see the dog tags himself, then promised to confront Erin when he had a chance.

Now, he approached his daughter. "Hi, Daddy," she said innocently.

"Erin," Terry asked, "did you give Charlie his ring back, like we talked about?"

"Yes," she responded easily.

"And the dog tags?"

"Oh, yes, I gave everything back."

Terry opened his palm and showed Erin the dog tags. "Then, what are these?"

Erin reddened. Terry later told police, "She got angry. . . . She was very upset we caught her in a lie. But I had no idea it could escalate."

Nor could he have ever fathomed that Charlie had called Waid earlier in the day to arrange a meeting to plan the murders. As Erin argued with her parents, Wilkinson and Waid were in a car together, charting out the night ahead.

After considering a variety of options, the two intended to sneak into the Caffey home and kill everyone in their sleep—except for Erin, of course, who'd manage to "escape" from the carnage. Charlie later told police that he was supposed to murder the parents, while Waid slaughtered Bubba and Tyler. Then, the cohorts would stuff the bodies in a van, and ditch the vehicle somewhere.

Charlie had Guard duty the next day at eight AM in Green-

ville. He planned to report as if nothing out of the ordinary
had occurred. When the Caffeys' bodies were eventually discovered, and detectives began probing the activities of those
who might have had a motive, it would appear that Charlie
was with his National Guard unit at the approximate time that
the crime had occurred.

No one would even think to search for Waid since he had
virtually no connection to the family.

Waid offered to bring along two swords, each three and a
half feet long, including an eight-inch handle embellished
with gold outskirts. Although the blades—diamond-shaped
with two edges—were sharp, they were decorative items
that he'd once ordered out of a magazine. "We used them to
play sword fight in the backyard," Charlie said. "We decided
to take them to the house because we didn't have a gun at
first.

"Then, I took my father's twenty-two." It was a Browning
pistol that used long rifle bullets. Charlie generally kept the
weapon at Waid's house in a black sheath. "We'd use it to
shoot cans and targets—you know, country boy stuff."

Charlie wanted to shoot everyone in the dark, barely looking at the victims: "We thought we'd go in there and—bam,
bam—kill everyone while they were sleeping." He presumed
that the kids would remain deep in slumber while the parents
were being murdered downstairs.

"A twenty-two is not very loud," Charlie explained.

The pair only had eleven bullets. So they opted to bring
the swords anyway—in case alternative weapons were required.

As they reflected on the challenge ahead, the duo concluded that the notion of abandoning a van full of cadavers
might be difficult. Terry and Penny would have to be wrapped
and dragged through the house to the vehicle, leaving blood-
stains and other forensic evidence. The boys' bodies would
actually have to be carried down a flight of stairs. Waid and
Wilkinson settled on instead setting the house ablaze after
the murders. Under ideal circumstances, firefighters arriving

at the scene would find the corpses charred beyond recognition. No one would look for bullet wounds or slash marks. After all, people died in house fires all the time.

Every day, Waid's mother dropped him off at the Pay-N-Serve convenience store in Alba, where he'd eat breakfast before someone else gave him a ride to his job. Sometime in February, the clerk told police, Waid had taken "a great deal of interest in the Zippo lighter display." Around Valentine's Day, he purchased a lighter adorned with blue dolphins. About a week later, he bought a lighter with the same style of Remington Realtree camouflage found on hunting rifles. The third lighter was made from silver pewter and embellished with a cow skull decoration.

Most likely, burning down the house would not require anything more than a single lighter. By the time firefighters turned up at the remote location, the building—and everything inside—would be scorched. With three lighters, Waid felt more than prepared.

Charles and Bobbi Johnson enjoyed what appeared to be an agreeable dinner at a Chili's chain restaurant in the town of Sulphur Spring. Then, Waid drove his girlfriend's car, a 2005 silver Dodge Neon, to Lake Fork, where he dropped her off at her job. Charlie was with Waid when they arrived at Bobbi's job at nine PM. Since she wouldn't finish her shift for another hour, the boys left, dressed like two young men whiling away the night in East Texas and attracting little attention. At ten PM, Waid returned alone and drove Johnson to his brother Matthew's house.

Matthew was lounging outside with his common-law wife, Emerald Blair, who was in the midst of a difficult pregnancy. Emerald was feeling nauseous, but noticed that Bobbi was in a very good mood, mentioning a raise she'd received at her new job.

Bobbi also made it a point to state that she was very happy with Charles.

The conversation didn't last long; Emerald was about to throw up. Before she vomited, she caught a glance of Waid.

"Charles looked preoccupied," she later told police, "but not upset."

Waid's facial expression was no different than what Emerald noticed close to every day.

That kid always seemed to have something on his mind.

CHAPTER 7

Although Erin had been a challenge the last few months, Terry and Penny went to sleep feeling optimistic. Terry had recently interviewed for a higher-paying job and apparently impressed the employer. As the couple lay in bed, Terry informed his wife that the man "basically said I could have it if I wanted it."

Penny was encouraging, as Terry's eyes began to droop. He and Penny would pray about whatever decision he made—and calculate whether a new job, and the challenges it entailed, was best for the family.

With the Caffeys, the children always came first.

After visiting his brother, Charles Waid and Bobbi Johnson drove over to the Maxi-Mart to grab something to eat, then stopped by her apartment in the town of Point, where the Caffeys had lived when the kids were growing up.

Earlier in the night, Breanna Bright—Bobbi's friend from Dairy Queen—had run into Matthew Waid while shopping, and Charles's older brother mentioned that a group of people would be hanging out at his house later that night. Breanna was invited by stop by. Just after eleven PM, Breanna was driving when her cell phone rang.

It was Bobbi. "She asked me what I was up to," Breanna

told police. "She didn't really sound like Bobbi, so I asked her what was wrong, and she said she was just tired."

Breanna didn't like talking on her cell phone while steering her vehicle around the dark country roads, and promised to call back later. But she became sidetracked, and decided not to stop by Matthew's after all.

Even if Breanna had called back, though, it's unlikely that Bobbi would have been able to chat. Soon Charlie joined the couple, and everyone's attention shifted to the murder plot. The boys had long-sleeved shirts and rubber gloves—the latter a contribution from Bobbi. At two AM Erin called Charlie's cell and told the group to meet her at the end of her driveway. She slid into Bobbi's car, and the four drove around, working out the details.

During the hourlong ride, Charlie said he made one last effort to convince Erin to run away with him, but she ardently argued for killing her parents instead. "She said, 'It has to be done,'" Charlie said. "'It's the only way we can be together.' The same thing over and over."

In an interview with *Texas Monthly*, Bobbi reinforced this account: "Charlie kept saying, 'Are you *sure* you want to do this? And she said, 'Why are you asking me this? If you love me, you'll do it.'"

He later complained that the murders had been Erin's idea, but all responsibility for the crime "got pushed off" on him and Waid.

He maintained that he was still disturbed by her insistence that her brothers be killed.

"Why do we have to hurt the kids?" he claimed he asked one more time.

"Little ones talk," Waid allegedly answered. "I came to kill tonight and I want my money, so let's do it."

The presence of Bobbi bewildered the others. She *knew* Erin, after all, but they were hardly more than acquaintances. Waid had a profit motive, and Charlie and Erin wanted to end the interference in their relationship. But Bobbi really didn't belong anywhere near the crime scene.

When police later investigated the crime, Charles Waid's

rationale was quickly apparent. "There was some loyalty that Charles Waid had for Charlie Wilkinson," said Texas Ranger John Vance. "He wanted to help him out, saw an opportunity to make some money. You've got to wonder if the fantasy was there, too—'What is it like to kill a person?'"

Bobbi Gale Johnson's motives were more perplexing. Enraptured by Waid, Bobbi was eager to soil her hands alongside her lover. Noted Vance, "I kind of liken it to Bonnie and Clyde—'We're going to carry this all the way through, and we're not going to get caught.'"

Before doubling back to the Caffey house, the group pulled into a cemetery. There, Charlie said, the others tried to convince Bobbi to leave.

"We all told Bobbi that she didn't have to come with us. But she said she wanted to be there for Erin, to comfort her when her family wasn't around anymore."

Said Charlie's lawyer Ron Ferguson, "She didn't want to be left out of it."

Bobbi painted a different picture, telling *Texas Monthly* that Charlie was not the thoughtful friend he depicted himself to be. "I just wanted to go home," she contended, "but Charlie said it was too late, that I was already involved. He said that if anybody said anything to anyone, that person would be taken care of. I was scared shitless."

Charlie started to psych himself up. He'd been in the Caffey home enough to know its layout by heart: a 624-square foot, one-and-a-half story, single-family dwelling with a pier beam foundation. There were two points of entry—one on the east side of the home, near the southeast corner, the other on the north side, near the middle wall. Terry and Penny slept in the bedroom located downstairs, in the northwest corner. As always, the two doors, leading into different sides of the bedroom, were closed.

The upstairs loft section of the building extended the same approximate distance as the lower portion. But because of the slanting, barnlike roof—covered with sheet metal—the north and south walls of the upper section limited the amount of space that could be utilized as living areas. Just inside the door on the northside of the building were the stairs leading to the children's rooms.

The plan, Charlie said, was "to walk in like you own the place . . . tap, tap, tap, cut, cut, cut." Authorities would be chilled by his comment that he intended to take care of business "like any ole gunslinger would do when he was robbing a bank."

Bobbi and Erin drove a short distance away and parked, waiting for the call to return to the house. Johnson told the *Times* of London that Erin excitedly mentioned that she "couldn't believe it is actually going to happen."

While Bobbi turned off the ignition, Charlie and Waid were lumbering through the Caffeys' front door. There was no need to break a window or pick a lock; Erin had left the entrance open. Waid and Wilkinson carried two samurai swords and the .22 that belonged to Charlie's father. There were ten rounds in the clip and one in the chamber.

Whatever uncertainty Charlie claimed to have harbored had to be pushed aside. With Waid beside him, there was no way to turn back or change his mind. Still, Charlie admitted that he was scared, as his eyes adjusted to the darkness. "Who wouldn't be?" he said. "But I told myself, 'This is what I have to do for us to be together.'"

The pair moved through the house, entering the utility room located just south of the bedroom. Suddenly, they burst through the bedroom door, startling the sleeping couple. "I remember the doorknob hitting the washing machine and making a loud sound," Terry said. "There was a little bit of light from the kitchen, and I saw a face, but didn't realize it was Charlie at the time."

In his confusion, Terry had initially wondered if one of his children had woken up from a nightmare. Now, he thought that burglars might be raiding the home.

Penny was on the south side of the bed, closest to the

intruders. Charlie fired, then his gun jammed. He handed the .22 to Waid, who aimed at the Caffeys and blasted off two more shots.

"I can still see in my mind the horror that unfolded that frightful night," Terry wrote in a memoir published on his ministry's website. "I can hear Penny's screams as we were both riddled with bullets. I can hear the shots and sounds of that night as we both fought for our lives."

Charlie gave little thought to Terry's feelings; the teen was too consumed with his own thoughts. "I was thinking, 'It's over now,'" Charlie said. "'We can be together now.' That's pretty much what was going on in my head. This is what Erin wanted done so we could be together. I don't know *how* I got to that point."

But it wasn't as easy as Charlie hoped. When he envisioned the murder beforehand, he'd imagined the parents dying instantly. The next phase would be moving upstairs to take care of the boys. Now, as he surveyed the scene, he realized that Penny was still alive.

"She wasn't dead," he said. "I knew she'd been shot, but it wasn't a fatal wound. None of her major arteries were hit. And there weren't that many bullets left in the gun."

Penny was bleeding, and in agony. Neither boy derived pleasure from the sight. They left the room for a quick conference. Terry would later tell police that although he never saw a partner with Charlie, he heard another person in the house, and a conversation, in both whispered and normal tones, coming from the living room.

"Finish her off," Waid said. "Don't make her suffer."

When Charlie reentered the room, sword in hand, he saw that Penny had made it out of the bed, and fallen to her knees. He stood in front of her, rearing back his arm, then slicing forward, cutting her throat. Her body dropped at the foot of the bed. According to the coroner, the sad, lonely boyfriend who just wanted acceptance from the Caffey family had hacked Penny so hard that she'd been nearly decapitated.

Charlie and Waid had no idea that Terry was still alive; he would later tell police that he heard Penny gurgling before she expired. Just before the attackers left the bedroom, Terry said that he felt someone kick at his feet, for any sign of movement. "I remember them breathing real heavy," he said. "I thought they had to hear me breathing. Then, I heard the gun being reloaded. *Click. Click.* I clenched my eyes and said, 'God, make it be quick.' I was waiting for the back of my head to be blown off. But I just heard those boots walking off."

As Charlie and Waid headed upstairs, they were also listening to footsteps—the panicked sounds of Bubba and Tyler attempting to find a safe place to hide. Erin's younger brothers were supposed to be slain in their sleep. Now, the boys were awake, and aware that something dire was occurring downstairs. The strategy was falling apart.

"It didn't exactly work," Charlie reflected. "The boys woke up and ran into Erin's room. So then, we had a whole different situation."

Wilkinson quickly looked at Waid. "Go get the kids," Charles ordered.

Why couldn't they just grab Erin's clothes and flee? "I don't want to do this," Charlie claimed to have said. "I can't do this."

"You have to," Charlie said that his partner demanded. "We can't leave any witnesses."

Charlie said that Waid threatened to leave his accomplice alone in the house if he wasn't willing to complete the mission.

Holding his sword, Charlie opened the door to Erin's room, with Waid following behind him on the stairs, grasping the .22. "It was at that point, when I saw both of the boys, that I said, 'I shouldn't be doing this,'" Charlie stated. "'This is wrong.'"

Charlie noticed that Bubba was carrying a knife, but he was tentative about it; the thirteen-year-old clearly lacked the capacity to thrust the weapon through another human's flesh.

Charlie never had an issue with the Caffey boys. They'd built bonfires together, and he enjoyed their company. If

Terry and Penny hadn't been so obstinate, Bubba and Tyler would have eventually become Charlie's brothers-in-law. He knew he had the aptitude to love them the way he loved the children in his own family.

Now, he claimed, he couldn't even look in their faces.

"Get out of that room," Charlie commanded. "Get in your beds." If the kids were lying down, it would be so much easier to get this thing done with. But the brothers refused to cooperate. As they left Erin's room and stood in the balcony area, a frightened Bubba kicked at his sister's boyfriend, hitting him in the arm, and Waid fired upward from his vantage point on their stairs, striking the boy in the head and splattering blood everywhere.

It was a direct hit. Bubba hit the ground hard and didn't move.

Charlie said that Waid followed this up by stabbing Tyler with the sword. But Wilkinson admitted thrusting his own sword through the eight-year-old as well.

The intruders turned, leaving the bloodied children for dead.

Charlie maintained that he immediately regretted hurting the youngsters: "Of course, I feel bad. They were younger than me. They didn't get a chance to live. They didn't get a chance to understand what's really going on out there. If I could go back, I would rather give myself up than them."

After his assailants went upstairs, Terry tried to push himself off the floor and crawl over to his wife. The timeline is uncertain because, from the moment he'd been shot out of the bed, he'd drifted in and out of consciousness. Blood flowed from his jaw, nose and mouth. He couldn't feel the right side of his body. He was horrified by the gory scene and too weak to help his wife—Terry would write that he knew she was "already gone"—or pursue the killers.

Before he lost consciousness again, he claimed to have heard Bubba screaming, "No, Charlie! No! Why?! Why are you doing this?!"

The child's pleas were followed by more gunshots. Terry

desperately wanted to rescue his children, but was practically dead himself. Remarkably, he managed to rise to a kneeling position. Then, instead of standing and halting the massacre upstairs, he passed out.

Charlie and Waid had more to do—robbing the house, then setting it on fire. But first, Charlie borrowed Bobbi's cell phone from Waid and called Erin.

"Drive up to the house," he told her, "and kill the motor. And don't come in. Just stay outside and wait for us."

According to Bobbi, Erin had one pointed questioned for her boyfriend: "Are they dead? Are they dead?"

Earlier that day, when Erin was certain that this was the night when her parents would die, she'd packed a small bag. It was exactly where Erin said it would be, and Charlie gathered it up. As per Erin's instructions, Charlie found a jewelry case and opened it, removing necklaces and earrings. Wilkinson and Waid had the combination to Terry's lockbox—stored under the parents' bed—and procured $160 in cash. In Terry's wallet, there was another hundred dollars. Approximately $115 were located in Penny's wallet. Change was grabbed—even the Caffey sons' allowance. A safe that belonged to Erin's grandfather could not be infiltrated; it needed a key. Waid took it, hoping to open it later.

For whatever reason, the duo neglected to seize the few weapons the Caffeys kept at home: Bubba's pellet gun, and a BB gun Terry had received for a Christmas gift a few years earlier.

All in all, the take was far lower than the $2,000 Waid had been promised.

In a highly symbolic gesture, Charlie made sure that he rummaged through Penny's purse until he found his dog tags—the same dog tags Penny had swiped from Erin during their argument, earlier in the night. As distasteful as he found the crime, he looked forward to handing the tags to Erin with the knowledge that her parents could never wrest them away again.

According to Charlie, Waid went upstairs one more

time to verify that Bubba and Tyler were indeed dead. Charlie entered the downstairs bedroom to check on the parents.

Wilkinson claimed that when he entered the room, he was stunned to discover that Terry was still alive. The man lay on the ground, making slight gasping sounds.

"What have I done?" Charlie allegedly thought to himself.

Charlie said that he couldn't muster up the vigor to finish off his girlfriend's father; the guy looked like he was going to die in a few minutes anyway. If not, he'd certainly be consumed in the fire. Wilkinson said that he looked away from the man, and left the room.

Waid was waiting outside. "Are they dead?" he allegedly asked.

"Yeah, Charles, they're dead."

Holding the lighters that Waid had purchased at the Pay-N-Serve, the intruders began setting fires. Bedsheets, clothes, furniture, even food items in the pantry were ignited.

The boys left the home, their arms filled with Erin's belongings and the items the pair had stolen. As they stepped onto the gravel driveway, according to Charlie, they were surprised to see Bobbi leaving the vehicle, as if she wanted to cast a glance inside the house and see how everything was going.

"Get back in the car," Waid demanded.

Bobbi looked at the boys, and noticed a bloody sword. "It's something I'll never forget," she said. "They put it in the trunk. . . . I was freaking out, but Erin was jumping up and down in her seat, excited."

In fact, Bobbi told *Texas Monthly,* Erin wanted to get out of the car and check on all the bodies herself—gushing that she was finally "free."

Said Charles Waid, "She was happier than a kid on Christmas morning."

Erin would later dispute this, claiming that, while she

and Bobbi cried, Waid and Wilkinson were high-fiving each other.

The fire spread quickly, and the perpetrators took off. On the east side of the house, flames engulfed a 1971 Chevrolet pickup registered to Terry and a 2004 Chevrolet van registered to both parents. The 2006 Ford van Terry used for his job met the most dramatic end when the radiant heat surrounded the cylinders used to administer oxygen to home health care patients. The tanks blew up, rattling the leaves, the trees and the grass, and casting a startling glow in the sky.

The emergency workers who'd converge at the scene never imagined that the secluded dwelling had been the sight of a mass murder. Nor could any of the perpetrators—including Charlie, who claimed that he'd seen his girlfriend's father grasping for life—have conceived that Terry would possess the fortitude to take flight.

With his arm hanging limp, the result of a bullet that pierced a nerve, Terry snapped to his senses, as the picture window in the living room detonated. Flames inched across the floor and up the walls. Laying on the bedroom floor, between the bed and the wall, he pulled himself to his knees and, then, to a standing position. His first instinct was to help Penny, and he threw himself across the bed to awaken her. Instead, he saw his wife drooped against the wall with her throat cut.

"It was a horrific scene," he told *The Dallas Morning News*. "I had never seen so much blood in my life."

Terry took stock of his surroundings. The tip of the bed was ablaze, as well as the closet on the eastern wall. The bitter smell of fire stung Terry's nostrils. He attempted to breathe and gulped down smoke. It was impossible to see through the black haze. Stepping over his wife's lifeless body, he staggering forward through the south bedroom door into the utility room, then the bathroom, pressing his hands across the hot walls. There, too, the closet was on fire. He thought about racing through the door leading to the kitchen area and getting his children. But when he closely observed the setting, he was shaken by the image of a "rolling fire" in the living room.

At that point, Terry believed that Erin was also upstairs with her brothers. His mind raced, trying to conceive a way to help his kids. As the flames grew, he resigned himself to the fact that the task was impossible.

Terry knew that Charlie Wilkinson had shot him, and he was determined to live long enough to tell the authorities. He turned, his fingers grasping the shower curtain, but his feet gave way below him. Terry fell into the bathtub, but continued to scramble for some type of escape, running his hands up the wall until he found the window above the tub.

"I pushed . . . the lock," he said. "I couldn't get it to open. So I'm pounding on it, and pushing up, and all of the sudden, it shoots up."

He stuck his head out the window and let the cool morning air sweep the smoke from his lungs. Perhaps this was the rejuvenation he needed to turn around and save his family. But when he looked back, reality again set in. "It was no use," he said. "I pushed my body out the window, and let the weight carry me to the ground."

Later, he would contemplate the fact that he'd been surrounded by flames, but never burned, and equate his experience to that of the slaves escaping from Pharaoh's Egypt on a strip of land while the seas parted on both sides. Landing near a propane tank, he deliberated his options. At any moment, he feared, the killers could slink up behind him and put a final bullet in his head. Suddenly, there was another blast—more windows blowing out. How long would it be before the propane tanks exploded, too? He couldn't stay near the house. Crawling under a barbed-wire fence, Terry decided to go west until he landed in Tommy Gaston's doorway.

"Even though I saw my wife dead, and there was no doubt the kids were gone," he told the *Times* of London, "I just thought that if I could get to Tommy and Helen's, they could get help, and everything would be okay."

He shifted through the woods, but couldn't move for long. "I thought my lungs were collapsed," he said. "I couldn't breathe. I had blood coming out of my nose, my ears, my mouth."

Finding a log, Terry rested, leaving a coat of blood for the investigators who would re-trace his steps. Looking back, he saw the flames rising, devouring the house. Where were the firefighters? Where were the police? Inside, Penny's body was burning. His children were probably also dead, he thought. He was the only one left to tell their story.

If he stayed in one place, he wondered, would he pass out again? Then, would wolves eat him? How long would it be before someone discovered his body? Would Charlie Wilkinson and the guy who helped him slaughter a household ever be found and brought to justice?

Terry kept going, falling and rising, slipping into the creek and fighting his way out, peering over his shoulder to see that the flames were now rising above the treetops. The Gaston home wasn't that far away. And Terry was getting closer.

"I remember standing up and looking back at the house one more time," he said. "And then, I turned my back, and never looked back again."

A groggy Tommy Gaston answered Terry's knock on the door. Tommy and his wife had lived on and off in the area since 1951, and never witnessed anything as disturbing as the sight of their neighbor bleeding from so many places that the older man couldn't detect specific wounds. Tommy looked outside and saw flames shooting up from the Caffey residence.

"He told me Charlie had done it," Tommy said, "and that there was somebody else with him—he didn't know who. I asked about Penny and the kids. That's when I went out of it. I was thinking, 'Is this really happening? No, Lord, not Penny.'"

Just as the Caffeys always called the Gastons Ma and Pa, the Gastons loved Terry like a son. Vowing not to let his boy die, Tommy picked up the phone and dialed 911.

"This is Tommy Gaston. We have a man that's been shot. He's out here at my house now."

"Okay," the operator answered. "Stay on the line." The call was forwarded. Beeping, then ringing was heard, before another voice came over the receiver.

"Nine-one-one, what's the address of your emergency?"

Gaston was feeling frenzied, fearful that his friend would pass away right in front of him, and not much in the mood to follow instructions. "This is Tommy Gaston," he repeated. "I've got a man that's been shot out here at my house."

"Okay, so he's been shot?"

"Yes."

"Where are you?"

"2320." Tommy glanced at Terry, becoming more fretful by the second. "Wait a minute, hang on. It's 2063 County Road 2320, 2370 . . ."

By now, the emergency appeared so grave that other dispatchers joined the call. "County, are you on the line?" asked the operator.

"Yes, ma'am."

The operator concentrated on Tommy again. "So you're in Alba?"

In the background, Tommy could hear a conversation: "The complaint is that he has a victim in his house that's been shot."

"Sir, are you there? Hello?"

"Hello?" Tommy replied.

"Sir, can you hear me?"

"Hello?"

"Sir, can you hear me?"

Tommy raised his voice slightly. "Yes!"

". . . I have a few questions that I need to ask you, okay? We're going to get you an ambulance. I need you to stay on the line with me. Okay? Are you with the patient now?"

"Yes."

"How old is he?"

Interestingly, the question did not fluster Tommy. He knew the Caffeys well enough to instantly provide a response. "He's forty-one."

"Is he conscious?"

"Yes."

"And is he breathing?"

"Yes."

The operator wanted to make sure that Tommy was still engaged. "Sir?"

"Yes."

"Okay, I'm sorry. When did this happen?"

"I don't know. Just a little bit ago. We've also got a house on fire out here?"

The statement was confusing. Was Tommy's house burning down while a gunshot victim lay on his floor?

"And the house is on fire?" the operator repeated. "Is the assailant nearby?"

Terry let out a pained moan. Tommy didn't know how long his friend could endure. "Uh, I think . . ."

"Is the person who shot him still nearby, sir?"

Tommy's mind was racing. Why couldn't they just send an ambulance and ask questions later? "Yes," he answered in an exasperated tone, having not fully listened to the question. "He's right here with me!"

"You shot him."

Tommy was incredulous, and he was starting to get angry. "*No!*" he proclaimed loudly. "I didn't. I don't have any more details! I've got to hang up and help him!"

"Sir, I have to ask you these questions," the operator tried to explain. "Okay, is there any serious bleeding?"

"Yes, he's bleeding."

Once again, Terry moaned.

"Is he completely awake?"

"Yes. He's awake!"

"Okay. What part of the body was injured?"

Tommy looked at Terry—blood on his face, and stained

into his clothes with mud, grass and dirty water from his 300-yard trek from the burning home. "I don't know!" Tommy shouted. "I don't know! But I've got to go because . . ."

"Sir," the operator insisted, "I need to know where he was shot."

"Okay. What?"

"I need to know where he was shot?"

Tommy wasn't a medical professional. Why all these questions now? When was somebody going to show up to help Terry? "*I don't know!*" he hollered over the phone.

The operator was persistent. "He's right here, and you don't know where he was shot at?"

"Yes."

"Where is he bleeding?"

"*He's bloody all over!*"

"He's bloody all over?"

"Yes!"

"Okay. Do you know what he was shot with?"

Now, Tommy was supposed to be a detective *and* a forensics specialist? "*No!*"

"Is there more than one wound?"

"I don't know!"

"All right, sir."

If nobody was going to show up, Tommy would tend to Terry's injuries himself. "Give me the towel, Helen," he told his wife.

The operator asked Tommy to examine Terry's injuries. Terry moaned again.

"Helen," Tommy repeated, "give me my towel." He hung up the phone.

"Sir?" the operator asked. "Hello?"

"This is county," said the other voice on the line.

"Did they hang up?"

"Yes, ma'am."

"You got officers en route?"

"Yes, ma'am."

Within minutes, the Caffey property would transform

from a desolate outpost to a crime scene so noteworthy that newscasters as far away as Dallas, Atlanta and New York would familiarize the public with the names Terry Caffey and Charlie Wilkinson.

CHAPTER 8

When Rains County sheriff's deputy Charles Dickerson finally arrived at Tommy's home, Terry used every reserve of strength he'd saved to stress that his family needed help. There were four people inside the burning house, he emphasized, Penny, Bubba, Tyler and Erin.

Detective Richard Almon met Terry as he was being placed in the ambulance. In a barely audible voice, Terry told the officer, "I think I'm going to die, and I need to tell someone who did this—who killed me and my family."

Terry said he'd woken up to someone standing in the bedroom with a shotgun. He claimed that when he lifted an arm to protect himself, both he and Penny were shot. Terry spoke about blacking out, then waking again to hear Bubba shouting the name Charlie before more gunshots were fired.

It was important that law enforcement knew the identity of Charlie, Terry said—Charlie James Wilkinson, a young man he described as Erin's "ex-boyfriend."

As Almon listened, Terry recalled passing out another time, then coming to in a smoke-filled house. His first priority was saving the children, he asserted. Only when he realized that this effort was futile did he burst through the bathroom window into the woods, heading toward the lifeline the Gastons provided.

In the midst of the confusion, emotion and general chaos, Almon, a self-assured Navy vet, seemed to be the one person able to block out unnecessary distractions and take control of the crime scene. He immediately ordered the start of a crime-scene log. The name of every person who set foot on the property was to be documented, and crime-scene tape would secure the entire area. Officers were dispatched to major intersections to control traffic and direct arriving authorities to wherever they were needed.

Of course, the most important job at the moment was ensuring that Terry remained alive. Before the ambulance doors closed, Helen Gaston climbed in next to her neighbor, promising not to leave him. He held her hand, and she clutched it as a mother would a son's all the way to East Texas Medical Center.

Despite the fact that he was admitted to the hospital in critical condition with blood seeping from his back, right upper arm, right cheek and left ear, Terry was conscious and alert.

"Caffey was in a lot of pain," Tyler police officer Donald Malmstrom wrote in his offense report. "I was informed by hospital personnel that the gunshot wound to his face had penetrated the sinus cavity, which was causing him a lot of pain and his face was beginning to turn purple and swell. . . . He was in a lot of pain from the gunshots in his back and his arm. He told me at one point that his hand was numb."

Terry's mouth was dry. But because of the tubes running in and out of his body, physicians had yet to allow him to lubricate his throat with liquids. The man was obviously a victim. Still, investigators had to be cynical. He'd also survived. It was not uncommon during a crime of passion for, say, a husband to inflict an injury on himself in order to allay suspicion that he played a role in his wife's demise. Was Charlie Wilkinson really the perpetrator? Or was Terry Caffey involved in the massacre of his family?

Officer Malmstrom was asked to take nail scrapes from Terry's fingernails. But his fingernails were too short to accomplish this. To document their dilemma, police photographed Terry's fingertips. Malmstrom then used a sterile swab, one for each hand, to scrub the fingertips, just below the nail. The swabs were then placed into a container and sealed.

Yes, Terry was weak. But investigators had interviewed people in his condition who'd used whatever energy they had to attempt to cover the truth. In Terry's case, there were no such efforts. It was obvious that he wasn't worried about what the DNA evidence would yield.

Charlie said that he wasn't happy when he reentered Bobbi's Dodge Neon. "I was feeling down," he maintained. "I didn't want to think about what I'd done. When I got into the car, I told Erin, 'It's over. It's over. We can be together.' She said, 'Thank God.' I wouldn't say she was happy, but she wasn't sad. I guess she was happy it was over."

As the two couples drove away from the burning house, Charlie said that Erin studied his features. He was pondering the events of the night, trying to grasp what had occurred inside the Caffey home, and the extent to which he'd gone to preserve his romance. "She talked me into going along with it," he claimed. "I don't know how to explain it. You can't explain how other people feel."

Erin seemed concerned about Charlie's demeanor. Although she'd been the catalyst of the massacre, he said, she now worried whether Charlie would think less of her.

"You're not going to be different now, are you?" he claimed Erin asked. "You're not going to change because of this?"

Charlie remained introspective. But he managed to blurt a less than reassuring, "No."

The co-conspirators agreed to drive around for a while because they didn't want another motorist to notice the car going directly from the Caffey home to Matthew Waid's trailer. Yet no one in the vehicle really expected the police to come looking for them. The closest neighbors, the Gastons, were an elderly couple who were probably asleep, Charlie surmised, and lived far enough away not to hear the gunshots. By the time they woke up, the house would be burnt to the ground, and Charlie would be in Greenville with his National Guard unit. The other neighbors were barricaded from the Caffeys by woods. It was highly unlikely that anyone saw Charlie and his accomplices pull up, or the two couples leave.

If the Caffeys weren't all dead when Wilkinson and Waid left the house, they were dead now. As difficult as it had felt to murder the family, the strategy of leaving no witnesses had been the best one.

Who was going to talk, after all? Waid was good for his word. Bobbi was too involved—and too loyal to Charles—to say anything. And Erin—well, Erin knew how to charm, and tell a story with sincerity. Whatever she came up with, people would believe her.

Texas Ranger John Vance would later find himself bewildered by this cavalier attitude. "That's the one thing I questioned—what were their plans afterwards?" he said. "Because they did work out a lot of details. Some stuff they had to do on the fly, but the majority of stuff they had pre-arranged. I wondered, 'What was your next step? What were your plans for tomorrow?' They didn't have any. Everything was thought out up until that point. The 'what if' afterwards was not."

Vance had noticed this pattern with other offenders who, their felonious intent notwithstanding, lacked the requisite criminal experience to ponder the long-term repercussions of their actions: "Most of these criminals—especially the younger criminals we come across—think only of the crime itself, and not either how to hide themselves, or how to hide the crime, or how to blend into society afterwards. That just isn't thought through."

Nonetheless, Charlie took the minimal precautions to separate himself from the crime scene. Tanis Condit was one of a group of friends crashing in Matthew Waid's battered blue trailer that night. Tanis woke up at 4:30 AM to get ready for his railroad job and stepped into the living room. There, Charlie's housemate, Michael Dickinson, was asleep in the love seat, and Charlie and Erin were hanging out. Charlie handed Tanis the .22.

"Could you clean this?"

Tanis nodded. "Sure. When I get home from work."

Charlie's eyes glinted. If police ever tested the weapon, they'd find Tanis's prints.

Despite the hour, Matthew Waid was also awake. As Charlie and Erin headed for a bedroom, Wilkinson asked Matthew to wake him up for Guard duty.

"I missed last month 'cause I slept late," Charlie said. "I really can't miss two months in a row."

"Don't worry, Charlie. I'll wake you up."

Soon, Matthew returned to his bedroom, where, after a night of feeling queasy, his pregnant girlfriend had finally fallen asleep. "Nothing seemed wrong with anyone," he told police. "Nobody seemed jumpy or anything."

Charlie grabbed a bottle of bourbon and took a few swigs to numb his memories. The liquor quickly delivered its desired effect. He was proud of the fact that he wasn't using up whatever alcohol Matthew might have stashed in the house. Matthew was already providing a place to stay; it would be poor manners to drain him of bourbon.

"It was mine," Charlie recalled. "I had my Ezra Brooks. That's what I drank *all* the time."

When police found a condom in the bedroom where Charlie and Erin repaired, much was made of the fact that the two had sex that night. Their harshest detractors depicted them as vicious and cold. Was Erin aroused because her parents and brothers were dead? Was Charlie reveling in the power channeled into his loins through the act of stealing away life?

Wilkinson appeared bemused by these theories. "It wasn't like that at all," he said of the sexual encounter. "It's just what we did."

At the crime scene, local police and firefighters were joined by emergency service personnel from neighboring jurisdictions, as well as statewide and even federal agencies. Members of the Emory and Point fire departments crisscrossed the Caffey property with the Texas Rangers and firefighters and sheriff's deputies from all over Rains, Hopkins and Smith counties. Longview fire marshal Mark Moore brought Nina, the department's accelerant detection canine. Because the intruders had left a living witness, investigators knew that arson was used to cover up the homicides. As a result, the ATF was called in to sort through the debris. From his room in East Texas Medical Center, Terry signed a consent form, allowing authorities to search wherever they wished.

Detective Ira Earls from the Smith County Sheriff's Department photographed what remained of the Caffey home, and took careful notes of the scene. "I noted that the residence had burned down to the sub floor and there appeared to be approximately between two and three feet of burned debris in the location," he reported. "As I took the overall photos I noted what appeared to be a burned body near what would have been the east wall of the location. The body appeared to be carefully covered by a burned mattress. Continuing on I noted a bone sticking out of the debris on the northwest corner of the location and also what appeared to be a chunk of flesh."

After climbing into a bucket truck and shooting down at the site from a height of about thirty feet, Earls began tracing the steps Terry had taken as he escaped from his home. "I noted that just southwest of the residence there was a fallen tree that had pushed down the barb wire fence," the detective wrote. "I walked to this location and as I approached I noted a reddish brown substance on the tree which I believed to be blood."

It was the place where Terry had stopped to rest and rebuild his strength while inching toward the Gaston house.

"I crossed a fence and further noted blood on the ground in the area," Earls continued. "Having been advised that Terry Caffey had fled out of a bathroom window to a neighbor's residence, I believed that this was most likely blood from the wounds he had received." Earls motioned for Noel Martin, another Smith County sheriff's department detective, to join him and confirm the sighting. "We back tracked the blood to a fence directly beside the residence and then to the house. We then followed the trail westward and it went toward the neighbor's house where we were told the 9-1-1 call had come from. The trail crossed another fence, and then a small creek. The trail then died. I continued toward the residence and found the trail before it died out was heading to a small bridge in the pasture. . . . Det. Martin and I marked 18 locations of suspected blood."

Like lawmen everywhere, Earls had heard the tales about small-town police departments losing, polluting or simply overlooking DNA evidence. As long as he was on the job, though, no such calamity would occur. He quickly collected swabs of suspected blood at six random locations. In each case, the sample was tested with leucomalachite green (LMG), a chemical used to confirm the presence of blood. All six tests came back positive.

When the case went to trial, and a defense attorney questioned the veracity of the victim's narrative—after all, how well could a man recall the aftermath of an attack after he was shot in the face?—these tests would bolster his words, modern-day stations of the cross with DNA endorsement.

The first cadaver Earls could unequivocally identify was that of eight-year-old Tyler. "I believe this was due to the small stature of the subject," the detective wrote. "I noted that the body was face down . . . that everything below the subject's knee was gone."

The investigator asked his colleagues to retrieve a body bag. As Earls and Smith County detective Joe Rasoc spun the corpse onto the object, the top part of the little boy's head fell off, exposing brain matter. Despite this ghastly sight, Earls understood that, with every police finding generally questioned by judges, juries and defense attorneys, it was crucial to maintain a clinical detachment. "I observed the body and noted that was unclothed or that possibly the clothes had been burned off," he wrote.

As Earls completed his search for evidence below Tyler's

scorched carcass, an ATF agent nearby shouted that he thought that he'd uncovered another body.

Wrote Earls, "I noted on the right side of the body in the rib cage area what appeared to be a possible puncture between two ribs. I continued to clear ash and debris away from the body. I used a small shovel and hand rake to move debris away from the body." Among the items unearthed was a chain adorned with a pair of miniature *nunchaku*, or martial arts weapons, presumably a keepsake of one of the Caffey boys. "Rasco and I then were able to turn the body onto its back. I noted what appeared to be breasts and on the left side of the chest what appeared to be the remains of a bra. I believed this to be the body of Penny Caffey.

". . . I then returned to the location where the body had been and searched for the area for any further evidence. I was able to locate two cartridge casings which appeared to be .22 caliber."

The arson had apparently failed to obscure the particulars of the crime. Earls had already found the blood trail Terry had made after escaping the fire, all but identified the bodies of two of the victims, even located the casings of the weapons used in the shootings. With this evidence alone, the story of the Caffey tragedy was close to written.

And the investigation was only beginning.

Pastor Todd McGahee was with his family at their retreat in Lake Palestine—"It's where we go to hide away," he explained—when he received a call from a fellow minister, Wayne Wolf. The man told McGahee that he was sitting with Tommy Gaston. It was so early in the morning that McGahee knew the news couldn't be good.

Terry Caffey was in the hospital, McGahee was told. Before he even heard details or the name of a suspect, he wondered if Charlie Wilkinson was somehow involved. "Not that I thought Charlie would do that," McGahee said, referring to the murder. "But, I mean, there were problems."

According to Wolf, Terry had crawled over to Tommy's

house and informed his friend that Wilkinson had invaded the Caffey home in the middle of the night, and killed the entire family.

McGahee recalled hearing that "nobody was left."

The pastor's wife eyed him with concern as he ended his phone call. "I'll say I was in shock," he said. "And all I can truly remember about it is she asked me what had happened. And if I remember correctly, I told her, 'You don't want to know.'"

Hesitantly, McGahee retold the saga. Then he rushed over to Tyler to see Terry in the hospital.

He found Terry in a building swarming with law enforcement. Terry seemed relieved to see the familiar face, and the two prayed together.

"I'm sure they were giving him lots of painkillers," McGahee said. "But he was still very emotional."

News was starting to trickle in to the hospital. The bodies of Penny, Tyler and Bubba had been accounted for. Erin—well, that was another story.

The pastor thought back to Wednesday night, push-starting Charlie's truck out of the church parking lot. The congregants were all so certain that Wilkinson was venting his rage after the breakup with Erin, but the minister still had his doubts:

"I kind of thought the whole thing Wednesday night was probably them putting on a show for her mom and dad, and for the church to think that they were [broken up]. Because he certainly didn't act like he was upset out in the parking lot."

Still, it was one thing to deceive some adults about a forbidden romance, and quite another to walk into a church and ask a pastor to push your truck—when you're planning to murder the former youth leader. Despite the tensions between Charlie and the Caffeys, McGahee never imagined this. "Not to this magnitude," he said. "It came as a great shock that it happened."

Terry was also reminiscing about the events of the recent past, as investigators probed him about how he came to know Charlie Wilkinson. "When we first met this guy, I had a funny feeling," Terry recalled in a near-whisper, as his sister, Mary Horn, hovered by his bedside. "At first, I thought it was just because he was annoying. He talked *all* the time, as if he just knew everything about anything, just got on my nerves. . . . And the more I pushed him away, then I was afraid they were going to run off together. So I tried to give a little slack there, keep an eye on things, but . . . we could tell she started changing in the last few months. She was always particular about keeping herself made up . . ."

"Very beautiful," Terry's sister added.

"And she wouldn't keep her hair washed half the time. And I remember the other day . . . I'm going to work, getting ready to go, and I said, 'Do you have deodorant?' She started leaving her hygiene, even my wife noticed it. We talked about this yesterday . . . keeping herself clean . . . She just started . . . changing, and we would make little hints. 'Don't you think you could do better?' "

To use Terry's terminology, Charlie had broken Erin down, calling her dumb and telling her that she was too skinny one day, too fat the next, until her sense of self had been reduced to nothing. The investigators asked Terry when he first noticed his daughter's apparent disregard for her appearance.

"It was in the last month . . . something wasn't quite right. [Charlie] seemed to be controlling. He wanted to know everywhere that she was, and he showered her, showered with roses all the time, real protective, gifts . . .

"And we were at church one night, and my wife came up and said, 'Did you see what Erin got on her finger?' And I said, 'No.' And she said, 'She's got a wedding ring.' And I said, 'No, she doesn't.' So I looked and, sure enough, she did.

"So I pulled him to the side, and I said, 'She's just sixteen, you realize. Y'all realize you're going too fast.' And he said, 'I know that, *Terry*.' Just like that. I said, 'You don't show me respect. If you're going to date my daughter, you're going to show me some respect.'

"A couple of days after we found the ring, we had him come over, and handed the ring back to him. We said, 'This is not appropriate,' and that was disrespectful for him to talk to me like that in church. And then, I said, 'If you're not going to respect me, how will you respect my daughter?' And he was being all apologetic, and pouring on the charm. And we were so afraid that they were going to run off . . . so we thought, 'Well, we're going to let you still speak to him, but on a limited basis.' Because he was coming over every day. That's too much."

Despite his exhausted condition and frail voice, Terry was eager to speak more, now telling detectives about probing Charlie's MySpace page: "My wife says—we don't have a computer at home—she said, 'You got to see stuff on that MySpace.' So we went to the library on the computer, and she always said he was a good Christian boy because she just started dating . . . we told her she couldn't date 'til she was 16 . . . we said, 'When you do date, it's not going to be just anybody. It's got to be a Christian young man.' We brought her up right. And she was like 'Okay, yeah, I undertstand.' "

Terry claimed to have been shaken by the contents of Charlie's MySpace page—obscenities, references to smoking and drinking, blasphemy and other passages a young man who possessed Wilkinson's alleged Christian beliefs would never conceive—and the fact that Erin continued to wear Charlie's ring after she'd purportedly returned it.

"And she used to not lie," Mary Horn interceded.

"And she lied to us," Terry said despondently, "always honest, a good girl."

The detectives asked if Erin eventually broke up with Charlie on her own.

"That's what she told us," Terry replied. "But . . . I don't know."

On Friday night, Terry said, he'd awoken in the middle of the night to the sound of a dog barking. He fell back asleep, he continued, until the gunman entered the bedroom. Initially, he maintained, his bleary eyes did not have time to adjust long enough to identify the intruder. Within seconds, the gun was discharged and Terry assumed, because of Penny's proximity to the shooter, that his wife was hit first. As before, he spoke about passing out after the first fusillade.

But when he came to, and heard Bubba shouting out Charlie's name, Terry had a moment of clarity, and realized the face he'd seen firing at the bed belonged to Wilkinson.

"How sure are you that Wilkinson was the one who shot you?" he was asked.

"If you put it in percentages, it would be in the high nineties."

In every interview with authorities, Terry repeated the same general information. During one bedside discussion, he was asked if he'd heard Erin in the house. Terry responded that he only heard screaming from the children's rooms, then silence.

Not once did Terry attempt to evade a question or retract a prior statement. One after another, each official deduced that it was not in his nature to tell anything but what he believed to be the absolute truth.

"Based on his injuries and the fact that the facial wound could account for him drifting in and out of consciousness I did not think he had any part in the homicide but was a victim," wrote Tyler police officer Malmstrom.

With that out of the way, detectives could pursue the people they perceived as the real perpetrators.

CHAPTER 9

Danny Walker, the editor of the Greenville *Herald Banner*—the daily newspaper headquartered closest to the crime scene—felt a dual sense of purpose after digesting the early details of the massacre. Naturally, he wanted to report the murders. But there were many unanswered questions, and he suspected that some of his readers might be able to assist.

Authorities told the *Herald Banner* that Erin was missing and asked the newspaper to spread the word that anyone who had any information about her whereabouts should contact the sheriff's department. Said Walker, "I believe even they made the statement, 'She's not considered a suspect at this time. She's just a missing person. We're concerned about her welfare and safety.' "

Walker had covered a similar case before while working for a newspaper in Vinita, Oklahoma. On December 29, 1999, in the nearby community of Welch, Ashley Freeman was celebrating her sixteenth birthday with a friend named Laura Bible. Laura's parents had given her permission to spend the night. At about five AM, a passing motorist noticed that the mobile home was burning. When firefighters finally arrived at the scene, they found a badly charred body with a number of gunshot wounds, facedown in bed. It was Ashley's mother, Kathy. Authorities concluded that the fire was set to cover up the murder.

Initially, there was speculation that Kathy's husband, Danny, had committed the crime and vanished with both teenagers. But a day later, while searching the property themselves, Laura's relatives uncovered Danny's body.

For the next several years, Oklahoma state investigators received tips that the girls were sighted in various parts of the United States. Every lead turned out to be bogus.

Then, in 2004, Jeremy Bryan Jones, a convicted sex offender charged in the murder of a sixteen-year-old Georgia girl, suddenly began confessing to a variety of crimes, including thirteen homicides in six states. Jones, who'd lived in northeastern Oklahoma at the time Ashley and Laura disappeared, claimed to have killed Danny and Kathy Freeman in their trailer. In the turmoil, he told investigators, he convinced the teens to run out of the home and into his truck. He said he drove them to Kansas and killed them,

Based on this information, authorities exhaustively searched a collection of sinkholes and mining pits in Kansas's Galena region, using radar equipment and cadaver dogs. But nothing was ever found. The detectives who'd expected to close the case began to wonder if Jones's confession was motivated not by truth, but a deranged need to outsmart law enforcement and frustrate the victims' loved ones.

Now, as Texas officials urged the Greenville *Herald Banner* to ask its readers to support the search for Erin, Danny Walker thought about the teenagers in Oklahoma. "I guess your reporting is colored by things that have happened in the past," the editor reflected. "Another sixteen-year-old girl was missing, and we wanted to help. I wondered if drugs were involved. We speculated that some drug deal went wrong, and they took the daughter as compensation or whatever. Again, I didn't know the family or their circumstances. But your experience as a reporter always affects the way you look at a story."

For those who knew the Caffeys better, the notion of Terry and Penny becoming embroiled in a drug dispute was almost comedic. Still, the crime was too fresh for the people who cared about the family to laugh. As police parceled out the elements in tiny pieces, even members of Miracle Faith Baptist were forced to invent scenarios involving Erin's whereabouts. "What we heard," said youth leader Sarah Meece, "was that she jumped out a two-story window or something, and was alive in the woods."

Lynne Sullivant, weekend reporter at CBS-19 in Tyler, heard some rumblings about a murder-arson case in the Emory area when she arrived in the newsroom at nine AM. "Nobody knew what was going on because they weren't releasing the names of the family," she said. "They weren't releasing details other than three people in a family had been killed. We didn't know if they were shot, stabbed, anything. And their house was burnt down. So we were trying to call to figure out exactly what happened. And we weren't really getting anywhere on the phone."

Despite the tightening budgets at local news operations, Lynne and her colleagues lived by the philosophy that you couldn't report a big story from your desk. You might get the generalities on the phone—the equivalent of a press release prepared by some public information officer, maybe even a mug shot or victim's graduation photo e-mailed in time for the broadcast—but the texture of the story, the gritty specifics, the personal anecdotes, the flavor of the community, could only be conveyed by the reporters on the ground. Lynne and a cameraman were soon in a news truck, heading up U.S. 69 North to Rains County.

"I had never even heard of Emory before this happened," Lynne said. "I didn't know Rains County. I mean, we have a beat list that we check, and I don't even think Rains County was on it.

"Not much happens there. You have these small towns. Houses are spread apart. Everyone has their own pasture. You see horses out there. It's very country. I wouldn't call

Tyler a metropolis, but compared to Emory, it seems like a big city—well, a big small city."

Once they neared Alba, the crew found their way to the crime scene primarily by following the smoke emanating from the Caffey residence. But they didn't have a chance to get close to the embers. Yellow crime scene tape confined reporters to the roadside.

Because of the rarity of this type of felony in Rains County, Lynne expected to encounter hordes of neighbors craning their necks to watch the emergency service personnel. But she found the area strangely devoid of gawkers. When people did show up at the crime scene, they came to grieve, not gape.

"I tried looking to see if there was a shell of a house and there was *nothing* there," Lynne said. "Not even a resemblance of a home. Nothing but smoke. And really, not a lot of people to talk to."

After asking a number of sheriff's deputies for information, Lynne was finally directed to Rains County sheriff David Traylor. "He was very vague," she said. "He didn't give us any names of suspects, mention their relationship to the family, nothing. We didn't know if the daughter was still alive, if the dad was still alive, which family members had been inside the home."

Yet Lynne didn't feel like turning around and heading back to Tyler. The sheriff was simply being a pro, protecting his investigation instead of grandstanding to the media. And there was a solemnity to the crime scene that the crew could immediately read. Something terrible had occurred. In a small community, the emergency service personnel likely knew the victims, and the looks on the faces of the police and firefighters told a great deal.

Even though Lynne grew up in a more populated section of the state, she shared the Texas roots of the people she saw. She understood the culture of church and livestock auctions and homecoming queens. In fact, Lynne was a former beauty queen herself.

Lynne's father was born in Beaumont, the son of an oilman.

Her mother was raised in Chicago by way of California. Although Lynne was born in Seattle, the family relocated to Texas during her childhood to The Woodlands, an exclusive planned community outside Houston. At age sixteen, she entered her first pageant.

Nonetheless, she never considered herself a "pageant girl," a female who bounced from contest to contest from early childhood onward in the shallow pursuit of a title. "There's definitely the pageant mom, the hairspray, the fake boobs—all of that is true," she noted. "But when I thought of pageants, I remembered Heather Whitestone, who couldn't hear her name announced as Miss America because she was deaf. I remember Miss Texas pointing at her to say, 'You're the winner.'"

In high school, Lynne studied dance, and lost seven classmates to drunk driving accidents. At a certain point, she decided to combine her talent and raven-haired good looks to create a platform to speak against alcohol abuse by teens.

"I loved being on stage," she said. "I loved performing. I loved talking in front of a crowd. I kind of got hooked."

On four separate occasions, Lynne competed for the title of Miss Texas. Even so, before she graduated high school, she knew she was interested in TV journalism. At Texas A&M, she worked in the athletic department doing television production. Her vision was to cover sports in the Lone Star State. But just before graduation, she heard about a news reporter slot in Tyler.

The tragedy in Alba hit her hard, and brought back memories of those seven students who died. Ironically, their misfortune may have inspired Lynne to overcome her initial shyness and put herself out in public. Were it not for those deaths, she might not have been spending a Sunday morning watching fire inspectors sift through the rubble outside the Caffey home.

During her trips back and forth to Emory, Lynne would develop a close friendship with the cameraman, a spiritual man who always listened to the K-Love Christian Radio

Network. As the strains of Jars of Clay's "Love Song for a Savior" or Newsboys' "God Is Not a Secret" came over the radio, the two would talk about the images they'd seen that day—rope-hewn crosses neighbors had left on the fence, toys that had been charred in the fire—and feel the loss of the Caffey family.

"We'd just take the time to remember how precious life is," Lynne said.

Chief Deputy Sheriff Kurt Fischer had been woken up at 4:15 AM by Detective Almon. After hearing a quick description of the events at the Caffey house, Fischer dressed and rushed out to Country Road 2370 in Alba. Fischer arrived to see the house completely engulfed in flames. He recognized the home next door as Tommy Gaston's place.

"Almon approached me and said he just spoke to a victim that was in an ambulance," Fischer said, "and was told that Charlie Wilkinson broke into his house, and shot him and shot his family. Almon said the weapon appeared to be a shotgun, possibly because of the wounds the victim had to his head. I asked him how the victim knew it was Wilkinson, and was told that the kid was dating his daughter until they made her stop seeing him."

Fischer was stunned. Not only was he familiar with Charlie Wilkinson, but the boy had gone out to the chief deputy's house to discuss his problems with Terry. It was Fischer who Charlie asked about the feasibility of running away with Erin, and it was Fischer who advised the young man to slow things down.

"I know Charlie Wilkinson," Fischer told the detective. "He's a family friend."

The deputy only lived a half mile from Matthew Waid's house and knew that Charlie occasionally slept there; Fischer had visited the place himself. In fact, Fischer was fairly sure that Charlie was there right now: On the way to the crime scene, the chief deputy had recognized Wilkinson's 1991 Ford Explorer backed up in the driveway outside Matthew's place, facing the road.

A call was made to dispatch with Charlie's vehicle information; all deputies were now officially looking for him. But this was simply a formality. Fischer and Deputy Ed Emig left the crime scene to drive over to the intersection of Farm to Market Road 779 and Rains County Road 3274 and knocked on the Waids' door.

Michael Dickinson got up from his spot on the love seat to answer. He and Fischer nodded at one another.

"Hey Michael, is Charlie here?"

"I don't know."

"Well, could we come inside and look for him?"

Dickinson opened the door wider, and motioned the officers in. "Okay."

Fischer knew Charlie well enough not to fear him. But the kid was now a murder suspect, and the chief deputy exercised appropriate caution. He immediately opened a bedroom door to his right. Matthew and his common-law wife, Emerald, were asleep. The officers shined their flashlights around the room—and directly at the couple.

"Do you know where Charlie is?"

Emerald rubbed her eyes. "I don't know."

The officers left, and returned to the living room, stepping over piles of clothes and beer cans.

Down a narrow hallway, the deputies spotted another bedroom, its doorframe obscured by a blanket. Charlie had heard the officers traipsing through the trailer, and knew exactly what this was about.

He roused Erin awake. "The police are here," he said. "Go hide." He turned his focus to the approaching officers. "Who is it?" he yelled.

When Fischer pulled the blanket back from the doorway, he saw Charlie on his stomach, shirtless on a mattress, his arm hanging over the side of the bed. A holstered handgun lay on the ground about a foot from Wilkinson's grasp.

"Charlie," Fischer announced. "It's Kurt. Let me see your hands."

Charlie acted confused. "What's going on?" he replied,

feigning innocence. The moment of hesitation made Fischer wonder whether Charlie was reckless enough to reach for the weapon.

"Let me see your hands," Fischer repeated more sternly. The deputy noticed a bolt-action rifle leaning in the corner of the room. For everyone's safety, Charlie was handcuffed and taken outside. The officers told him to sit down on the porch steps.

The weapons were secured and placed in Emig's cruiser. Fischer told dispatch that the suspect was in custody.

"The whole time, Wilkinson never asked me . . . why we were there," Fischer noted.

The chief deputy removed a card listing the Miranda warning, and read it to Charlie: "You have the right to remain silent. Anything you say can and will be used against you in a court of law. You have the right to an attorney present during questioning. If you cannot afford an attorney, one will be appointed for you. . . ."

Most officers could probably repeat the Miranda Warning by memory. But it wasn't worth taking a chance. If in the course of securing a suspect and processing a crime scene a clause were inadvertently omitted, a killer could walk on a technicality.

"Do you understand each of these rights I have explained to you?"

"Yes," Charlie said.

"Having these rights in mind, do you wish to talk to us now?"

"Yes, sir."

Fischer had had long conversations with Charlie in the past. Now, the young man had "a very quiet disposition," the deputy said. "And when I told him about the Caffeys, he showed no emotion."

Charlie simply lowered his head.

"Were you involved in this?" Fischer asked.

Charlie shook his head. "No, sir. I got drunk last night and passed out."

Fischer called Almon and repeated the assertion. Almon reminded the chief deputy that Terry had claimed that *two* intruders were responsible for the murders. Fischer shifted his attention to Michael Dickinson.

Unlike Charlie, Dickinson appeared genuinely curious. "What's going on?" he asked.

When he was told that the Caffey family had been slaughtered a few hours earlier, his eyes widened with surprise.

"Do you know anything about it?"

Dickinson shook his head. "I wasn't with Charlie last night." He claimed to have returned to the Waid trailer at 11:45 PM and fallen asleep.

"Well, you need you to come with us, also."

"Am I under arrest?"

"No, but we need to talk to you."

Dickinson grabbed his coat. Charlie watched Michael's interactions with the officers, but wasn't too concerned for his friend. "He didn't know anything about this," Charlie later claimed. "I didn't want to tell him because he would have knocked some sense into me. And after that, he would have knocked Charles [Waid] in the head, and talked *him* out of it."

On the porch, Charlie appeared to be chilly. "Do you want a shirt and shoes?" Fischer asked him.

"Yes, sir. They're inside."

Charlie's shirt was retrieved from the bedroom, his western boots from the living room. "Deputy Emig was about to let Wilkinson put his boots on," Fischer said, "when he observed what looked to be blood droplets on the top part of the boots. Emig did not let Wilkinson put them on."

Instead, the boots were saved as evidence, and Charlie was placed in the back of the cruiser, saying nothing as he was driven to the Rains County Sheriff's Department. He and Dickinson were each placed in separate holding cells. Fischer involved himself in paperwork, drawing up a search warrant for Matthew Waid's home. Rains County justice of the peace Don Smith swiftly signed the document.

* * *

Detective Almon and Texas Ranger John Vance read Dickinson his Miranda warning, and asked him to detail his activities on Friday. Michael described a relatively mundane day. He said that he was having problems with his truck and, after school, he and Charlie went to a repair shop to work on it. Then, they drove over to the Wilkinson house to clean up, and headed over to see Charles Waid at his brother's place.

Eventually, Wilkinson and Waid left to pick up Bobbi at her job, while Dickinson and a friend drove to Billy's Beer Store in the town of East Tawakoni to purchase some alcohol, then the Maxi-Mart in Emory, then Matthew Waid's place again. At 11:30 PM, Michael went to another friend's house to meet a tattoo artist. Dickinson told police that when the artist didn't show up, he returned to Waid's for the final time that night, to crash.

A short time later, he heard Charlie at the front door with Waid and Bobbi Johnson. Matthew Waid had been sleeping, but he went outside to join them. About ten minutes later, Matthew came back inside, and the other three drove off. Dickinson told investigators he fell asleep, and didn't wake up until the police arrived.

"How well do you know Erin Caffey?" Michael was asked.

"Not very well. She has an attitude toward me." He explained that Erin was jealous of him because he lived with the Wilkinson family, and hung out with Charlie. He also mentioned that Erin's parents "hated Charlie's guts" because they thought he was "rude and disrespectful" to them.

"Charlie always talks about Erin," Michael said, "how great they are together, how much he loves her." Dickinson theorized that, regardless of what her parents decreed, Charlie and Erin would continue to sneak around without the Caffeys' knowledge.

"Was Charlie drinking last night?"

"I don't think so. He had Guard duty. He already missed last month, and he had to be in Greenville at eight o'clock this morning. So I can't see him getting drunk."

The investigators asked about the weapons in the house. Dickinson replied that Charlie had a rifle that was likely at his father's house. He also had a shotgun, but it was currently in the credit union building in Alba because Charlie was using it as collateral. Tanis owned two Japanese war rifles and some swords. Oh, and there was also the sword that Dickinson believed belonged to Matthew Waid—the one Wilkinson and Charles Waid liked to use in their playful duels.

"It was the craziest morning," recalled Teresa Myers, the woman who'd begun to look at Charlie as another son. "We woke up, and Michael Dickinson and Charlie are in jail, and we hear they killed the Caffey family."

Teresa knew Michael fairly well; her niece was dating the eighteen-year-old's older brother. "So there was this whole connection thing going on," she said. "We literally sat on my porch the entire day, trying to figure out what had happened. And there were all these rumors. Erin was killed with her family. Everybody was killed except Erin. Erin was in on it. Erin was missing.

"And I remember we all sat and cried, thinking of Charlie and Michael doing something like this, and saying, 'There's no way.'"

Teresa's son, Justin, who'd come to look up to Charlie as a dependable mentor, was particularly dismayed. At some point on Friday night, he'd contemplated getting together with Charlie. "He's talking to him on the phone," Teresa pointed out, "and the next thing you know, it's the next morning, and you wake up, and the whole world has changed."

Throughout the day, Teresa found her sadness mixed with feelings of helplessness and guilt: "I was thinking, 'My God, was there anything that I could have done or said that would have made it any different?' I kept going back to that conversation I had with Charlie about Erin—'She's trouble.' That's truly how I felt. But I kept thinking, 'Did I not follow through?' I kind of felt like a parent, thinking, 'Did I not do enough for this kid?'

"It was devastating. And I've spent a lot of time running all those possibilities through my head, and shedding a lot of tears over it."

CHAPTER 10

The *Tyler Morning Telegraph* received its initial tip from a reader in Alba.

"She said, 'Somebody's been murdered,'" said reporter Lauren Grover. "She thought it had to do with a boyfriend-girlfriend situation."

Had Alba been a little closer to Tyler, reporters at the newspaper would have had a long-established network of contacts at the sheriff's office and nearby fire departments. But the seclusion of Rains County meant that media sightings were rare. This was fine with the locals; in fact, one of the incentives for living in the area was the fact that outsiders—and outsider concepts—stayed away. Unfortunately, this crime was too significant for the usual rules to be applied.

Now, Grover's assistant editor was calling her at home, asking her to look into the report. What was unusual about this was that Lauren didn't even cover the police beat. Her family was in health care, and she was a medical reporter. And she was supposed to come in at night. But a story like the Caffey massacre meant that every spare hand was needed. And, with some ten months on the job, Lauren wasn't quite a newbie anymore.

Nine days after graduating from Hillsdale College in Michigan, Lauren walked into the newsroom in Tyler to officially launch her career. Although she'd grown up in Phoenix and interned in Washington, D.C., she felt surprisingly little culture shock. She attributed this to fact that she'd been born in Beaumont and her mother hailed from Louisiana. "We kind of have some Cajun, Deep South traditions in my family," she explained. "I grew up with a drawl. So it's easy for me to flip back into that when I'm out in the country."

Because of this, she felt comfortable blurting out comments that a Yankee would never dare. "I've called Tyler the armpit of the Bible Belt," she joked. "Very, very conservative. Very old traditions. If I'd grown up here as a young girl, I would have gone through lots of 'what you do as a Southern girl' kind of stuff. We've got the Rose Festival, which is a huge deal. There's a Rose Queen, and a Rose Court, and pretty much every young person who's anybody is part of it."

Yet, there was much about the region she loved: "It's got some quintessential country elements, Texas elements, that are great. Barbecue is a big deal. You don't come here if you don't eat barbecue. And if you don't have some homemade coconut cream pie, then you haven't had your experience.

"The people are just nice and super-friendly. You'll never find another place where you can have twenty-minute conversations in the produce section, and that's not a joke."

Like reporters everywhere, Lauren could hold the community at arm's length—examine it from the bottom, twist it to the side, and find comic relief in the institutions her subjects embraced without question. In the course of exuding this skeptical aloofness, however, she found herself celebrating many of the same things herself.

The request to rush to Alba had occurred so quickly that Grover didn't even have an address. So she pulled up at the sheriff's department and asked. No one there would venture to say anything on the record. Lauren, like the other media members starting to assemble in the small town, would have to wait for the sheriff's press conference.

She spent much of the day behind crime scene tape, breathing in the ashes from the smoldering home and chatting with the volunteer firefighters. One confided, off-the-record, his apprehension about coming face to face with his deceased neighbors.

"It's so weird because we're fighting this fire, and we know there are bodies inside," he revealed. "So we're trying to be careful, to do everything right. But this is a small town, and we've never had to fight a fire with bodies that haven't been removed yet."

Some of the firefighters had been on the scene since long before daybreak, when Terry's medical van had exploded. "It just blew up right next to them," Lauren said. "It was a huge explosion, the roof peeled back like a tin can and, fortunately, none of them were injured. I don't think a lot of volunteer firefighters have dealt with something like this, ever. Then, at seven or seven-thirty that night, when the road opened up again, these same guys were finishing up. They'd been at there the whole day, standing out on the road, blocking traffic after fighting the fire."

Before his interview with investigators even started, Charlie made an unsolicited statement: "I'm in a lot of trouble."

Neither Detective Richard Almon nor Ranger John Vance confirmed or denied the comment. But Charlie admired and respected the police. All things considered, they were treating him well. "I think it had to do with the fact that I already knew a bunch of them," he later opined.

Perhaps this is why Charlie admitted to the type of character traits a Texas jury typically savors before imposing the death penalty.

"I ain't got no conscience."

"I'm a psycho maniac."

"I joined the Army to do whatever needed to be done without thinking."

"What happened, Charlie?"

"Erin called me Friday night. I was still pretty pissed off about her parents telling us that we could not see each other. So Erin said, 'I want to kill them.'"

Charlie claimed that he'd told Erin to just run away with him. Her alleged reply: "No, kill them."

Later that night, at 1:30 AM, Charlie said he went to the Caffey residence with another person. When investigators asked him to identify his partner, Charlie politely refused: "I have a code, and won't give people up."

No one pressed him on this matter, figuring they'd get it out of him soon enough; he seemed to be in a particularly talkative mood. When Charlie and his accomplice arrived at the house, he continued, the family dog barked, and Terry apparently woke up and got out of bed. The pair decided to leave.

A short time later, Erin called her boyfriend on his cell: "Where are you?"

"The dog was barking, and someone was moving around in the house, so we left."

"Look, come back in an hour. I'll keep the dog quiet."

At two AM, Charlie said, he received another call from his girlfriend. "I can't stand being in the house any longer. Meet me at the end of the driveway."

The car returned to the home, where Erin was waiting outside in her pajamas. She climbed into the vehicle, Charlie alleged, and drove around with him and his partner for the next hour, plotting the crime. Once again, he insisted that he'd told Erin to pack her clothes and run away with him. After a year and a half, when she turned eighteen, she'd be free to do whatever she pleased. According to Charlie, Erin reiterated that she "just wanted them killed."

"What happened next?" Almon asked.

"We went back."

Charlie said that he and his associate entered the living room, then the ground floor bathroom, looking for money, before the bedroom. "I shot at Mrs. Caffey, but did not kill her," he said. "She did not wake up. I shot at Mr. Caffey twice, and left the room. I told the other person that I could not do it."

Almon inquired about the weapon. Charlie replied that he'd used his father's pistol—the same gun that Chief Deputy Fischer had confiscated that morning.

"How many rounds in the gun?"

"Ten in the clip and one in the chamber."

Returning to the story, Wilkinson contended that his partner expected him to shoot the boys. When Charlie went upstairs, he said, Bubba and Tyler had locked themselves in Erin's room. Avoiding eye contact with the kids, he told them to get out and go into their own beds. Wilkinson's partner was coming up the stairs, as Bubba kicked at his sister's boyfriend—and, Charlie said, that's when the accomplice shot the older boy in the head.

He admitted stabbing eight-year-old Tyler with a sword.

Almon and Vance were careful not to show disapproval—just yet, at least—not when Charlie was on this kind of roll. The detective calmly asked what Wilkinson and his partner planned to do after the murders.

"We were going to put the bodies in a van, ditch the bodies, and burn the house," Charlie answered. He thought for a moment, and added that, after going upstairs, he'd heard two shots from the Caffeys' bedroom—suggesting that he wasn't the only one who'd fired into Terry and Penny.

Almon stared at Charlie, and pointedly asked him to name his partner. Charlie confessed to entering the home with Charles Waid, while Bobbi Johnson sat in the car with Erin.

Johnson would be easy to identify, he assured police. She still went to Rains High School—"tall, blonde with big breasts."

The suspect filled in a few voids for investigators. The weapon was a .22-caliber Browning pistol that used long rifle bullets, and was kept in a black sheath. The fire was set "with a couple of Bic lighters." After the murder, the conspirators removed a bag of Erin's clothes, two pairs of shoes and her purse. Because Charlie's truck had to be push-started, the killers used Bobbi's silver Dodge Neon.

Then—after blaming Erin for inducing the scheme—he asserted that his girlfriend did not know what was about to occur in the house that night. Yet, he also said that Erin had a "big smile" on her face afterward, and declared, "I am glad that is over."

The investigators stepped out of the room, but left the

video camera running. The tactic yielded exactly what they'd anticipated. They later watched the footage of Charlie sitting alone, mumbling to himself.

"They got my boots," he said in an audible tone.

When Almon and Vance returned, Charlie recalled a conversation he'd had with Erin the day before the murders. He claimed that he'd made it clear that the crime was her idea so that it wouldn't "fall back on" his conscience.

"Was that the first time Erin had mentioned something like that?" Almon asked.

"You mean, the first, second or third time she said that?"

Wilkinson told the police that Erin had been talking about killing her parents for about a month and a half.

Not long afterward, Charlie said, the cash-strapped Waid agreed to participate. But there was some question about whether the murders would actually occur. On Friday morning, Charlie told police, he called Waid and informed him, "She wants it done."

The pair made a nominal effort to avoid detection, meeting to discuss the scheme rather than plotting over the phone. The two considered sneaking into the house and "slitting everybody's throats." Charlie would kill the Caffeys, Waid the kids. "Tap, tap, cut, cut."

"Why did the kids need to be killed?" Almon said.

"Charles said that little ones talk."

In this version of the story, Charlie claimed that the barking dog had changed their plan. "The gun got involved," he said, "because the dog did not shut up." Between stops at the Caffey home, the pair took a trip to pick up the .22, in case the animal caused another distraction.

"What did you do after that?" Almon asked.

"Walked in like any ole gunslinger would do when he was robbing a bank. I wiped the gun down with alcohol wipes so it would only be my prints on it. I gave it to Tanis at the house to clean so his prints would be on it."

"When you were shooting at the parents," Almon said, "what was your intent?"

"I intended to kill them because I thought I was in love."

As before, the deaths of Bubba and Tyler seemed to upset Charlie the most. After shooting Terry and Penny, he maintained, he handed the gun to Waid because "I could not do it [kill the children]." Still, Charlie admitted to carrying a sword. Tyler "was stabbed four times," he said. "I think I stabbed at least once."

In the midst of the description, he looked at the detectives, and implored, "Why did he have to die?"

Vance had felt a fondness for Charlie when the suspect was first brought into the sheriff's office. "He looked to be a kid that you would see on the baseball field, or at the drive-in," the ranger recounted. "When we started the interview process, you could tell that he was hiding some information. Then, he started explaining what took place. And that's kind of when it turned from talking to the local kid to looking at the face of the killer."

During the interrogation, investigators realized that they'd missed Erin by seconds. "I remember hearing Chief Fischer coming down the hallway," Charlie said of his morning in the trailer, "and I told Erin to hide."

Vance wondered if her mood had changed once she'd gone back to Matthew's home and had time to digest the enormity of the murders. But Charlie responded that Erin remained happy.

"Did the two of you make love?" Almon asked.

"Yes."

"Was it consensual?"

"Yes, we both wanted to have sex."

The thought of indulging in intercourse so soon after the massacre unsettled virtually everyone who discussed the case with Charlie. Still, few police believed that they were talking to a kid completely devoid of a heart. Although detectives were quickly able to break through his refusal to name Waid or Bobbi, he wanted his questioners to understand that Michael Dickinson was faultless. He was oblivious to Wilkinson and Waid's plans, Charlie stressed, and was only picked up because he had the misfortune of falling asleep on Matthew's love seat.

"I did not tell him anything," Charlie insisted, "because I did not want him to get into trouble if we got caught."

With that one gesture, Charlie sustained a tatter of morality. But it did little to bolster his spirit. The evil of committing the mass execution—including the slaughter of two children—was so enormous that Wilkinson wondered not only about his fate in the American penal system, but the next world, as well.

While queried about the aftermath of the murder, Charlie ignored a question about what he did once the grandfather's safe was removed from the home.

"I hope that God forgives me," he remarked instead.

The phone in Bobbi Johnson's apartment rang at nine AM.

"Do you know Charlie Wilkinson?"

It was the apartment manager. "Yeah, I know Charlie. Why?"

"He went into his girlfriend's house last night, and shot up her whole family."

A shaken Charlie was allowed to call his father after the interrogation. Charlie was looking for some type of reassurance, but his father couldn't offer any. As always, the suspect felt very much alone—even with the familiar voice of Bobby Lee Wilkinson on the other end of the phone. Said Charlie, "I could hear the disappointment in his voice."

"I don't know what you did and why," Bobby uttered bluntly. "I'll ask you one question. You shot her dad, right?"

"Yes."

"Did you shoot the kids?" Bobby asked pointedly. The story of the murder of the two Caffey boys was now circulating around the community, and it was clear that Bobby had divorced himself enough from his son to feel the same wrath as everyone else.

"No," Charlie answered in a voice choked with tears.

"They just got caught in the fire?"

"No, but I'm not the one that did it."

Bobby wouldn't let it go. "Did somebody shoot them, or did they get caught in the fire?"

"Somebody shot them." There was a long pause. "But it wasn't me."

The elder Wilkinson appeared mildly reassured. "I could see you shooting her dad. You're a hothead. But I don't see you shooting the little kids." Having resolved the matter for himself, Bobby switched topics. "I think you need to see about letting me get you a lawyer. Have you already written out a confession or something? Otherwise, they wouldn't be letting you talk to me probably."

"I never signed anything," Charlie sobbed, "anything at all."

". . . I don't know what they can do for you or what, but you've got to at least get somebody that knows the system enough to explain things to you."

It was obvious to both father and son, though, that there was nothing Charlie could really do to reverse his actions.

"I love you," the younger Wilkinson cried.

"I love you, too. See you later on. Okay?"

"Okay. Bye."

As reporters tried combing the region for any useful quote, Lauren Grover inadvertently bumped into Bobby Lee Wilkinson at the sheriff's office. "He didn't want to talk," Lauren said, "but he was very polite. I felt terrible for him. He couldn't believe what was happening. He just looked very distraught and solemn, like any caring father would.

"I can't imagine being the parent."

CHAPTER 11

After their interview with Charlie, Rains County detective Richard Almon and Texas Ranger John Vance came to a realization: holding Michael Dickinson was probably a waste of time. There was little reason to doubt Charlie's allegation that Charles Waid and Bobbi Johnson played major roles in the massacre. Rains County chief deputy Kurt Fischer and deputy Ed Emig were told to search for Bobbi's Dodge Neon.

If they could find Bobbi, it was reasoned, they could find Waid.

Less than twenty-four hours after the murders, Waid called his estranged wife, Diane, presumably to discuss their children. In the course of the conversation, though, he suddenly stated, "I want to tell you something before you hear it somewhere else."

"What is it?"

"Charlie's in jail. He went and killed his girlfriend's parents and two brothers."

He also mentioned that cops were looking for another shooter, but, as of now, the identity was a mystery.

Diane never liked Charlie. But, like everyone else who knew him, she found it difficult to imagine the brooding young man with the occasional wry smile butchering Erin's family. As for the other shooter, the first name that occurred to Diane was Michael Dickinson. She claimed that he followed around Charlie "like a puppy."

She questioned Waid about when he last heard from his friend.

"Last night at eleven o'clock." Then, perhaps resigned to the fact that he'd soon be staring at the cinderblock walls of a jail cell, he asked for a photo of Diane and the kids.

Fischer called Almon from the field. He had a lead on Bobbi Johnson. His sources had given him the name of the restaurant where she was recently hired, in Wood County. While the chief deputy and Emig were driving toward Lake Fork, he spotted a silver, four-door Dodge Neon moving in the opposite direction. It was Bobbi's car, and a white male was at the wheel. "That looks like Waid," Fischer said.

From the passenger seat, he managed to read the last two digits on the license plate. The numbers matched the vehicle police were seeking.

"Turn around," he told Emig.

The cruiser made a U-turn and fell in behind the Neon. The driver accelerated. The cruiser caught up to the car on U.S. Highway 69, just south of Country Road 2350. Yes, this was definitely Bobbi's car. Emig threw on the lights and sirens, and the driver pulled over.

The officers removed their weapons, and Charles Waid came out with his hands up. There were no other passengers with him. He was handcuffed and read his Miranda warning.

"I told him we were investigating the murders of the Caffeys," Fischer said, "and asked him if he was involved."

Waid denied any participation. But the officers noticed that he betrayed nothing resembling emotion.

"Do you have any weapons in the vehicle?" Fischer asked.

"There's a sword in the trunk."

Fischer went to the rear of the car, and procured the blade. The hilt of the sword was wrapped with black electrical tape.

As the sun rose on March 1, 2008, firefighters sifted through the smoldering remnants of this Alba, Texas homestead, finding the charred bodies of 37-year-old Penny Caffey and her sons, Bubba and Tyler, ages 13 and 8.

Texas Department of Public Safety

While studying for the ministry, Terry Caffey delivered medical supplies to home health care patients. As the fire spread from the home, the oxygen tanks in Terry's van exploded.

Texas Department of Public Safety

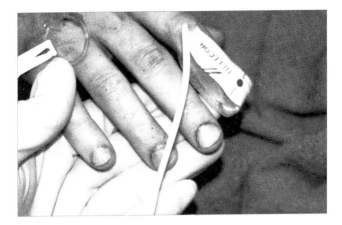

In order to rule out Terry as a suspect, authorities attempted to take nail scrapes from him in the hospital. The purpose of this photo was to document the fact that his nails were too short for the procedure.

Texas Department of Public Safety

By the time police found Erin Caffey, hiding in a fetal position in her pajamas, some in the community believed she'd been killed. She then told a curious tale about being held in a smoky room by two men with swords.

Texas Department of Public Safety

Although time went into planning the Caffey murders, little thought was apparently devoted to what the co-conspirators would do afterwards. As a result, Bobbi Johnson, her boyfriend, Charles Waid, and Erin Caffey were quickly taken into custody.

Texas Department of Public Safety

After initially hesitating, Charles Waid led police scuba divers to a creek where he claimed to have disposed of evidence related to the slayings.

Texas Department of Public Safety

Following Waid's instructions, police sifted through the area around Elm Creek for two hours, solidifying the case against the suspects.

Texas Department of Public Safety

This safe was found floating in a foot of water in Elm Creek. Inside were a number of items belonging to Terry Caffey's recently deceased father.

Texas Department of Public Safety

Charlie Wilkinson claimed that the group brought along two decorative swords purchased from a magazine advertisement. Prior to the killings, the items' only purpose had been harmless sword fights in the backyard. Texas Department of Public Safety

Charles Waid's brother's home was such a popular hangout for the group that Matthew Waid had a difficult time keeping track of the people who passed through. Likewise, when a pair of rifles was discovered in a car outside the residence, police believed Matthew's explanation about not knowing who brought them there.

Texas Department of Public Safety

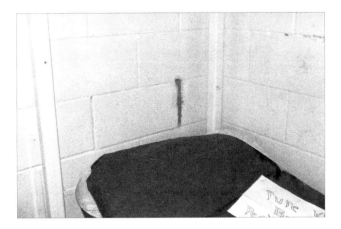

The tedium of jailhouse life, his insulation from nature, and the public fury over the crime apparently led Charlie Wilkinson to attempt to carve his way out of his cell.

Texas Department of Public Safety

According to his jailers, Charlie attempted to use a handmade tool to burrow a small hole into the wall of his cell. Said Erin's lawyer, "I think he took a spoon to the wall."

Texas Department of Public Safety

Even in his prison whites, Charlie Wilkinson could appear friendly and sympathetic. To this day, he insists that he only killed because of his desperate need to maintain his relationship with Erin Caffey.

Keith Elliot Greenberg

Terry Caffey's quick recovery from the attack was considered a miracle by neighbors, who marveled at his sense of Christian forgiveness, when he stood beside his daughter, Erin, in court, and asked for leniency.   *Rains County Leader*

"Where's your girlfriend Bobbi?"

"I just dropped her off at work."

Waid did not struggle as he was placed in the police car and transported to the sheriff's department. A tow truck was called to bring the car to Parmer Automotive and Towing in Emory, where it was impounded.

"Why do you think you're here?"

Charles Waid looked over at Detective Almon and Ranger Vance. "Because I heard that Charlie Wilkinson killed his girlfriend's parents."

Not realizing what Charlie had already revealed, Waid attempted to create a timeline for Friday night: he and his girlfriend had hung out at Matthew's house, then, at about eleven PM, headed back to Bobbi's place in Point.

Almon pointed out that Bobbi's car had been spotted on Country Road 2370 at 2:30 AM. "I want the truth," the detective said.

Waid apologized. "Okay, I'll tell you the truth."

He claimed to have been with Bobbi and Wilkinson at midnight, when they left Matthew's place to go to Erin's house. "Charlie needed help," Waid said; "but I didn't know with what."

The lawmen shot Charles a knowing look. Remembered Almon, "I told Waid I felt that he knew why he was going over there. . . . Waid replied they were going to kill Erin's parents and the brothers, and to hide Erin. I asked Waid why. Waid replied that he was financially strapped and this was a quick way to make some money."

At 12:30 AM, the suspect said, he and Wilkinson walked up to the Caffey home, while Bobbi slept in the car.

"Did Bobbi know what was going on?" Almon questioned.

"Yes."

Like Charlie, Waid said that the dog was barking and wouldn't stop, and the intruders noticed some movement inside the home. Charlie suggested getting close enough to the dog to stab it, Waid recounted, but the goal was elusive, and the pair drove off.

"Waid stated that Erin called Wilkinson and asked where they were at," Almon wrote in his report, "and that Wilkinson told Erin about the dog. Erin told them to come back around 2:30 AM. Waid stated they left and went back to Matthew Waid's house. I asked Waid who all was in on the planning. Waid replied that he and Wilkinson had discussed it while Johnson was at work, and Johnson did not know about it until later in the evening. . . . Waid stated that it was a way to make good money."

Vance later pondered Charles Waid's motives for becoming ensnared in the plot: "He was facing some financial obligations with his child, and he was promised $2,000, and $2,000 wasn't going to solve his financial problems. And to weigh out the odds, and say, 'Yeah, I'll do this for $2,000,' it just doesn't make sense. In reality, he ended up with a couple of hundred dollars that he spent basically the next day, and didn't have the opportunity to spend on his child."

Apparently, Waid also noted the futility of his involvement. Contemplating the fact that he was just as destitute as he'd been the day before the crime, Waid reflected on Charlie's vow that there was cash in the Caffey house.

"That was a lie," Waid told his interrogators.

At about two AM, Waid continued, Erin called and told her confederates to meet her at the end of the driveway. For the next hour, the group drove around, Waid said, planning the murders. Despite his desire to protect Bobbi, he admitted that his girlfriend played a role in the discussions, as well.

When they returned to the Caffey home, Waid said Charlie instructed him to "just walk in the house and do the job." He confirmed Charlie's allegation that that plan was for Wilkinson to shoot the parents, while Waid would "do the kids." But Waid insisted that he told Charlie that he would not kill the children.

The door was open when the pair entered the house, and Charlie went through the entranceway first. "Waid stated that Wilkinson was the first through the door," Almon wrote, "and then into parents' bedroom, and fired five or six, maybe seven shots at the parents. . . . Waid stated that Wilkinson thought he was out of shells, but the gun was only jammed. Waid stated that he fixed the gun. Waid stated that Wilkinson took a sword and 'finished the mom off.' "

Charlie had blood on his hands, according to Waid. When Waid was asked if his hands were also bloody, he responded that he'd been wearing gloves. He later left those gloves behind in the house. Presumably, they'd burned in the fire.

In Waid's account of events, the children were upstairs as their parents were slaughtered, shouting for Terry and Penny. From downstairs, Waid yelled to the kids to remain where they were. It's at this stage that Charlie started to panic, confiding that he couldn't kill the kids, and Waid threatened to leave. Wilkinson responded to the threat by going upstairs.

"I asked what happened next," Almon wrote. "Waid replied that he remembers Wilkinson stabbing the little boy. I asked which one did he kill. Waid replied 'the big one.' Waid stated that the big one was 'shown to be a threat.' Waid stated that [Bubba] charged toward Wilkinson several times, and that [Waid] pulled the gun and shot him. I asked if [Bubba] dropped right there. Waid replied 'Yes.' Waid stated that Wilkinson killed Tyler."

It was getting harder for the investigators to hide their disdain for what occurred. Referring to Bubba by his given name, Almon asked, "Do you know how old Matthew was."

"Twelve years old."

"Do you know how old Tyler was, and does it matter?"

"No."

"This was just a job for money?"

"It didn't turn out that way. First it was a job for money, and to help a friend out."

Waid next described robbing the house, following Erin's instructions by locating the lockbox next to the dryer in the bathroom, looting Terry's wallet and Penny's purse, and pilfering jewelry from various spots. He called Bobbi, he said, and demanded, "Get up here, kill the car, but don't get out." Bobbi complied, and it took "two or three trips" to transfer Erin's belongings and other items into the vehicle." When the fire was set, Waid told cops, he did his share by igniting the comforter in the master bedroom.

Almon asked about where Terry had been at the time.

"He was facedown between the bed and the wall on the floor." Penny, Waid added, was on the ground, with her feet extending into the bathroom. Charles said that he checked the mother and the kids to verify that they'd been killed. It was a gory scene, but no one appeared to be moving. Charlie told his friend that he'd examined Terry, and he, too, was dead.

As far as Waid knew, there was no reason to assume otherwise.

After the blaze started, Waid told police he drove his girlfriend's car away from the crime scene, turning down different roads to release tension. When Almon asked what, if anything, was said in the car, Waid quoted Erin.

"Holy shit . . . that was awesome."

His total take of the night: slightly over $200.

After dropping off Charlie and Erin at Matthew's trailer, Waid and Bobbi returned to her apartment. While his girlfriend was getting ready for work, Charles said, he threw all the evidence he had into the Sabine River.

Almon asked about the sword found in the trunk. Waid denied that it was the weapon used to kill the family. Rather, it was a matching sword from the same set. The foil from the massacre had been tossed into the Sabine, on the west side of Highway 80, between Grand Saline and Mineola. Waid had placed the sword in a bag—unzipped so it would fill quickly and sink down.

The investigators made note of the detail, then switched back to the aspect of the crime that most disturbed them.

"Did the kids ever do anything against you?" Almon asked.

"No."

"Did the parents ever do anything against you?"

"No."

Vance interjected. "This was just a financial opportunity?"

"Yes."

In another era, Waid might have received a kick to the stomach and a broken nose on the spot. Instead, the lawmen contained their emotions, and simply concluded the interview.

When police pulled off Highway 154 and parked in front of the Oak Ridge restaurant, they found Bobbi Johnson sitting out front, speaking on her cell phone. Chief Deputy Fischer, Deputy Emig and Shanna Sanders, the chief of police for the Rains Independent School District, politely impressed upon her the need to end her conversation.

Bobbi told Sanders about her recent pay raise. "She acted very nonchalant about us being there," Fischer remembered.

He asked if she'd heard about the Caffey murders.

"Yeah, that is so sad. Can you believe what happened to that poor family?"

"It is," Fischer answered. "Bobbi, do you mind coming with us to the sheriff's office? We have some questions to ask you."

"Sure, just let me tell my boss."

She re-entered the restaurant, then came out quickly, sitting down in the passenger seat of the police car, feigning a cheerful demeanor. "It's just terrible, isn't it?" she said of the murders.

"Very tragic," Fischer replied from his spot in the back seat, watching the girl delete items off her cell phone.

At the Rains County Sheriff's Department, Bobbi was met by Detective Almon and Ranger Vance. Their tone was grim as they began questioning the young woman.

"Bobbi," Almon said. "Your car was seen at two AM on County Road 2370. We know that Charles Waid and Charlie Wilkinson were with you. We need to know what happened—and we want the truth."

Bobbi claimed that Erin had called Charlie around midnight, claiming that Penny was yelling and hitting her. Because Erin appeared to be frightened, Bobbi said, she and Waid drove Charlie to the Caffey house, parking down the road. The boys left the car, she continued, but, because she'd taken some muscle relaxers, she fell asleep. She estimated that the pair was gone between ten and fifteen minutes. Then, they re-entered the vehicle and headed over to Matthew Waid's house.

They returned to the Caffeys, Bobbi said, after another phone call from Erin. Now, she wanted her parents murdered. Picking up Erin at the end of her driveway, Bobbi corroborated the story about driving around, attempting to talk the girl out of the murder plot. In Bobbi's version, she was the one counseling Erin not to resort to violence.

According to Bobbi, the teens came up with a compromise: they'd *all* go to Erin's house, and mediate some type of accord with Terry and Penny. When they returned to the home, the front door was open. The males entered "checking to see if the parents were awake," allegedly to initiate the dialogue. For some reason, though, Charlie happened to have a gun.

Once again, Bobbi contended, the muscle relaxers induced a nap. This time, Bobbi approximated, she was out for ten to twenty minutes before Waid came up to the car and informed her, "We got to go."

She quoted her boyfriend as saying that Charlie shot Terry five times and Penny "three times or so." There were flames coming from the second floor.

"Did you call the fire department?" Almon asked.

"No."

"Why not?"

"I was scared of Charlie."

"Why were you scared?"

"Erin's parents didn't do anything to him, and they got killed. So just think what he could have done to me."

The investigators asked her to clarify a number of points, and the tale about the effort to negotiate a truce between Erin and her parents melted away. Waid had initially been carrying two swords, Bobbi said, but when the boys left the Caffey residence, Charlie was holding the foil with the bloody blade, as well as a gun and some money. Bobbi depicted her boyfriend as playing a secondary role, hauling out Erin's boots and other personal items.

"Did you know what was going to happen?" Almon asked.

"Yes. I knew what Charlie was going to do." After all, Erin had implicitly told him that she wanted to "get rid of" her mother and father.

Bobbi said that she'd heard Erin complain, "I'm tired of getting beat by my parents"—a charge that would later be denied.

While Charlie murdered the Caffeys, Waid was supposed to keep watch, and hold the dog, Bobbi said.

Both investigators knew this contention was a fallacy, and they chipped away at Bobbi until she could no longer maintain the farce.

"So Charles helped Charlie?" Almon asked.

"Yes," Bobbi replied apprehensively.

The cheerful girl who prattled on to the cops about her pay raise and surprise over the slayings now considered the severity of her circumstances. "I think I need to talk to my mother," she said.

"Why?"

"I might need a lawyer."

"Are you requesting a lawyer?" Almon asked, not willing to blow the case over a Miranda breach.

"Yes."

The detectives looked at one another. Legally, she could no longer be questioned. Nonetheless, police were gaining an accurate sense of what occurred in the Caffey household. "You had three different suspects," Ranger Vance noted, "and their interviews just mirrored each other. They were almost cookie cutter, to the point that you'd almost think they were rehearsed. But that much detail coming from three different people cannot be rehearsed. We knew we were getting the correct information."

Instead of sending her home, Vance arrested Bobbi for capital murder, and walked her over to the jail. Meanwhile, Deputy John Wallace inspected Bobbi's purse. He found several latex gloves turned inside out, as well as the hull of a spent shotgun shell.

Meanwhile, the reporters working the story were starting to uncover small details about the participants, most notably that Charlie Wilkinson—the young man accused of viciously killing his girlfriend's mother and two younger brothers— was well-liked in some quarters. If he had the predisposition to commit mass murder, few of his acquaintances noticed.

"There was nothing too remarkable about him," said *Tyler Morning Telegraph* reporter Lauren Grover. "He was kind of quiet, kept to himself, attended church with Erin, went to youth group. We knew he had some family problems but, at school, he didn't stand out as a bad kid—nothing worse than some tardiness, and some absences.

"His classmates said he was not a cool kid. He was not popular. He was kind of on the fringes of the high school, didn't have a lot of friends. And then, when Erin got there, they spent all of their time together."

Similarly, Bobbi Johnson was characterized as a student who allowed her romance to eclipse the other interests in her life.

The only difference was that, while Charlie seemed cheerless and stagnant to a certain extent, Bobbi was a kid with interests, a work ethic and the potential to branch out from the small town dormancy.

"Everyone said she was a really sweet girl," Lauren recalled. "Apparently, she was very outgoing. I talked to a teacher of hers at a café one night who was so shocked [about Johnson's involvement in the murders] because Bobbi wasn't like that. She was a good student, a hard worker, someone who showed a lot of ambition in school. Then, she met Charles Waid, and started drinking and going downhill.

"Bobbi just dropped off the face of the earth when she started dating Waid, and spent all her time with him."

* * *

Ranger Vance could barely remember the last time he slept. In his fatigued state, the images of the crime—Terry crawling through the bathroom window with a bullet in his face, Penny on her knees, having her throat slashed, Tyler watching his brother get shot in the head moments before a sword infiltrated his eight-year-old body—played over and over. Just after processing Bobbi Johnson's car, he decided to drive home.

"I'd been working this thing through all day long, eighteen to twenty hours," he said. "And I kept my composure because this is a job that I'm doing. I'm out working for the victims. I've got one shot to get all of this, and I wanted to make sure I had everything."

As he approached his home, the ranger would generally drive past a little corner church, round a corner and enter a tunnel of overhanging trees. At the end of the passageway, the trees parted and gave way to open country. Through the windshield, Vance could see his house.

But on this day, something was a little bit different. Under the trees, parked in the center of the road, was a car with its lights out. "It was just past the church, before you get to the opening, before you get to my house," Vance said. "And it all comes flowing back to me, man—Terry Caffey, sleeping in his house, with that car sitting just down the road."

The ranger swiftly rolled up on the vehicle and jumped out, finding not a group of co-conspirators in a mass murder, but two lovers, frantically struggling to pull on their clothes, as they faced the vigilant—and slightly jittery—officer.

CHAPTER 12

Matthew Waid stood in the doorway of his home, surrounded by piles of beer bottles and trash, beleaguered by recent events and deferential to the police officers displaying their search warrant. "You don't need it," he said. "Search anywhere you want."

As Chief Deputy Fischer and Deputy Greg Stout entered the living room, they noticed that Matthew's pregnant, common-law wife, Emerald Blair, appeared to have difficulty breathing. "I'm not feeling well," she explained. "Could I please sit down on the couch?"

The deputies granted her request. Matthew sat down beside her, telling police that after a night of drinking he'd fallen asleep at about eleven PM on Friday night. But it had been anything but a quiet evening for Matthew and Emerald; it never was. He told investigators that his brother Charles, along with Charlie Wilkinson, Michael Dickinson and Tanis Condit, had also been around.

"My brother's friends come here a lot to hang out," he said.

Fischer's eyes scanned the trailer, and stopped on a small, camouflage-colored purse. "Whose is this?" the chief deputy asked.

"I don't know," Emerald answered.

Fischer opened up the pocketbook and looked through it, quickly finding Erin Caffey's driver's license.

The officers now headed to the back room, hoping to find evidence of the crime: blood, smoky clothing, guns, boots matching the footprints left by the suspects in Bobbi's vehicle. Because there was no overhead light, Fischer removed a blanket from one of the windows and let the sun seep into the room. Stout took photographs, while Fischer moved slowly in a counterclockwise direction, examining everything he spotted.

Spread out on the carpet were several shell casings. A box of ammunition stood alongside the mattress. Fischer motioned at his subordinate: "Let's take all of this in as evidence."

The chief walked over to a black and white western shirt and lifted it up, scrutinizing the item for blood. As the shirt left the ground, a used condom fell onto the floor, a trickle of semen leaking out—evidence that Charlie and Erin had had sex, if nothing else.

Moving over to the closet, Fischer reached in and began to move objects around. "I lifted a blanket up and saw what I thought to be some type of large doll," he wrote in his report. When he grabbed the hair, however, the eyes suddenly opened. It was "a small female," he said, "in a fetal postion, sitting against the wall."

He'd just seen the face minutes earlier, gazing out at him from Erin's driver's license.

"Show me your hands," he commanded, drawing his gun.

Erin didn't move. "She appeared to be in shock," he wrote. "Her eyes were open wide, and she just stared at me."

The chief asked the pajama-clad girl to identify herself. In a tiny voice, she replied, "Erin."

Somehow, he managed to get her off the ground and march her into the living room. Both Matthew and Emerald ogled the teen in disbelief.

Matthew sidled up to the deputy and spoke to him in an incredulous tone: "I was told she was dead."

Later, Fischer remembered, "It appeared to me that she was under some type of drug. Her eyes were wide, and I could see her pupils were very large. We called EMS to check her out. I asked her again if she was Erin, and she nodded yes."

Matthew and Emerald remained transfixed, as bewildered by the scenario as the officers.

"How did you get here?" Fischer asked.

"I don't know. Where am I?"

"Do you remember anything?"

"Fire."

Erin was wobbly, and the investigators worried that she was about to throw up. She was taken outside into the chilly air, then brought back inside the trailer.

"Do you remember what happened?" Fischer asked.

"Two guys with swords yelled at me to get on the floor. I remember smoke."

"What else do you remember?"

"Nothing."

Noted Fischer, "She appeared to be very disoriented, and mumbled things that could not be understood. EMS arrived and, after evaluating her, decided she needed to be transported. . . . When the ambulance arrived, [Emerald] began to get sick, and another ambulance was dispatched for her. She was also eventually transported to the hospital. Mr. Waid stayed behind with the officers for the search."

Outside, the officers found two long guns—an older "Mauser-type" rifle, along with a twelve-gauge shotgun—in a Cadillac.

"What are these?" Matthew was asked.

"Honestly," he responded. "I didn't know they were there." Apparently, so many people passed through his home that he barely paid attention to their possessions.

In a shoebox on the backseat, Fischer discovered a pair of used boots. The officers confiscated the footwear, in case the boots matched any of the footprints found at the crime scene.

When the search was completed, Matthew asked if he could meet up with Emerald at the hospital. He'd been a gentleman from the moment the officers arrived—not even a perfunctory effort had been made to cover up for his brother—and he appeared to have been excluded from the crime plot. "Go ahead," he was told.

Back at the sheriff's department, Detective Almon contacted Fischer and asked him to describe the evidence found in the home. "Did you see any swords?" Almon asked.

"Yes, I did. There were two samurai swords in the back room. One was in the closet. One was by the bed."

"I think we need to take these in, too."

Because the house had been released back to Matthew Waid, police were required to type up a second search warrant for the trailer and have it authorized by the justice of the peace. Matthew made sure that he was at the home to accommodate investigators.

"Whose swords are these?" Fischer asked.

"One of them is mine. The other belongs to my roommate, Tanis."

"What's your sword doing in Tanis' bedroom?"

"I don't know."

Once again, Matthew wasn't being evasive; people and objects simply tended to move freely around his residence. As police left with the swords, Matthew reminded them that they could return whenever they wished.

In the hospital, Terry was told that his daughter was safe. But police were still extremely guarded. Piecing together the few scraps of information he had, Terry believed that Erin was found wandering somewhere close to the house. He wasn't sure if she'd escaped during the massacre, or been kidnapped by her boyfriend, then released.

"When can I see her?" Terry asked.

His sister, Mary Horn, told him that the family would bring Erin to his bedside, after doctors examined her at Hopkins County Memorial Hospital in Sulphur Springs.

Terry's allowed his nerves to settle for a moment. The news that Erin was alive was the most heartening information he'd received. At this stage, satisfied that he'd endured long enough to identify Charlie as the killer, his own future had become secondary.

It was Erin's fate that was most important.

Penny's mother, Virginia Daily, noticed Erin's peculiar frame of mind as police spoke to her in the hospital. The girl seemed puzzled by even basic questions. When Shanna Sanders, the chief of police for the Rains Independent School District, asked Erin her age, the teen stated that she was fourteen. Virginia was quick to correct this.

"So she's not fourteen?" Sanders said.

"She's sixteen!" Virginia emphasized, out of Erin's earshot.

"She told me she was fourteen."

"She's got a driver's license, she's got a truck," the grandmother pointed out, noting that Erin purchased her vehicle with money that she'd earned at Sonic.

Just a few days earlier, Virginia reminded police, everything had seemed so ordinary. It had been the grandparents' anniversary, and the couple was planning to take a short trip. They needed someone to watch their dog and, on Friday, Penny had stopped by her parents' home to pick up their Boston terrier. Now, Penny was dead, and Virginia was sitting alongside her confounded granddaughter, inundated by misfortune.

"I don't even know where my daughter would want her grave in the cemetery," Virginia sobbed.

"Well, I just want to answer the questions that you have for us," Sanders replied reassuringly. "I'll do anything that I can to help you."

Virginia's thoughts shifted to Charlie. Was Erin's relentless boyfriend really capable of such terror? And, if so, could he get to Erin, or hurt other family members?

"Has he been arrested?" the grandmother questioned.

"As of right now, he's being detained."

"Okay, so he's not on the street?"

"No, ma'am."

Like Terry, Virginia imagined Erin fleeing from the

house, as Charlie perpetrated the crime. "You see this on TV but, my God, when it happens to you, it's terrible," Virginia said through tears. "And she ran . . . I'm sorry, you're more into this than me . . . Was he going to get her?"

"I don't know. I don't know the details."

"My God, she ran."

"Did she tell you she ran?"

"Oh no, that's what I thought. They said they found her in the woods."

"I don't . . . I hate to say because I'm not a hundred percent sure. But I think they found her in the house, in the suspect's house."

Virginia gasped in shock. "The suspect's house? Oh my God."

"But I'm not real sure right now."

"Oh, dear."

In the emergency room, Erin whispered something urgent to her cousin, Courtney Daily: "There were two people. They're after me."

"Who?"

"I'm scared. They're going to get me."

"Who, Erin? What did they look like?"

"I don't know."

After moving Erin to the hospital's trauma room, police ordered that the girl be given a full toxicology screen, specifically to check for date rape drugs. A nurse also conducted a sexual assault examination. When asked if she'd had sex within the last week, Erin answered affirmatively, claiming to have engaged in relations with two separate males—one white and one black. In the days that followed, police questioned Erin's associates to determine the identity of the African-American male, but were never able to come up with a name. As a result, authorities concluded that Erin, in her less than rational state, had conjured up this lover or, given her history of manipulating the truth, managed to keep yet another secret from not only her family, but Charlie.

Erin repeatedly asked Sanders about her parents, but not

her brothers. At different times, her grandparents, as well as other relatives and a pastor, passed through the room. Police noticed that the girl showed little emotion unless a family member was present.

Sanders attempted to decipher the nature of Erin's affiliation with Wilkinson. "You said that Charlie is your boyfriend," the chief asked. "Is he your boyfriend, or was he?"

"He was."

"He was? Why isn't he now?"

"I don't know. I guess . . . my mom really didn't like him, so she made us break up."

"Okay, she didn't like him, so she made y'all break up."

"She didn't make us, but we decided that it was best."

"Okay, y'all decided it would be best for y'all to break up. How did he feel about that?"

"He was kind of mad."

"He was mad?"

". . . But he decided we'd just be friends."

"When was that about?"

"A couple of weeks ago."

"Okay, so he was mad?"

"He wasn't mad . . . I guess . . . upset."

"He was upset? How long had y'all gone together?"

"Ever since November."

"Since November? Did y'all get along pretty good when y'all went together?"

"Yeah."

"Why didn't your mom like him?" Sanders suddenly shifted to the present tense, to imply that Penny was still alive. "Why does she not like him? You said that she didn't like him?"

"He was, he was too old."

According to Erin, though, the Caffeys continued to condone the friendship, as long as it stayed platonic. "We were planning on hanging out this weekend," she said.

"Who?"

"Me and Charlie."

"You and Charlie planned on hanging out? What were your plans?"

"Just going to the bowling alley."

"To go to the bowling alley? Were your parents going to let you do that?"

Erin nodded.

"They were? Did you ask them?"

"Yeah, I told them. She said it was fine."

Erin proceeded to tell a story about waking up in a smoke-clogged house, while two men with swords held her hostage. As far as Erin could tell, neither had a gun. After an indeterminable amount of time, they released her—no reason given.

"You don't think you were at your house last night?" Sanders asked.

"I was when I got home from school, but I don't know how I got to the other house."

Sanders was having problems constructing a logical sequence of events. "Can you think of anything else that can help us?"

"I drank some stuff."

"You drank some stuff? At your house, or at this other house?"

"At that house."

"At that house? You drank some stuff?"

"Yeah."

"Do you know what you drank?"

Erin shook her head from side to side.

"No?"

"No."

"Did somebody give it to you?"

Erin claimed that one of her sword-wielding captors handed her a drink, after she'd mentioned that she was thirsty. "He had blond hair," the girl said, "long blond hair. He was really tall."

The description fit neither Charles Waid nor Charlie Wilkinson. Cops would later wonder if this was deliberate.

Was Erin attempting to steer them away from the actual killers?

"And this was at the other house?" Sanders queried, in a kindly voice, hoping to keep Erin talking. "Okay. So that was good. You remembered that. Is there anything else you can remember?"

"My head hurts."

"Your head hurts? Okay. Well. There's nothing you can remember that can help us? Okay . . . we're here for you. We'll help you through this as best we can."

In a barely discernable tone, Erin mumbled, "They're coming back."

"Huh? They're coming back? Why?"

Erin said something so quietly that it was impossible to understand.

"Can you think of a reason why somebody might do anything bad to you? Is there anything going on that we need to know about? What makes you say that they're coming back?"

"I just know that they are."

The story just didn't make sense. Investigators noted that, in contrast to other victims found in smoky homes, Erin's clothes lacked the smell of burnt wood or phosphorous. She displayed none of the symptoms of smoke inhalation. And when her toxicology tests came back, detectives saw that Erin's body contained neither Rohypnol, GHB or other drugs capable of inducing memory loss. As a result, police began operating from the premise that either Erin had been doped by an unfamiliar narcotic, or she was flat-out lying.

Every new development seemed to find its way back— in some form or another—to the congregants at Miracle Faith Baptist Church. "When [the police] said they'd picked her up, I was like, 'Did they have to put a cast on her? Is she okay?'" youth leader Sarah Meece remembered. "And they were like, 'There's not a scratch on her.' And then, I was like, 'Wait a minute. Whoa.'" It was then that Sarah and her husband decided to resist the mounting press inquiries about the Caffeys.

"We didn't have a clue, but we thought, 'Okay, there's something really fishy . . .'"

Just before Erin was released from the hospital, Sanders and Rains County deputy Serena Booth offered to remain close to the girl for the rest of the day. Erin accepted the invitation. "Where are you going now?" Sanders asked.

"I want to see my father."

The officers told Erin and her grandparents to follow them to East Texas Medical Center in Tyler. As the caravan was leaving the Sulphur Springs city limits, traveling south on Highway 154, Chief Deputy Kurt Fischer called Sanders on her cell phone. After speaking to Charlie Wilkinson, Charles Waid and Bobbi Johnson, authorities believed they had reasonable cause to arrest Erin Caffey.

Although Erin's story was certainly disjointed, Sanders had begun to feel protective of the befuddled blonde who'd just lost most of her family. Sanders was silent for a few seconds, then handed the phone to Booth, who listened to Fischer's instructions to place the girl in police custody.

"You want us to do that now?" Booth asked, surprised.

"Yes, I do."

Sanders and Booth pulled into a parking lot. The Dailys parked there, as well. Sanders motioned Virginia over, and explained the circumstances. Not surprisingly, Virginia burst into tears. First, her daughter and two grandsons were murdered in their home. Now, her granddaughter was about to be charged in the multiple slaying. Just when the situation seemed like it couldn't become worse, Virginia had to stand there helplessly, and watch Sanders place Erin in handcuffs.

Sobbing uncontrollably, Virginia grabbed Erin's face and looked her in the eyes. "Did you have any part in this?" the grandmother demanded.

"No, Grandma," Erin cried.

Virginia stepped back and looked on as Erin was placed in the police car and transported to the Rains County Sheriff's Department. Since she was younger than the other suspects, she was locked into a juvenile holding area, where Justice of the Peace Don Smith read the girl her Miranda warning.

Ranger Vance later told *Texas Monthly,* "I was picturing a monster, for lack of a better word. Here was someone who dreamed up a scheme to murder her family and manipulated people into carrying out her plan. And then, in walks this tiny, meek, blonde-headed girl who couldn't fight her way out of a wet paper sack."

The judge asked Erin if she wanted to speak with detectives. She refused, choosing to explain her actions in writing. As before, she insisted that she'd been kidnapped, and bore no responsibility for the carnage.

In Erin's booking photo, her smooth skin was punctuated by signs of teenage acne. Her hair, pulled back, appeared greasy, loose ends dangling around her ears. Erin's eyes were wide and her lips thin, betraying neither guilt nor innocence.

"She looked like a child more than anything else," Vance recalled. "I had already witnessed the crime scene, seen the burned up bodies, and heard the interviews where this was calculated and planned—the original plan hatched from her. The one thing I did expect from her was fear, for her to have a little anxiety about what was about to happen. And she just had this blank stare. I think she honestly felt, 'If I close my eyes and open them again, maybe all of this will be a bad dream, and it'll be over with.' I don't think the severity had sunk in.

"She was holding to her story. She was told a story—if you get caught, this is what you are to say. And she was sticking hard to that story."

With the formalities completed, deputies drove Erin to the Greenville Juvenile Detention Center. As with her associates, the charge was capital murder.

Kurt Fischer, the man who'd spoken with Charlie about his girlfriend problems, then arrested the young man who'd socialized with his sons, also found himself in the awkward position of notifying Terry about his daughter's part in the massacre.

Gauze covered the hole in Terry's cheek, but the material

was discolored. He regularly cleaned the bloody liquid seeping from his nose. In between sentences, Terry coughed up fluid. Still, his desire to get some answers was strong.

With his sister, Mary Horn, listening intently, Terry beseeched the lawman, "I guess I want to know how my daughter is. . . . They won't let me watch TV or anything. They say it's all over the news. Is she okay?"

"Yes, she's doing fine. She's going to be in a juvenile facility in Greenville."

Terry braced himself. "I don't want a whole lot of details. But," he paused, "what kind of involvement did she have?"

"Her involvement was great."

Terry broke down, choking with sobs.

"Take a deep breath," his sister softly urged.

The normally composed Terry continued to wail. What more could the world do to him?

Mary struggled to come up with a reassuring remark. The best she could do was, "You have nothing to feel sorry for."

"*Why?*" Terry begged. "I don't understand why."

Coincidentally, Ranger Vance was also on hand to witness this heart-wrenching scene. "A father's love," the ranger observed, "you know, it's there. And then, to hear that she had full knowledge—his wife was gone, his boys were gone, his house was gone, and she had a hand in it—he was just devastated."

CHAPTER 13

"Momma," Bobbi Johnson cried over the phone, "I love you. I miss you."

Bobbi had gotten herself into a hell of a mess. But her mother, Theresa, realized that this was no time to let her dissolve. The girl had a tendency to be gullible and trusting. And, even in a detention facility as small as the Rains County Jail, she had to be wary of the vipers who stood a chance of cutting themselves a better deal at Bobbi's expense.

"You don't talk to nobody, okay?" Theresa counseled.

"Yes, ma'am."

"I'm getting an attorney. It's going to be the top criminal attorney in Texas, okay?"

"Okay."

"But whenever I get this attorney, I want you to tell him everything."

"Yes, ma'am."

"Anything you know. And if anybody's in a cell with you, and they're trying to be nice to you, and they're trying to chitchat when it comes to this subject, you don't say nothing about *one* thing, okay?"

"Yes, ma'am."

"Even if they're being so nice to you, Bobbi, and you think

they're your friend or something. You don't tell nobody about anything."

"Yes, ma'am."

"Something innocent can be misconstrued, and they can turn it around and make you look guilty about something."

"Yes, ma'am."

". . . Are you okay?"

Bobbi wept. "Yeah."

"I mean, I know you're not okay. But, I mean, are you okay?"

". . . I've been having anxiety attacks."

". . . If you start feeling like you're panicking, you just close your eyes and take some deep breaths, okay?"

"Okay, I can't eat anything. I can't."

"I know. Just try to nibble because it's better to throw up a little something than nothing. And just drink."

Bobbi sniffed. "Okay."

". . . Everybody that knows you, baby, knows that you had nothing to do with this. Okay?"

"Okay."

"And I want to ask you questions that I've had on my mind. But I don't want you saying anything, okay?"

Bobbi sobbed that she was willing to disclose whatever her mother wished.

"Well, they could be recording or listening in on the conversation, and I don't want them to have anything to incriminate you, or have any question about you or anything. Okay?"

"Yes, ma'am."

Nonetheless, Theresa tried to ask just enough to assure herself of her daughter's blamelessness. "Where was your car at . . . you were at work?"

"Charles had it . . . he dropped me off at work."

"And that's what he did Friday night also?"

"Yeah, and then he came and picked me up."

"And then, y'all went home that night?"

"Huh?"

"Then, y'all went home that night?"

Bobbi would not provide a detailed response, switching topics by expressing her love for her mother. But she also wondered what people were saying on the other side of the jailhouse walls.

"Is it on the news?" Bobbi queried.

"Well, no names have been said, but . . . they showed footage of the house and the cars that had been burnt. They just said that four people had been arrested. . . . I have not found one place where they've named names. They can't do that."

Bobbi cried. "I think my time's up," she said.

". . . I love you. You stay strong, and you pray."

"Yes, ma'am."

As soon as public defender Roland "Ron" Ferguson heard that he'd been assigned to represent Charlie Wilkinson, he rushed over to the jail to caution the defendant about betraying too much to the authorities. "I was hoping to get in there before they got all the confessions and written statements and everything," the attorney said. "But, of course, as we all know, that didn't happen. They got that before I was even aware of how the attack went down."

Ferguson had worked a full day in court, and had his mind clouded with other cases. As was customary, he brought along his wife, Stacy, his sweet-tempered, idealistic investigator/mitigator. Ron later admitted that he wasn't thrilled about his new client. Like others in the community, he was revolted by the attack on the Caffey family. And Charlie was doing little to win over the lawyer. The more the suspect revealed, the angrier Ferguson became.

"I was mad at Charlie for the senselessness of the act. It got to the point where I thought, 'It's time for me to leave. I've heard too much.'"

The meeting took place in the jail's visitation room. A collection of mattresses rested on one side. On the other was a bank of phones for inmates to call friends and relatives. Charlie positioned himself on a stool in the center of the room, and, as he spoke, Stacy sat down on the floor, looking up at him. Like other maternal figures in Charlie's life, she harbored little fear of the murder suspect. Instead, she found his wretched circumstances drawing her closer.

Remembered Ron, "She was almost at his feet, asking him about what happened then and what happened next and what happened next. She does this a lot—she got *way* too close to him real fast."

The attorney maintained his reserve. No jury was going to be sympathetic to this kind of story. He told Charlie that he was facing a charge of capital murder. "At this point," Ferguson informed his client, "there's several things that can happen—the worst being the death penalty."

The best possible outcome the attorney could envision was life without parole.

"I don't want that," Charlie replied. "I don't want to live the rest of my life that way."

The already irritated lawyer shot back, "That's too bad. We can't plead guilty to capital murder. We can't do that. My job is to keep you alive. And at this point, the best that I can see happening is for me to try to save your life."

Tall, graying and even-voiced, Ron had a focused demeanor inside the courtroom. But the moment the day ended, he could sit back and tell stories, a skeptical smile creeping across his face, the tone of his laugh indicating a certain incredulousness about the system he'd sworn to defend.

Ron had been born in Roswell, New Mexico, in 1955, eight years after UFO proponents claim the U.S. military covered up the discovery of a crashed flying saucer and the recovery of several aliens, some of whom were still alive. Ferguson's father was in the Air Force and gave the allegation little credence. The family changed addresses regularly, relocating to Japan and the Philippines, among other places. When Ron was four and living in Greensboro, North Carolina, he was hit by a car. As the family story went, the stress caused Ron's mother to go into labor with his younger brother.

"I ran out in front of the car," Ron said, "and the driver carried me to the hospital. I wasn't hurt seriously, just some scrapes and bruises. But that's one of my first memories, waking up after being hit."

Because the life of a military child eliminated the likelihood of long-term friendships, Ron threw himself into academics. "If I wasn't in school," he recounted, "I was hauling hay or cutting pulpwood. In high school, I played on three different football teams. It was kind of strange growing up that way, but my best friend was always the public library. I read a lot."

In 1978, he graduated from Texas A&M's campus in Commerce—then known as East Texas State College—with a degree in accounting. He'd initially been a photography major, but decided to switch specialties after realizing that he was "not color-blind but color deficient." "I was looking around at psychology, sociology, when I went to a career seminar and asked the headhunter, 'If you had to start all over again, what would you study?' He said accounting, because it prepares you for any field of business you're interested in. So I changed majors, and I found this to be very true."

The career fit at first. Ron became comptroller at a corporation, and the job was challenging. But Ferguson began to feel that there was little opportunity to advance toward the CEO's position. So at age thirty-five, he enrolled in law school.

"My mother said, 'Boy, are you crazy?'" Ron said. "'Do you know how old you are?' I said, 'Mom, I'm doing it because I want to help people.'"

For two years, Ferguson served as assistant county attorney—or prosecutor—in Hopkins County. The county attorney at the time was Robert Newsom, a friend who'd once encouraged Ron to go to the law school. Later, Newsom would be a judge in Texas's Eighth District Court (and the magistrate in the Charlie Wilkinson case) while Ron went into private practice as a criminal defense attorney.

"I've been asked more than once why I try these cases," Ron noted. "People say, 'How can you sleep at night? How can you do this?' And my thinking is that it doesn't matter what kind of case this is. My job is to make sure that my client's rights are preserved. I'm going to try to get that jury to start out with a presumption of innocence."

The assumption has never come naturally—particularly when members of the jury pool stare across the room at the person sitting in the defendant's chair. "Their first thought is usually, 'I wonder what he's done,'" Ron pointed out. "And it should be, 'I wonder what he's accused of.' An officer once told me, 'Ron, he wouldn't have been arrested if he wasn't guilty,' and that's just not always correct.

"I usually start a case with the viewpoint of the appeal, trying to preserve the record so he has a chance of appeal, if I lose. And then, I work backwards to show jurors why he's not guilty."

Nonetheless, through the years, there have been moments when Ron's wife Stacy has struggled with her own suspicions. "I will say this: It hurts when you're sitting at the table next to a person that you have reason to believe is guilty. You're looking at the victim's family, and your heart can't help but go out to them. And then, sometimes, you don't know, and you're questioning yourself, 'Are they guilty, or are they not?' Because most of the time they say they're innocent. They convince themselves of a story and stick to it. Then you go to trial and, suddenly, the prosecutor's pieces fit together. And Ron and I will look at each other and go, 'Oh, no.'"

When the verdict is guilty, the trial shifts to its punishment phase, the segment of the case when Ron's performance can literally determine life or death. Under Texas law, the jury has two options in a murder case: life without parole or capital punishment. "The jury has to examine the evidence to determine whether or not the person will be a continuing threat to society," Ron explained. "And society has been defined to include prison—the prison staff, the doctors, the other people there. So the jurors have to consider if there's any type of mitigating evidence that justifies sparing the defendant's life.

"What we have to do is educate the jury that they never

have to sentence someone to death in the state of Texas. Because many people, after reading the jury instructions, will think, 'This is my only choice.' The jury's not compelled to make that decision."

Nonetheless, Ron conceded, by the time a trial reaches the closing arguments, most of the jurors have already made up their minds.

Stacy's appreciation for life—including that of a person convicted of murder—may be linked to her own experience battling cervical cancer between 1996 and 1998. "They gave me a year to live," she said. "I went through all the legal paperwork and everything. I was going to give my children to my sister. I was prepared, you know, to not make it."

When the cancer was finally eradicated, she never took lightly the gift of surviving another day. In October 2008, shortly before Joseph Ries—convicted of killing a sleeping man during a burglary—became the twelfth prisoner executed that year in the country's most active death penalty state, she wrote a protest letter to Governor Rick Perry.

"Too many Texans on death row are suffering from mental illness, left untreated," she said. "We live in America, a country that should help save and rehabilitate those that are mentally ill. . . . Mental illness is a disease. If one has a terrible disease, such as AIDS, HIV, hepatitis, T.B., etc, these diseases are contagious. . . . Mental illness is no different. . . . Mental illness affects others. Texas really has no place for the mentally ill, long-term, except prison.

"It is unconstitutional, not to mention 'un-Christlike,' to put to death those that are ill."

The inequalities in the justice system also became a theme of Stacy's blog, periodically sent to friends and colleagues. Along with specifics about various cases and judicial rulings, she'd remind readers of a quote from Dr. Martin Luther King Jr:

"Injustice anywhere is a threat to justice everywhere."

Ron and Stacy met in 1998, after an alcoholic neighbor suddenly moved out of town, leaving behind two children and a note requesting that Stacy raise them. Stacy, an attractive blonde who, even in business attire, seemed like a bit of a hippie, agreed to the woman's request, and hired Ron as an attorney.

"The state wanted to take the kids away," he recounted, "and I had to argue the case. And at that point, we lost one and kept one."

The child taken by the state later dropped out of school and battled homelessness, Stacy said. The one who remained in Stacy's home went on to dental school.

At the time, Ron was sharing an office and splitting expenses with an attorney named Phil Smith. Both were involved in pro bono work for battered women in the area. When Ron and Stacy decided to marry, Phil, an ordained minister, performed the ceremony.

Because of the origins of their relationship, work and leisure quickly blended together in the Ferguson home. Cynicism was addressed with humor. The melancholy surrounding many of the cases was alleviated by analysis about the psychological impetus behind the crimes. Stacy grew to admire Ron's erudition of the fine points of American law. Ron came to see Stacy as the sociologist of the pair.

"I tend to get tunnel vision," he said. "If someone says 'black,' I assume it's black. Stacy sees gray. I don't always question everything the way she does."

In 2003, the Sulphur Springs police pulled over a car on Interstate 30. A drug interdiction officer found $270,291 in cash in a backpack in the trunk. Passenger Roland Means insisted that the money was being transported from Milwaukee to Dallas to pay for the production of a rap video; in his community, he contended, everything was done with cash. But authorities placed him under arrest, accusing him of laundering drug funds.

The court appointed Ferguson as Means's attorney. Ron had never tried a money-laundering case before, but applied the same techniques he employed in other criminal trials. When a fellow passenger, Marece Milton, testified that the money was actually going to be used to purchase twenty kilograms of cocaine, Ron invoked the witness' criminal history, and chipped away at his credibility, implanting enough reasonable doubt in the jurors that Means was acquitted.

Just before the verdict was read, Stacy was asked to leave the defense table and move to a section of the courtroom flooded with officers. Meanwhile, the bailiff, John Hipkins, took a position between Ron and the judge. "I really didn't understand why," Ron said. "And I said to John, 'I can't see the judge. Would you step to the side?' And John has these cold blue eyes, and he looks at me, and he steps to his right, about an inch and a half. And it dawns on me that he was worried about a violent incident, and he'd put himself in the line of fire between my client, the people in the courtroom and the judge."

Means headed home toward Milwaukee after the trial. But he stopped off at a home in Mississippi's rural Panola County first. Milton, the man who'd testified against him, followed the same route and allegedly waited outside. When Means left the house, the pair had a confrontation.

"I hear you're going to kill me," Milton allegedly said.

"That's right."

"Well, I'm going to kill you first."

Police said that Means turned to run, and Milton fatally shot him in the back of the head. (Milton was ultimately convicted of manslaughter.)

Interestingly, although Means was acquitted, the $270,291 remained classified as contraband. Eventually, the proceeds were divided to fund various charities.

Rightly or wrongly, in East Texas, authorities tended to operate by their own code.

Like many small town lawyers, it was not uncommon for Ron to know the parties on both sides of a dispute, and the Charlie Wilkinson case was no exception. Ron had met both of Erin's parents while representing Penny's brother in his divorce—from Terry's sister.

"We'd actually sat at the kitchen table, drinking coffee

and sharing muffins or something like that," Ron said. "So then, when I had to defend Charlie, it wasn't as if I was looking at photos of a victim I'd never seen. I'd spent time with Penny Caffey and her family.

"Penny was a very nice, very kind, very pleasant person, and she was careful not to be overly critical of her brother's wife. She didn't like some of the things she thought her sister-in-law was doing, and she was willing to testify about it, and so was Mr. Caffey. Terry was definitely on Penny's side in this. They came across as a very Christian, very strict couple who thought the sister's dresses were too short, she wore too much makeup, she let her daughter go with people they didn't approve of."

Later, when Ron was placed on the Wilkinson case, he was asked if there might have been a pattern running through the family. After all, if the Caffeys imposed their austere standards on their niece, how rigid—or unreasonable—had the couple been with their daughter?

"That would be a good inference," he answered cautiously. "I won't say anything about how they judged their children."

The attorney was far more comfortable evaluating the young people involved in the case: "These were teenagers. Charlie was a child—just a few weeks past his eighteenth birthday. Kids make very poor decisions. They're naïve. They don't understand the consequences of what they're doing."

He believed that this theory pertained to the haunting comments Charlie made to investigators: "I ain't got no conscience . . . I'm a psycho maniac."

"When I saw the police report," Ron said, "and I read how he told the detectives that he walked into the house like 'any ole gunslinger' ready to start shooting, it was so callous. The first time you hear that, you're just thinking, 'What?' You can't say stuff like that! I mean, a whole family's been murdered, and you're talking about it like you're in an Old West movie. It's just crazy!"

Yet, very quickly, the defense attorney began to warm

toward his client. "He's a very engaging person," Ron said. "He told me about his childhood. He spoke about going into the Army and being in the National Guard program for high school students. He told me about his ten-year plan. I'll be honest with you, I was very impressed with his thinking, his thought processes. I just really didn't understand why he'd do something like this. And, of course, I don't know if I understand it today."

Neither did Stacy—although her bond with the murder suspect was instantly stronger: "From the moment our eyes met, I lost all anxiety [about his crime]. There was a lot about Charlie you'd never know from what you'd seen in the media. I did not see him as a cold-hearted murderer. I saw him as a very sad teenager, a kid who needed love, affection, acceptance and nurturing."

She sensed that he trusted very few people, particularly women, and wondered if this had to do with his mother's decision to move so far away from where Charlie was raised. Since November, he'd allowed Erin to become the dominant female in his life. He claimed that he loved her so much that he'd allowed himself to kill for her. Now, once again, he'd been defrauded by his emotions.

"When we first began talking, Charlie was very protective of Erin," Ron said. "Then, we let him know that, when she'd been found in the closet, she told police she'd pretty much been kidnapped, and all she could remember was smoke. When Charlie heard that, he was kind of astounded, and told us real quick, 'That's not how it happened.'"

Nonetheless, he appeared hesitant to get Erin in any more trouble.

"Listen," Ron pointed out, "we can't protect Erin. We're here to protect you."

Toward the end of their first meeting, Ron went ahead to address some paperwork issues, while Stacy remained behind in the cell. "I was starting to feel like a mother, rather than a professional," she recalled. "I wanted to hug him and tell him that we'd get through this, but something told me not to."

Instead, she placed both of her hands on his chest, over his heart, and looked him in the eye.

"Charlie," she began, "what you did was absolutely horrible. Yet it's not unforgivable. I'm a Christian, and I believe everyone can be forgiven. I listened to everything you said in the interview, and I do not see you as a mean person. I see you as someone who is really hurting and crying out. Deep down in your heart, I know you're a good kid who had a lot of bad things happen to him growing up. And I'm so sorry for that.

"We all make mistakes, Charlie. Some worse than others."

CHAPTER 14

Charles Waid was assisted from the patrol car and led to a small body of water. The Sulphur Springs Fire Department dive team was gathered, ready to retrieve a black, double-edged sword similar to the one found in Bobbi's trunk. They were also instructed to search for a safe—the one the suspects couldn't open—and a duffel bag. Waid would remain at the shoreline with deputies, guiding the divers in their search.

During his interrogation with investigators, Waid had maintained that he'd hurled the items into the Sabine River, in the Big Sandy area. But while being escorted to the site, he admitted that he'd attempted to mislead detectives. Perhaps realizing that his cooperation might convince jurors that his life was worth sparing, he now promised to bring authorities to the proper location, off Highway 19, north of Emory, toward Sulphur Springs.

With Waid directing, the procession of vehicles turned onto Farm-To-Market Road 514, traveling several miles and crossing over Elm Creek. Several hundred yards from the Elm Baptist Church, Waid told police to stop on a dirt and rock access road to the creek.

The suspect was brought to the water's edge and introduced to diver Duane Sprague. "Show us where you were standing," Sprague said, "and what direction you tossed the items."

Waid gestured at a spot on the south side of the bridge, where he claimed to have discarded a pair of boots. The sword had been hurled in a westernly direction toward the middle of the creek. The duffel bag was thrown toward the northwest, drifted between the third pillars on the east end of the bridge, and sunk on the north side of the overpass. The safe was tossed toward the west, but floated north under the bridge. Waid hadn't seen it submerge.

As the divers slipped into their wetsuits, water boots, gloves and life jackets, sheriff's deputies announced that they'd spotted a grayish safe about a hundred yards north of the bridge, near the west bank. The divers entered the creek, finding the safe floating in about a foot of water. It was opened, and detectives confirmed that the contents belonged to Terry's recently-deceased father.

One member of the team, Charlie Vaughn, soon found the sword, as well.

As Sprague navigated the water, in search of the duffel bag, he grabbed a stick and poked at objects under the surface. He tried lifting one from underwater with his feet, but could only bring it so far.

"I'm holding something with my feet," he told the other divers. "I don't know what it is."

Vaughn held out his arm for Sprague to grasp while he attempted to bring the item up, securing it between his knees. When he reached down, he felt the type of wheel found on a suitcase. With the assistance of his teammates, a dark-colored "wheeled suitcase/duffel bag" with an extendable handle was pulled to the east bank.

"Is that the duffel bag?" Waid was asked.

"Yes. That's the one."

Detective Richard Almon opened the carrier and looked inside, finding Erin's clothes and two boxes of jewelry.

Under the bridge, investigators also found a yellow cardboard box, containing the boots Waid said that he'd worn during the crime.

As the box was photographed and logged as evidence, Almon looked over at the divers. "This is it, guys," he said. "I think we have everything."

It had taken less than two hours for Waid to help investigators build on what already appeared to be an iron-clad case.

Waid informed his parents that he'd helped his own cause.

"I'm being cooperative," he reported over the phone. "I just got back from showing them where I threw all the stuff."

Charles's father, Bruce, asked about the other defendants.

"I'm not allowed to be told." Charles' voice quivered. "The only person I care about is Bobbi."

He breathed deeply, while Bruce handed the phone to Charles's mother, Shirley. "Charles," she said. "You've got to be strong, babe. I know it's not going to be easy." Her eyes filled with tears. "Are you still in the holding cell or are you in . . ."

"I'm still in the holding tank."

"How long do you think you'll be there?"

"I don't know."

"Are you the only one in there?"

"Yep."

"I wish there was something we could do."

"There's not."

"I know. That's what makes it so hard. What happened?" Waid stated the obvious. "I screwed up."

"Did you know what you was doing?"

"I killed one person. . . . I needed the money."

"Was he going to pay you?"

"Yes, a lot. Supposed to . . ."

"Oh, my God."

"He killed two, and there's another one in the hospital."

"He killed two?"

"Yeah, but I got three counts. Three charges for murder."

"But you killed one?"

"Yep."

"That don't make sense."

"I know it don't make sense that I got three counts of murder when I only killed one person."

"I guess because you was there."

"Yep."

"Oh Charles, I know it's going to be hard. I just, it's so hard to even imagine. And me and Dad, we were waiting for your phone call, and I think we're going to leave because the media will probably be out here. We're not going to talk to them."

"If the media goes out there, tell them to go fuck themselves."

Like Bobbi's mother, Shirley tried finding some words of consolation: "We're here for you. I know it sounds bad. Even though there's not a lot we can do, we're still here for you. We'll always be there for you."

"I know."

"I mean, I just don't understand how it happened, and I never will, you know. But we can't turn the clock back. And I know you wish you could."

"Yep . . . I just hope Bobbi's going to be okay?"

"Do you know what she did?"

"I don't know what she's charged with."

"Did she even get out of the car?"

"No, she never once got out of the car."

"Okay, she'll be charged as an accessory probably." Shirley's own feelings of guilt tore at her. "I wish you had came and talked to us before you had gone and done something like that."

Charles did not respond to her comment, refusing to sorrowfully speculate over what could have been. Instead, he switched to other topics—like his car and cell phone bill.

"You've got to stay strong, okay?" his mother said.

"I know it. . . . I screwed up pretty bad. Things people do for money."

"And [Wilkinson] never gave you nothing, Charles. But that's all said and done now."

Waid felt rageful toward his accomplice: "I don't know. If I do stand face to face [with Charlie], I'm hoping I can keep my cool."

"You've got to keep your cool."

"Because if I don't, all that's going to do is make it worse on me."

"You've got to keep your cool, babe, because what's done is done."

"Yep, I made my own decision. I screwed my life up. . . . I tried to eat breakfast this morning and then I threw up."

"It's not going to get any easier, Charles."

"I know. All's I know is it's going to get a lot harder."

"But you've got to stay strong. You've got to pray. I know you don't want to think and hear that, but you've got to pray. God can hear you. You've got to ask God to forgive you. And he can do that, and he can keep his hands on you while you're wherever you're going to be."

On the Monday after the murders, reporters had the opportunity to view the suspects when each was arraigned on three counts of capital murder, and held on $1.5 million bond. Erin, sporting the same jeans and t-shirt she wore on the night of the murders, cried when she heard that she wouldn't be released from the juvenile detention center in Greenville. Because of her age, the media was barred from disclosing her name.

"Do you want to ask any questions?" said Justice of the Peace Don Smith.

Erin shook her head.

Her attorney, William Howard McDowell, told the press that he would use the time that Erin was in custody to investigate the charges against the teen. "There will be interviews with the probation department, as well as with a psychologist," he said to the Greenville *Herald Banner*. "We're still trying to find out the facts."

Before being escorted back to her cell, Erin hugged and exchanged a few quick words with her grandmother, Virginia Daily. Despite everything, the older woman was sticking by her blood.

The story was now national news. CNN quoted Alba mayor Orvin Carroll as saying that there hadn't been a murder in the town in eighteen years. But investigators, prosecutors and defense attorneys did not view the massacre as a one-of-a-kind incident.

They'd all seen the same type of crime in the past.

Early on Christmas morning in 1999, seventeen-year-old Stephanie Catherine Barron told police, an intruder burst into her home near Tyler, killing her parents in their bed. Stephanie was a decent student—her grades were mainly A's and B's—with no previous history of violence. Yet, police immediately knew that she was lying. In her closet, they found a bloody t-shirt and a recently-discharged .38.

That night Stephanie was arrested, and charged with murdering her parents with a gun stolen by her boyfriend, Dinario Jones, from another home. Afterward, police said, Jones set the house on fire, killing a woman and her three-year-old daughter in the process.

"We wound up clearing four murder cases off of this one case," J.B. Smith—the Smith County sheriff, who later co-authored a book on the crime—told KLTV in Tyler.

Jones was sentenced to forty years in prison. Stephanie Barron received seventy-five.

Smith described Stephanie as an attractive girl who "got into drugs . . . It's a story that many a parent can find horror in."

Because of the murder's Texas setting, as well as Stephanie's wholesome good looks, it was easy to make a parallel between the Barron and Caffey cases. Yet the tribulations of Daniel Petric of Lorain County, Ohio, also contained striking similarities. Like Erin, Daniel came from a religious home; his father, Mark, was a minister at the New Life Assembly of God church in Wellington. Daniel too decided to vent his rage against his parents after feeling constricted by their beliefs.

Mark Petric and his wife, Susan, disapproved of their son's fixation with the *Halo 3* video game—he apparently played between three and eighteen hours every day—in which players shoot monsters who've invaded the earth from outer space. When the Petrics took away their son's favorite diversion, the sixteen-year-old began planning their murders.

Several weeks later, on October 20, 2007, he used his father's key to remove the man's 9mm handgun from a lockbox—as well as the game. Entering his parents' bedroom, he announced, "Would you guys close your eyes? I have a surprise for you."

Believing the surprise would be a pleasant one, his parents observed the boy's wishes. Then, Daniel shot each in the head. As in the Caffey case, the mother died, and father survived.

Hoping to mislead investigators, Daniel placed the gun in his father's hand, expecting police to categorize the incident as a murder-suicide. He fled the home with one item—the *Halo 3* game.

Lorain County common pleas judge James Burge conceded that Daniel was probably so addicted to video games that "he had no idea . . . if he killed his parents, they'd be gone forever." Yet, despite this warped sense of reality, Burge rejected the argument that the boy was not guilty by reason of insanity, and sentenced him to twenty-three years in prison—pontificating about the evils of gaming technology for the assembled reporters.

"I feel confident that if there weren't such things as violent video games, I wouldn't know Daniel Petric," he said.

Nicholas Browning allegedly also tended to confuse real life with the flight of his imagination, according to the psychiatrist who examined the teen after he murdered his parents and two younger brothers in a Baltimore suburb.

"He was in a trancelike state," Neil Blumberg testified at the boy's trial. "He started fantasizing, 'Wouldn't it be nice if they weren't here? Wouldn't it be nice if they couldn't bother me anymore?' "

The Brownings lived in the town of Cockeysville, where Nicholas attended upper level classes and, while working on attaining his Eagle Scout badge, helped build a prayer garden at Epworth United Methodist Church. His father, John, a partner in a law firm in the town of Towson, was active in his sons' Boy Scout troop, while his wife, Tamara, worked part-time in property management while shuttling between her children's activities. Nicholas's younger brothers, Gregory, fourteen, and Benjamin, eleven, each attended Cockeysville Middle School.

"You cannot get any more normal than they were," Nicholas's uncle, Lee Browning, told *The Baltimore Sun*.

To neighbors, Nicholas was exceptionally polite for his age. But Blumberg claimed that, once the boy's grades started slipping in sixth grade, his parents bombarded him with abuse, mocking him as a "fuckup" with neither a moral nor intellectual compass. Convinced that he was a failure, friends said, Nicholas started behaving inappropriately, filching bottles from his parents' liquor cabinet, driving their car without a license, and badly beating his younger siblings.

Six months prior to the murders, Tamara Browning caught her son watching pornography and masturbating with another boy. Blumberg claimed that the other teen later alleged that Browning had raped him.

On the school bus, Nicholas joked about killing his parents, and inheriting what he perceived as his father's riches. As with the kids involved in the Caffey case, the boastful language set off few, if any, alarms.

On February 2, 2008—approximately one month before the Caffey slayings—Nicholas, several days short of sixteen, snuck up on his father, as the man lay on the couch asleep, with *The Da Vinci Code* playing on the television. Using John's own gun, the boy fired into his father's head, before one after another shooting the rest of the family in their beds.

He then attempted to fake a burglary—knocking over his mother's jewelry, and leaving the family's Xbox and Wii by the door—before throwing the gun in a collection of bushes and going to a friend's house for a sleepover.

He also invited his friends to a party at his home the next night, enabling him to enter the house in front of witnesses and feign surprise over the massacre. But detectives quickly broke him down, and he confessed to the crime.

Despite his age, Browning was sentenced to four life sentences. Nonetheless, the judge allowed for the possibility of parole after a minimum of twenty-three years, with good behavior. "The question of whether his actions were just diabolically evil," said Baltimore County circuit judge Thomas Bollinger, "is up to Almighty God."

The media hadn't featured Emory in a national dateline since 1989 when Debbie Tucker Loveless and her common-law husband, John Harvey Miller, were sentenced to life in prison for murdering Debbie's four-year-old daughter, April. Prosecutors claimed that the couple had tortured the girl with a hunting knife and curling iron. Debbie and John insisted that the child was mauled by a pack of dogs.

April had been allowed to play by herself on the couple's property, and both Debbie and John contended that they believed the other was keeping track of her movements. When they couldn't find April, they began a search, moving toward a sinkhole where April and the two older children in the house regularly played. While they were en route, April was spotted, naked and facedown beneath an oak tree.

Debbie claimed that the girl was still alive at that point, raising up to say, "Mommy, Daddy." At first, it appeared that April had merely been scratched in several places. But when she was rolled over, Debbie said that there was a massive hole on the child's inner right thigh; April's muscles, blood vessels, skin and femoral artery had been ripped out.

John, an unemployed construction worker who'd been certified as an emergency medical technician in Kentucky, said that he began administering first aid. As Debbie ran to the house to call an ambulance, the girl allegedly told him, "Dogs did it."

In addition to the couple's two dogs, April regularly played with an animal that belonged to a neighbor.

At Mother Frances Hospital in Tyler, doctors cleaned twigs, dirt, leaves and grass out of the wound, and used a graft of the girl's left leg to replace the femoral artery and femoral vein. Still, because of the trauma of the accident, April died on the operating table.

By that point, the Rains County Sheriff's Department already perceived the parents as suspects. In the house, police

found an electric curling iron, pushpins and thumbtacks—
items a pathologist said may have been used to scratch and
puncture the skin.

He later admitted that he'd never measured the curling
iron's teeth to determine if a match could be made to the
scratches. No traces of blood were found on the object,
either.

At the Tyler Police Department, two microscopic specks
were discovered on a hunting knife John had received for
Christmas. After testing the blade, police concluded that the
spots might possibly be blood.

Both parents were arrested. Prosecutors maintained that
John had beaten April to death, and Debbie did nothing to
stop him. In their effort to delude investigators, the pair allegedly concocted the story about the dogs.

It took one hour for jurors to find John Harvey Miller and
Debbie Tucker Loveless guilty of murder.

"There was a theory that the incision was made in April's
leg to take a chunk of her thigh and bleed her, and use the
blood for devil worship," recalled Laura Ardis, the legal assistant for her husband, Robert, who filed an appeal on behalf of the couple. "And all that thing was just rampant. The
district attorney had gotten together a search group, and they'd
gone through the house, and found things they thought were
satanic, such as peacock feathers and a carving that John had
brought back from some island.

"There was a definite rush to judgment because people
are just like dogs with that pack mentality."

Robert Ardis, a colorful figure who traced his roots to the
founders of Hopkins County, and worked out of a law office
abutting a Western ware store, was given access to the emergency room and autopsy photos that he claimed were previously withheld from the defense. "My daughter was a
technician in the forensic lab in Dallas, and she said, 'Come
and bring your pictures to the head of the whole forensic
center,'" Laura recounted. "So we did, and they got several
doctors together, and they looked at pictures, and then, they
showed us other wounds done by dogs, and compared them

to wounds done with a knife, and it was very clear that a dog had done this."

The majority of scratches consisted of "four nearly parallel converging or diverging lines," Dr. Charles Odom, of the Southwestern Institute of Forensic Science, told *The Dallas Morning News*. "Domestic canines . . . have four claws on their forefeet, and these marks are typical of the scratches that they leave on the skin when they attack."

A state crime lab chemist revealed that when a more thorough examination of John's hunting knife was conducted, not a trace of blood could be found. Shockingly, the test had taken place more than two weeks *before* the couple was indicted for murder.

In 1993, the Texas Criminal Court of Appeals dismissed the convictions. A judge eventually ruled that the couple would not have to endure another trial.

Fifteen years later, when the media began reporting on the Caffey massacre, Laura Ardis revisited the April Loveless case. Had the isolation of East Texas, she wondered, produced the mentality that made it so natural to brand John and Debbie child killers—or, for that matter, enabled four seemingly harmless young people to plot a family's death?

"They live in such a remote place," Laura said, "and they practice this fundamentalism. They're not part of the mainstream of society. They just have their own little rules."

CHAPTER 15

In downtown Emory, a florist noticed a precipitous drop in business after the murders, not unlike the respite experienced by New York shopowners following 9/11. "Traffic stopped," the merchant noted. "People didn't want to shop anymore. You didn't see people out and about. You didn't see people talking. Everyone just pretty much stayed to themselves—and they definitely did not want to buy flowers."

Yet the East Texas pioneer spirit continued to burn. "Last night, I was sleeping like a baby," Alba resident Gary Bohannan told the *Tyler Morning Telegraph*. "My door was unlocked. And it's going to be unlocked again tonight."

Anticipating a long series of trials, blood specimens were taken from the bodies of Penny, Bubba and Tyler. DNA samples also came from Terry and all four suspects. The test results confirmed that Penny's DNA had been on Charlie's jeans and each of his boots. "The probability of selecting an unrelated person at random who could be the contributor of these stains," read a report from the Texas Department of Public Safety, "is approximately one in 4.737 sextillion for Caucasians and one in 15.07 sextillion for blacks, and one in 441.5 quintillion for Hispanics. To a reasonable degree of scientific certainty, Penny Caffey is the source of the stains."

The criminal investigations division of the Texas Attorney

General's office did a forensic search on eight computers, targeting such terms as "kill," "murder," "parents," "death penalty," "capital murder," "little brothers" and "sword."

"Obviously, we seized everyone's cell phone," Ranger John Vance said. "Whenever we catch a bad guy, and he has a cell phone, we think that cell phone may have been used in the committing the crime."

One morning, while investigators sorted through evidence at the sheriff's department, a confiscated cell phone started ringing to the tune of the song "Find Out Who Your Friends Are" popularized by country artist Tracy Lawrence:

When the well runs dry
Who's gonna be there?

Vance instantly thought back to the interrogations, when Wilkinson and Waid quickly pointed fingers at one another.

"This was one of them moments," he said. "I look down at the box with the cell phone in it. It's marked 'evidence' from a heinous crime. And the ring tone is 'Find Out Who Your Friends Are.' And I thought, 'Man, that couldn't have been more real, right here."

Despite the incomprehensible nature of the crime, virtually everybody in the area had a theory about why it occurred. Some blamed Terry and Penny for being insular, strict and overprotective. Others blamed the world "out there"—humanism, rap music, the media.

On Texas Street, Emory's strip of small, one-story businesses, a pedestrian placed responsibility on video games and the Internet. "It's kind of like the Columbine killing," the woman opined. "There've been copycats ever since. And it's because kids watched it on TV, and went out and done the same thing."

When reporter Lauren Grover ventured into an Alba café to interview the locals, she found a group of older men eating pie and speculating about whether alcohol or methamphetamine played a role in the attacks. It was the only explanation that made sense, given the fact that the killings seemed to come out of nowhere, and authorities estimated that nearly 50 percent of all crime in the area had some type of drug link.

It almost seemed that, behind the pious terminology and oratory about clean, country living, methamphetamine lurked as a type of dirty family secret.

"The paradox," Lauren observed, "is that rural communities are very religious. You don't find a lot of atheists here. And you don't find a lot of people who don't go to church. Even if they're not real devout, they go to church because everybody goes to church. But there's also this disease out in the country—meth. It's cheap, it's destructive and it's out of control. Obviously, not everyone uses, but it's kind of the underbelly of the small towns, where you have good farming and good folks."

A few years earlier, when meth use was even more prevalent, Emory residents claimed, so many people were cooking up the drug in the country that they were "blowing themselves up all the time." Although the anecdote was exaggerated, the perception was based on stories heard too often in East Texas.

"I think drugs were involved or alcohol or *something*," Rains High School student Vanessa Hendricks hypothesized about the murders. "Because it's not uncommon. There's parties all the time for teenagers. There's not a lot to do out here, so people go party and get wasted, or they snort up coke, or they'll smoke pot."

Vanessa did not want to believe that Bobbi, the nice but clumsy teen who enjoyed performing in school plays, could be involved in anything violent. "I was kind of hoping that the girls didn't know what was going to happen," Vanessa said, "that Bobbi just drove there and sat out in the car, that she had nothing to do with it. And then, we heard that she helped plan this, and I started to change my mind."

One memory that came rushing back to Vanessa was Bobbi breaking down in the theater room: "I kind of reflected on it, like, 'Is *that* why Bobbi was so upset—because she knew what was going to happen—she knew what was going on?'"

In the hazy days after the crime, some residents viewed Erin as a victim of a deranged boyfriend who became a runaway train, not stopping until the Caffeys were shot and butchered. Others were far less forgiving, even theorizing that she murdered her brothers herself.

In the parking lot of a convenience store, a large man in a cowboy hat looked across the roadway at the decorative windmills blowing lazily in front of Potts feed store beneath a clear sky and blue water tower with EMORY inscribed in large white letters. He'd never met the Caffeys, and was unsure about the fine details of the murder plot, but he was pretty positive that he knew what occurred.

"This little girl had her parents sticking their thumb on her so much that when she met a boy who could offer her something better, she decided to take the easy way out, stage a fire and live off the insurance money with her boyfriend."

But Jerry Carlisle, the private investigator and former police chief who'd been moved by Erin's solos in church, had difficulty envisioning anything close to this. "She never showed that side," he said. "We all have children, and I'm sure Terry and Penny had problems with their kids, like we all do. Absolutely. But not to the extent that anyone would shoot and stab and burn down the house with people in it. Where does that come from?"

The question coursed through Miracle Faith Baptist Church, debilitating the kids who, days earlier, had sat with Erin and Charlie in youth group. "Some had to be carried out of church," Tommy Gaston's niece Diane Dunlap told the *Tyler Morning Telegraph*. "They're emotionally drained. When you see seventeen- and eighteen-year-old boys in tears, it takes a lot. They needed their mothers today—to walk with them and hold them in their arms."

Another church member recalled Erin being well-bred and well-mannered: "She never caused problems. She was very, very close with her brothers. It just blows our mind. These were churchgoing people. They always did things together. I never saw the family when they weren't together."

Now, congregants were slowly adjusting their minds to the fact that they'd never see the Caffeys as a group again.

"It didn't really hit me until I came in Sunday and saw the piano, and saw where Bubba played the guitar, where the kids sat," recalled Pastor Todd McGahee. "It really hit me, and I think it hit a lot of people."

Dunlap noted that, had Penny lived, she would have spent part of Saturday preparing the meal she was supposed to bring to church the next day. "Unless she was sick, she didn't miss one service," Diane said. "I don't know if I could forgive the person who did this, but I think Terry will. He's just that kind of person."

As word spread around town that other students had heard Erin and Charlie devising the conspiracy, both adults and teens reacted with a mixture of bafflement and ire. "Why didn't somebody say something?" wondered Joey Weatherford, the Emory native and editorial cartoonist for the *Herald Banner* in Greenville. "They heard them talking about it, and no one got involved. It breaks your heart thinking about that. Somebody could have stopped this."

Pastor McGahee's wife, Rebecca, relived her conversations with Erin about the friction at home. "We had all talked about this boyfriend, and told her, 'Don't get swindled into something you're not ready for,'" Rebecca reminisced to *The Dallas Morning News*. "But we were thinking sex. We weren't thinking murder."

Her husband also pondered the exchanges he'd had with Charlie Wilkinson and Terry Caffey, but realized that it was pointless to torment himself about the past: "We can sit and wish we've done other things and saw signs, but it won't do any good."

At the *Herald Banner*, editor Danny Walker wondered if the newspaper could do anything to soothe the community, and asked Weatherford to come up with a cartoon. "The only thing I could think of," the cartoonist said, "was something that I felt would show some type of healing—three little flowers growing on the ground in front of a house that was burnt, and a little caption that read, 'Blessed are the meek for they shall inherit the earth.'"

Still, even after the cartoon was published, Weatherford found himself dwelling on the viciousness of the crime, particularly the murders of Bubba and Tyler. "I'm just shocked that these people could hunt down two little boys," he said. "I think about these two bigger guys jumping on the younger boy and stabbing him. I mean, what the hell kind of person would do that? And they were out here running around. If they were capable of this, what else could they have done to other people if they hadn't gotten caught?"

Stacy Ferguson, who'd gotten to know Charlie Wilkinson behind bars, was sensitive to the way people like Weatherford felt. But she also believed that she was growing to understand Charlie, as well as the factors that might have driven him in such a destructive direction. "I saw right away that the defendants' families had a hand in creating these broken-spirited children," she said. "I don't shift total blame to the parents—that isn't fair. But I do know that if things had been different in their childhoods, these kids would have been more secure.

"They all came from different environments, but yet shared a common ground—the low self-esteem, the hunger for love and acceptance."

In jail, the suspects learned of the rumors surrounding them, and in some instances tried to put their individual spins on the story. Charlie, for instance, resented the implication that he decapitated Penny. "If she was decapitated, I didn't do it," he'd later tell the *Times* in the United Kingdom. "It must have been something from the fire. I stabbed her in the chest and in the neck. All that did was cut off the oxygen."

In a jailhouse letter to his grandmother, Charlie wrote, "Don't believe anything [you hear about the case] unless me or Mom tells you. Unfortunately, I can't explain what happened until after I go to trial cause they'll use it against me."

He also described his solitude, and desire to connect with family: "I'm in a single cell so I ain't got anyone to talk to. . . . Tell everyone I said hi. . . . I don't know half of your grandkids. How many cousins do I have in Florida?"

Waid's wife, Diane, refused to be interviewed by the author of this book. "Not only is it a tragedy to the Caffeys it is to me as well," she wrote in an e-mail. "I have a child w/a monster and don't wish to discuss it with anyone."

Nonetheless, Diane did talk to the local media, as well as the *DailyBS* website. "I have so many things running through my mind," she said in an online interview. "I still ask myself, 'What if I stayed with him? Maybe he wouldn't have done this.' On the other hand, I ask myself, 'What if I had stayed with him. He could have done it to me and the children.' Honestly, I have no idea what I would say to him, if I were to see him." Diane also told the *DailyBS* that Charles's parents had never liked her and—ironically, as it turned out—considered her to be a "bad girl."

Not surprisingly, it was difficult getting the students at Rains High School to concentrate on their studies. Every time a new theory emerged about the case it was texted from pupil to pupil. "It was a big rumor frenzy," Vanessa Hendricks recalled, "people living off of rumors and stories and gossip. It was nonstop."

And the teachers seemed equally distracted, running their exchanges with Charlie, Erin and Bobbi through their minds and wondering if there'd been a signal the educators had missed.

"These were students who had not been in trouble a great deal," Rains County school superintendent David Seago said.

Seago had brought in counselors to tell the elementary and middle school children that Bubba and Tyler—two of the most recent arrivals to the Rains County public school system—were murdered in the place where they were supposed to feel most safe. Students wept and hugged one another in the hallway of Bubba's school. In Tyler's third-grade class, the teacher arranged the desks so there would be no conspicuously empty seats. If the children wanted to cry, they were told, that was okay.

Plenty of adults were crying over the tragedy, as well.

Counselors also made themselves available in the high school, where virtually every one of the 485 students could remember some type of interaction with the suspects. "A lot of them are friends, cousins or somehow related to the kids that are incarcerated," Seago said. "Our counselors have been busy today."

When the pupils asked Seago how a crime of this proportion could occur amid the quiet of Alba, he answered with honesty: "We may never know."

Chelsea Wright, who'd happened upon Erin and Charlie as they argued in the hallway on the Friday of the murders, felt like she was walking through a dream. "I never thought two people I trusted were like this," she told police.

Charlie's friend Brandon Brimer also expressed his bewilderment to authorities. "I'd seen Bobbi and Charles . . . Thursday or Friday night," he told Detective Richard Almon. "They were just happy as bluebirds, didn't show no signs of anything. When I saw Charlie on Thursday, he didn't show like he was going to do anything. He was just happy-go-lucky."

But Almon knew that Brandon had heard rumblings about disposing of the Caffeys. "Let me go back to one thing real quick," the detective began. "You said that a month or so ago, he told you that they had talked about . . ."

"No, he said that his girlfriend was talking about . . ."

"Okay, that his girlfriend was talking to him about doing something to her family?"

"Yes, sir. I would imagine she was trying to talk him into doing it. That's why he came to me."

"Okay, so this was talked about a month ago between them? And Charlie talked to you about it?"

"Charlie was telling me, he came over. It was just a typical hangout night. We hang out, you know, once or twice a week, or we try to. I said, 'What's new, Charlie?' and he said, 'Erin's talking about murdering her parents.' And I was like, 'No way.' And he was like, 'Yeah, she is.' And I was like, 'Is she trying to get you to do it?' And he was like, 'Yeah, but I can't do it. They got two little kids in the house.'

"And I was like, 'I know. If you ever need help, just come to me, Charlie. I'll keep you out of trouble.'"

The boy looked at the detective with resignation, continuing, "Sounds like it didn't work."

The murder of the kids also confounded Teresa Myers, the mother of Charlie's good friend Justin. She remembered Wilkinson coming over her home, and speaking warmly of his own younger siblings. "He loved kids," she said. "I can't fathom him coming up with such a horrid plan to destroy a family. He was not a hateful person. He was not deceitful. It's just not the kid I know. I cannot imagine him doing anything like that unless he truly believed that he was doing it for the good of something.

"I mean, I feel so strongly about this that if he were to walk into my house today, even after all this, I wouldn't be in fear of him. I'm not in fear of my family being around him. I would open my arms and hug him, and tell him I loved him. He's just not that kid."

Lauren Grover was not the only reporter who heard this characterization of Charlie, and while researching her stories she tried to find a way to relate to his mindset. Her only conclusion was that something truly malevolent had overtaken Charlie: "It seems like it was a power issue, but I also imagine you have some sort of outer body feeling. 'This isn't me. There aren't going to be any consequences.' I mean, even if you *were* to kill someone, if you thought about it for a minute beforehand, you might realize, 'Uh, this is going to be a really bad deal for me. I'll probably go to jail.' But when you get as far as Charlie did, I think you lose that."

In church, Pastor McGahee preached that the actions in the Caffey home were orchestrated by nothing less than the Prince of Darkness: "For too long, some of us, me included, have sat back and took the easy road. And while we've done that, Satan has been stealing away our children, and stealing away our loved ones. But I'll tell you, this ought to wake us up, and fire us up. We need to go out and give the devil a black eye."

The perspective was widely shared by area residents. Said Debbie Hendricks, while operating the vegetable stand in her front yard next to Miracle Faith Baptist Church, "When you're in trouble, you ask God to save you, you open the door and God comes rushing in. And I think these kids opened the door to evil, and Satan came rushing in. I'm a Christian woman, and I really believe that."

But were these people relying on the all-too-familiar country theme of God and the devil to avoid a truly thoughtful discussion of the crime? And was falling back on the religious argument a way of ignoring the true character of the children who grew up evil, amidst all the platitudes about Jesus and being saved and living righteously? Was Charlie simply a resentful kid from a dysfunctional background who snapped when he couldn't work his way into a family he'd personally described as "perfect"? When the Caffeys chose to shun him from their utopia, did he react the way a jealous psychopath does when he hurls acid at a beautiful ex-girlfriend—vengefully obliterating what he viewed as the family's domestic bliss?

Either way, the arrest plunged Teresa's son, Justin, into an emotional chasm. The boy he'd seen as an dependable older brother was now being derided as a reprobate. And every day was worse than the previous. Justin had been proud of his friendship with Charlie and, with each new newspaper article, students and even teachers began to ostracize the youngster.

"My husband and I had to go to the school one day because of something one of the teachers said," Teresa recounted. "We had told Justin, 'Look, you can't defend what

Charlie did. But you can defend the friendship, and stand up for the person you know.' I guess Justin was doing this, and the teacher waved some article at him and said, 'Well, now, here it is. Here it is,' and read vivid details about the killings out loud—in front of the whole class.

"My son came home devastated, and I was so appalled that the teacher would do something like this that my husband and I were at the school the next day, ready to rip people apart. I was so mad that I really wanted the teacher to lose his job. I said, 'How dare you take it upon yourself to educate our children on what is and what isn't right? You sat in a classroom and just read all of this out loud, without any consideration for the connection that my child had with this boy.' The principal got involved, and agreed that Charlie had never been a bad kid—a little bit of a smart aleck, but that's about it. But the whole thing was very upsetting.

"It was not a pretty sight."

While these types of tempests stormed all over the community, Pastor McGahee and his wife, Rebecca, visited Bobbi Gale Johnson in jail. There were no questions about the crime. Rather, the couple offered comfort to a person the minister described as "a scared little girl."

Later, in a television interview, he emphasized that he wanted the community to offer the accused the same support. "We have to understand that they're not monsters," he said. "They're kids, and they chose the wrong path."

No one spoke up to condemn the preacher; there was too much respect for McGahee, even when he uttered statements people didn't want to hear. But many believed that they didn't have to apply the minister's standards to themselves. McGahee's position in the community required him to see everything through the prism of his faith. It was an obligation he coveted, using his private moments to address the tragedy by opening his Bible and reading Romans 8:28: "And we know that all things work together for good to them that love God, to them who are the called according to his purpose."

"That's basically what our church and Brother Terry have to stand upon," he stated. "We believe that God is sovereign, and nothing is out of his control. And when something like this happens, while he didn't orchestrate it, he allowed it for a purpose."

The pastor also reread Paul's words in Corinthians, when "The Apostle to the Gentiles" proclaimed that it was wrong to seek salvation only "in this life." Said McGahee, "If this was all there was, our faith wouldn't mean much. But our faith does mean something because God blesses us in this life. It's not always perfect—we don't believe in wealth and prosperity—but he does meet our needs. But it's not about this life. This is just a place we're traveling through, and that's how we have to look at it."

With information scarce, acquaintances, neighbors and reporters pored through the MySpace universe—which, even in the traditional setting of Rains County, had become a primary source of teenage expression in those days just before the explosions of Facebook and Twitter—trying to gather some new insight into the suspects. Did Waid's screen name "True Rebel" suggest a love of southern culture, or a desire to tear down society? Had Bobbi's slogan "oh well, shit happens" indicate an indifference to the responsibilities of preserving human life?

In the course of these investigations, it was discovered that Bobbi also had a YouTube account, where visitors could post comments. Although the suspect herself now had no means of accessing the exchanges, online guests continued to send Bobbi messages.

"You and your friends deserve the death penalty," wrote a person tagged BlackSwordsman777. "But before it happens I would hope that you . . . find forgiveness from the Lord."

From xxxtina2284: "You have ruined many lives including your own. And for what? 2000 dollars? . . . I hope they put you away forever."

And there were more:

"Wow. One question . . . what possessed you to go and murder a family. AND OVER BOYFRIEND TROUBLE? . . . Did it ever occur to you . . . IT WAS WRONG??!! You must have been seriously drugged up or drunk to have done something like that."

"Not 2 B-R-I-G-H-T."

"Rot in hell murderer."

CHAPTER 16

For several months, one question loomed over the case: Would Erin be tried as a child or as an adult, and face the harsher penalties that entailed? In order to fully comprehend whether Erin's behavior exceeded that expected of a juvenile, a judge ordered a complete psychological evaluation of the pretty teen accused of conspiring to have her family killed.

The first analyst to meet with the teenager found her to be "somewhat guarded, with a dull and almost flat affect. Periodically, she would cry, saying, 'I don't know why I'm here. . . . I didn't do anything wrong.'" Because Erin appeared so "fragile," the examiner kept the visit brief, leaving in just under an hour.

But in that time, the subsequent report stated, "Erin verbalized that someone had killed her mother and two brothers. . . . She was not oriented to time, claiming she did not know if she had been in detention for two, or up to nine weeks. . . . Vegetative signs of depression were noted, with sleep disturbance apparently severe."

When the analyst returned eight days later, Erin's mental condition seemed to have improved. While lethargic, her posture, grooming and eye contact were better than before. Nevertheless, she responded to many questions with a simple "I don't know," leaving the visitor to theorize that Erin was "blocking" any substantive conversation about the crime.

"Not constantly but periodically, Erin cried when she started talking about the murders of her family," the report read. "Her overall mental grasp and capacity appeared within normal limits. However, retention and recall were poor. . . . Ability to abstract think using proverbs was poor. General fund of knowledge was poor. Judgment and insight were also poor. Overall, intellectual capacity appeared to be at best within the lower range of low average. Erin appears to be a very concrete thinker and tends to frame events around her in very simplistic terms."

Erin claimed to have loved her brothers, and expressed concern for her safety in an adult detention facility. Her boyfriend, she contended, had threatened her, but the report didn't specify when or why.

"I get scared a lot," she said.

At least one examiner described Erin's background as "highly suffocated," and concluded that she'd been misdiagnosed with attention deficit disorder "when in fact she suffered depression and anxiety."

Despite her attractive features and musical talents, Erin appeared to have a personality disorder that separated her from the more popular kids at school and church: "She shows signs of characterological inclinations to be complaining . . . a tendency to alienate her from most healthy and socially adjusted peers."

Questions about her sexual history induced a number of curious responses. Erin spoke about three encounters in which she passed out after drinking, and woke up vaginally sore and secreting semen. According to the report, "In each instance, Erin said she would go to a deserted place with her boyfriend and three to four other 17-year-old males. Nevertheless, Erin boldy and confidently . . . claimed her sexual encounter 'was a sure sign of sexual abuse.' Erin followed this with the assertion that she had been 'raped.' Yet, she reportedly repeated this behavior three times."

When the discussion ended, the examiners were uncertain about what to regard as truth, since—like the people at Miracle Faith Baptist—they suspected that Erin had a tendency to bend the facts to suit her agenda. This trait, the report deduced, may likely have swayed Charlie, Waid and Bobbi to participate in the murder scheme: "Erin appears to have truly convinced her peers of her own personal misery simply to get what she wanted. . . . This child is highly sophisticated, yet socially immature. . . . She can manipulate to a degree beyond her maturity level to get what she wants."

The findings were damning. Although Erin had no criminal history, the analysts were certain that, in an effort to accomplish her ends, she'd readily disregard the rules of society: "This child poses a threat to the public; efforts at rehabilitation, utilizing the resources of the juvenile system appear inadequate."

In jail, cut off from his daily access to alcohol, Charlie was forced to face his feelings and grew introspective, reading up on psychology and sociology, and describing himself and his current conditions to friends in letters.

"I love the outdoors and hate being stuck inside," he said in one dispatch, characterizing himself as a guy who enjoyed hunting, fishing, and working with his hands. "So you know this is the ultimate punishment the government can put me through. . . . I am the kind of person that wants to make everybody happy, or to help the needy. . . . All in all, I'm a really nice guy that got caught up in some really bad things. . . . I had everything set out for a good future and I threw it all away."

Although there was always the allusion to Erin causing his downfall, Charlie also took himself to task for deciding to conform to her whims. He said it was a test of a man's character "to choose right from wrong. Even when people are trying to get you to do the wrong thing."

He counseled a friend with children to spend quality time with her offspring. Drawing on his own painful experiences, he wrote, "As a kid, I regret not being able to spend much time with my mom and my dad."

More and more, he appeared to be filling this void by bonding with his lawyer, Ron Ferguson, and his wife, Stacy, conveying his dreams about doing over his life, and ending up in a tranquil domestic setting with a wife and pampered children. He told Stacy that he imagined himself in a nine-to-five job, spending every night and weekends with his kids.

"I mean that," he told Stacy. "I would be the perfect husband and father. I would come straight home after work. I wouldn't yell at my kids for leaving toys strung out in the yard. They'd have a nice play area, and I'd provide for my family. I'd never dump my kids on whoever would take them."

In other words, he wouldn't raise his children to feel as empty and abandoned as he had. Rather, he'd do his life over—vicariously—by raising a family of adjusted, wanted young people. "I'd do anything for that," he said.

Then he cried—as much for the present as the past.

During those periods when the Fergusons were busy with other cases, Charlie's spirits sunk. "I'm depressed, but other than that I'm fine," he said in one letter. "I haven't seen my lawyers in a long time, which really sucks cause I don't know anything about my case. I don't even know if they're working on it at all. . . . Maybe they will come up here soon and tell me something."

But others were willing to offer a lifeline. Just as Charle cried with Stacy, he shed tears with Teresa Myers the first time she visited him behind bars. "I'm so sorry," he told her.

Teresa had treated Charlie like a son, and he believed that he'd let her down.

"Mom," he said, "I'll have to pay for what I've done, and I know what I've done is wrong."

Then, he paused. "They don't know the whole story," he added.

"Then, tell them," Teresa pleaded. "Tell them what the whole story is."

Whenever Teresa received a Bible study e-mail from her church, she'd print the item, fold it into an envelope and send it to Charlie in jail. She'd also purchased the teen a Bible to appraise in his cell. He read it often, he told her, in his quest to find forgiveness for his actions in the Caffey house.

The concept of justice came up regularly when the pair talked about the circumstances that led to Charlie's incarceration. "There were many times," Teresa said, "when he told me that, if the tables were turned and he had to serve on a jury, he'd sentence himself."

Oddly, numerous acquaintances of Charlie now decided to reach out to him—not directly, but through Teresa's son, Justin. It seemed that every day, the boy would come home from school with another letter from a pupil wishing to contact Charlie in jail. "I always read through the letters to see what the student was saying," Teresa said. "And it was always 'Charlie, we miss your great sense of humor, we love you,' this, that or the other. But it got to the point that I told Justin, 'Look, if those kids feel that strongly about their friendship with Charlie, then they need to be telling their parents, and their parents need to be giving them permission to do this. I can't do it anymore.'"

In his responses, Charlie complained about the cost of living in jail ("The price for one long distance phone call is $18.00," he wrote. "Kind of expensive I think") and the fact that authorities refused to allow him to dip snuff.

He was wise enough to realize that he needed a change of venue; it was highly unlikely that jurors in the Emory or Sulphur Springs courthouses could divorce themselves from the emotions and gossip related to the case. Despite the international coverage of the story, he believed that he stood a far better chance in another part of the state, where the locals had their own notorious defendants to despise.

"I'm trying to get the law books out of the library here," he wrote. "But the last time I checked, the one I needed wasn't there . . . I don't want to be in court and not understand what's going on."

A year before the Caffey murders, a man in upstate New York started a true crime-themed website he called the

DailyBS. The name was deliberate—his own statement about the types of crime he saw relentlessly reported on twenty-four-hour news stations and other media outlets. "Whether it's a story about a murder or a pedophile, there's always consistent bullshit running throughout the day," explained Sean Krause.

Because, in the Internet age, anyone could start their own news operation, Krause decided to offer the public an alternative: "Instead of just somber, straight reporting you normally get with murder stories, I wanted to express outrage. People could write to me and talk about their hate toward a particular killer. I took this up originally as a place for people to vent."

In that regard, Krause was no different than hundreds, if not thousands, of bloggers and webmasters around the United States interested in issues of crime and punishment. When the Caffey story broke, however, the *DailyBS* became a forum for friends, neighbors and even people identifying themselves as relatives of the participants—so much so that police in Rains County eventually contacted Krause.

Within days of the crime, Krause had created a Caffey family tribute site, complete with photos of the victims and reverential music. Although there was little that readers could do to assist the family, Krause pointed out that Charles Waid had two innocent children, now being raised by a single mother with limited resources.

"People wanted to donate money to Diane [Waid]," Krause said. "A lot of people had old baby clothes in their basements, just sitting there, collecting dust, and they offered to rewash them and send them to her. People went to Wal-Mart and purchased gift cards for the kids."

For a period, Krause was one of Diane's primary liaisons to the rest of the world; when she needed to communicate a point, he was happy to express it for her. "The entire ordeal sickens me," she told the *DailyBS*. "When I first heard about it, I thought I was dreaming. But to find out [Waid] himself did actually commit the murders was unreal. Mr. Caffey surviving is great. I'm sure it will be hard on him because he has absolutely nothing left. And to live with the fact that his daughter wanted it done so she could be with a boy is awful. My heart goes out to him."

Interestingly, Diane admitted that she still felt some fondness for Waid, since the pair shared a biological child together. "But also a bigger part of me hates him for doing this to her," she qualified. "So if I were to see him, I guess my question would be, 'Why would you be so selfish as to make my child grow up and not know who you are because of the choices you made?'"

Not wishing to stigmatize her children, Diane vowed that she'd soon be changing everyone's last name.

When Krause asked about whether the defendants deserved the death penalty, Diane conceded that she felt conflicted: "I'll break this one down. If it was someone I didn't know, I guess I would say lethal injection because I have no ties to them. But I still have to think about the fact that I have a child with this 'monster,' and I think he should rot for what he did. Why pay taxes for that pretty needle when he doesn't have to suffer?"

These were the types of quotes that traditional news outlets—concerned about advertising dollars and public perception—occasionally avoided. But Krause, unencumbered by such concerns, endeavored to put it all out in cyberspace.

Regardless of the source, though, just about every online item on the suspects was met with commentary from readers from every type of background and every part of the United States, each, through the miracle of the Internet, assuming the role of eminent authority, in the tradition of the talking heads featured each day on cable television:

"Looks like Erin's parents showed good judgment in asking her to break off her relationship with Charlie."

"What do these kids think? They can kill off their entire family and live happily ever after? Like no one will notice?"

"Obviously, these monsters didn't think and probably can't think."

On Bobbi's MySpace page, a visitor identified herself as

the girl's mother, berated others for not knowing the facts, and attacked them personally:

"this is her mom . . . FUCK U QUEER ASS!!!!!!"

This triggered a chain of responses, all aimed at the reputed parent of the defendant:

"I don't mind her defending her murderer daughter . . . But why be a homophobe? And we wonder HOW her daughter could plan a murder????????"

"If you were watching your daughter ahead of time, she wouldn't be in jail for murdering innocent people. Maybe you should get off your daughters MySpace account and get to the jail."

In reality, Theresa Johnson *did* have better things to do than sit at her computer and bicker with strangers—finding a lawyer, caring for the rest of her family. Nor was she the type of woman to fling adolescent-level epithets on MySpace. Bobbi's online "mom" was an imposter. But in the pandemonium surrounding the case, many refused to acknowledge this truth, and the story of Theresa Johnson's Internet insults became one of the many fictions related to the massacre.

Cut off from the Internet, Bobbi was oblivious to this controversy, communicating to the outside world with pen and paper, and affecting a cheery outlook in a letter to an uncle. "I just wanted to write you and say hi and I love you," she stated on a page adorned with hearts and large, shaded bubble letters. "I hope you're not disappointed and ashamed of me. I miss everyone so much."

But in a neatly-lettered note to Emerald Blair, Matthew Waid's common law wife, Bobbi exposed both her loneliness and insecurity: "I know you've most likely been busy with everything or you don't wanna talk to me anymore (which I hope that's not the case!!) . . . Could you *please* write me back!! . . . I can't seem to control my emotions as well as before. . . . I think about y'all all the time and keep y'all in my prayers. I put a stamped envelope in here in case you wanna write me back!!"

Meanwhile, despite her mother's warnings, the forlorn

teen was seeking the companionship of her fellow inmates, and allegedly saying things that could be used against her in court. At least two cellmates apparently listened closely before writing out statements of the conversations for Detective Almon.

Misty Lewers told the investigator that Bobbi quoted Erin as shouting, "Kill them. Kill them," in reference to the Caffeys. When the murder was over, the statement continued, Bobbi claimed that only Charlie had blood on him, and the entire quartet was laughing.

Jana Combs said that Bobbi told her about Erin specifically. Erin initially described "little things," like the nature of the relationships between the four defendants. "She started by saying she loved the guy she was going to be married to," Jana stated, "and how much he loved her and was different from other guys who just wanted sex. Then [Bobbi] started talking about the daughter of the deceased, saying the daughter told them that she was being abused by her parents. . . . She went on to tell me that the daughter convinced them into killing them. On the ride to the [Caffey] home, the daughter reportedly kept on saying 'we have to just kill them' . . . over and over again in a rocking manner.

". . . I asked her why did she and her boyfriend get involved. She stated because she had been abused as a child and she felt sorry for the daughter. I asked if anyone was drinking or using drugs. She said no. . . . She said . . . her boyfriend . . . told her that everyone died except the father and then, she got angry that he was still alive because he could then point out his killers. . . . No tears, no remorse. All she wanted was to see her fiancé. Then, she got angry at the daughter, and said [if] she ever sees her, she will hurt her badly. . . . Now, she blames the daughter for it all, and she's scared her fiancé would get death for it.

". . . She repeated a few times that the neighbor must have seen her car, or the daughter must have snitched out all of them. . . . She also talked about them being seniors in high school, and how it is all over for them now. . . . Then [she] asked if she could get an education in prison. I said yes."

In terms of solving the crime, there was little about these statements that police didn't already know. Nonetheless, there was a degree of insensitivity in Bobbi's alleged comments that contrasted with the general portrayal of the girl as an emotionally frail, self-doubting follower: her disappointment over Terry's survival, the burst of laughter after the murders, the threats against Erin, the concern with educational opportunities in prison over sympathy for the victims.

If jurors heard this depiction of the least significant member of the conspiracy, Bobbi might appear to be as heartless as her accomplices—and worthy of the same type of punishment.

One of her boyfriend's primary preoccupations during this time was making contact with his children. From the Rains County Jail, Waid tried contacting his estranged wife, Diane, but Diane ignored him. Charles persisted.

"How is everything out there?" he wrote in one letter, attempting to mask his frustration with civility. "Everything is the same in here, just getting more and more bad news. . . . Since I haven't heard from you . . . please write me back and let me know how [the kids] are doing. I don't care if it's all you put in the letter. It just helps me a lot to get a letter from you saying how the kids are doing."

But Waid didn't hear from Diane, and kept writing, believing that—his crimes and relationship with his ex-wife notwithstanding—he had as much right to know his children as a father outside of captivity: "I guess you're not going to write me back and let me know how my kids are doing. I don't know what your reasons are for not doing so . . ." he said, complaining that she had alienated him from his kids even before his arrest. "I guess you're going to be like everyone else, and look down on me and judge me because of my charges.

". . . I miss the kids more than anything in the world. There is nothing I wouldn't do for them kids . . . I know that there is nothing that I can do in here but hope that you have a change of heart."

In the envelope, Waid included an illustration he made for his children on a piece of lined paper: a heart entwined with thorny roses, the kids' names and the message "My Life."

He begged Diane to remind the children that he loved them, and give them the drawing when they grew up.

Apparently, Diane remained unimpressed, so Waid took the fragments of information he received in jail to reinforce the image he had of the way his ex-wife and the kids were living. "Steve is in the cell next to me," he wrote in a letter he snuck to Bobbi, "and he said that he saw Diane and the kids a few days before he came to jail, and . . . the kids looked great, but someone done beat the shit out of Diane. He told me that on the rec yard today, and I couldn't help but laugh."

CHAPTER 17

All over East Texas, there was talk of "rebuilding" in the aftermath of the tragedy. But neighbors had grown tired of reporters, some with condescending, preconceived notions of country life, knocking on doors, stopping by churches and asking questions at the livestock auction. "The people felt that no one had heard of them until this, and that's not what they wanted to be remembered for—a sixteen-year-old girl trying to kill her family because her parents didn't like her boyfriend," said Lynne Sullivant of CBS-19 in Tyler. "It's like Columbine: One incident changes the whole perception of the community, and so many people are affected by it. That was one of the hardest things for us, as reporters, to see what the community was going through."

If people weren't appalled enough by the murders, the autopsy results set everyone over the edge. Preliminary findings released by the Southwest Forensics Center in Dallas suggested that Tyler was alive when the home was set ablaze; smoke was found in the eight-year-old's lungs. In other words, he was still gasping for air as the house was burning.

Tyler's cause of death was listed as "homicidal violence" that included stab wounds and smoke inhalation, while Penny and Bubba died from gunfire and "sharp force injuries."

The report stated that charring had preventing forensics specialists from evaluating most of Penny's body. Her corpse arrived in the morgue with a few scraps of recognizable garments—a nightgown, bra and panties—along with jewelry. On her left fourth finger, Penny wore a yellow ring containing two rows of small, clear stones surrounding a central, larger stone. On her right hand was another metal ring, this one with a clear central stone and two smaller black stones.

Prior to the murder, her worst physical ailment appeared to be gallstones.

Penny had been shot in at least two places, including the left temporal area, about four inches from the top of the head. A small-caliber copper bullet was also removed from a muscle in her right temporo-occipital region. There were stab wounds in the neck—a one-and-a-half-inch long "horizontally-oriented" gash left over from when Charlie said he attempted to finish the woman off—and in the right lateral trunk. "The direction of the stab wound is from front to back," the report said, "downward and slightly right to left."

Because of the fire, Penny's internal organs revealed "extensive thermal change," while there was focal charring on the right lung.

Bubba's injuries included perforation of both the right and left temporal lobes of the brain, as well as the face. At least one bullet had entered the right side of his face, moving right to left and upward toward the rear of his head. The stab wound in his right upper chest extended for five-and-one-quarter inches.

Tyler's scorched body arrived at the lab mixed with three different fabrics, most likely from his jeans and t-shirt. Fire had amputated his left leg at the knee and right leg at the ankle. His "thermally altered brain" was exposed and, in certain spots, crumbling outward. The soot deposits in the boy's airways, the pink discoloration of his blood, viscera (or internal organs) and soft tissue, and blood carboxyhemoglobin level of 79 percent were strong indicators of smoke inhalation.

After canvassing the high school, police heard that one of the students had an older brother who'd dated Erin. The information led investigators to a house in Emory, where they found a polite young man named Michael Washburn. Like Erin, Washburn had divided his time between home schooling and working at Sonic. The two initially met on a field trip with Miracle Faith Baptist Church and, according to Michael, dated for two months.

"What caused the breakup?" Ranger John Vance asked. "I'm assuming y'all broke up."

"Yes, sir. . . . She said her mom and dad didn't want me seeing her because we were at church and they said that I tried to stick her in a trash can."

Allegedly, several members of the church later told the Caffeys that the young couple's behavior appeared inappropriate. Since the incident itself—most likely a spurt of flirtatious horseplay between two kids unable to properly harness their hormones—didn't seem all that relevant to the case, Vance chose not to dwell on the topic.

"When y'all broke up, did she call you a lot, did she pursue you? Or when the relationship was over, y'all went both ways and didn't talk to each other?"

"When we broke up, whenever I looked at her, she didn't look at me. . . . She like didn't talk to me or nothing."

". . . What caused you to quit working at Sonic?"

"They fired me."

"What did they fire you for?"

"For not doing my job. When I was doing my job, I was listening to my MP3 player."

Michael had also stopped attending Miracle Faith, and, while avoiding any negative comments about the Caffeys, implied that they were largely responsible for this. Penny, he claimed, "had said some stuff, and had made my mom and dad mad. And my mom and dad told me . . . 'Don't go to that church. Otherwise, they were going to start some problems, and I don't want you to get into trouble.'"

"How did Mr. and Mrs. Caffey treat you personally when you dealt with them?"

"They were good people. . . . Whenever I went over there, they said 'make yourself at home,' and all that. Good Christians."

Michael was asked to characterize Erin. "Was she a quiet person, a happy person, a mad person?"

"She was always happy, like a good Christian." Because of this, Michael expressed surprise over the murders. "She didn't seem like the person that would do this. I mean, she was all, 'Yes, ma'am. No, ma'am. Yes, sir. No, sir.' . . . She got manners."

In fact, he emphasized, it was Erin who had led him to Jesus Christ.

"She told me she started going to church when she was a little kid," he recalled. "I mean, I want to know what possessed her to do this."

But the reality was that Michael had a pretty good idea. "She told me every time she dates a boyfriend, her mom tries to break them up," he admitted. "And she said that it happens every time. It happened with Charlie. It happened with another kid named Charlie—the two Charlies and me. She said that she could never have a boyfriend because her mom would try to mess it up for her."

Vance took on a compassionate, but serious tenor. "You have to understand that if I ask a direct or hard question, I need a grown-up man's response. Okay? What we have is a very serious crime that's been committed. And any information that you can think of, that you can give me, you may not think it means anything at all, but it may be something that I can use to . . . help figure out what truly happened that night."

"I'm going to tell the truth. . . . She told me that she was going to hire somebody to do it."

Vance let the words register, then carefully followed up with a short question. "To do what?"

"To go out there and kill her parents."

From an investigator's perspective, this was stunning news. If Michael was telling the truth, Erin was so committed to murdering her parents that she'd broached the topic with a prior boyfriend. In other words, Charlie Wilkinson may have truly been a pawn to Erin's manipulations.

The exchange with Michael allegedly took place one night on the telephone, while Erin was in her room and her parents were downstairs.

"Now, how long ago was that?" Vance asked

"When me and her was going out."

After establishing that the conversation likely took place in the summer of 2007—some three months before Erin began seeing Charlie—Vance switched the discussion back to Erin's motive. "Why would she want to have somebody go up to the house and kill her parents?"

"Because she told me that every time she gets a boy-friend that she really likes, her mom and dad tries to break them up."

"Did she talk to you about it just one time, or did she mention it several times?"

"She just said it one time."

". . . Did she ever ask you if you could do it for her?"

"No."

In the middle of the interview, Michael's cell phone rang. With Vance's permission, he answered, and had a brief con-versation with his mother. He explained that he was being questioned by the police, and the woman neither asked for details of the conversation, nor warned him to temper his words.

It was obvious that Michael had nothing to hide. Nor could he really grasp the fact that Erin was a very different person than the girl he thought he knew.

"Do you feel that Erin was serious when she was talking about killing her parents?" Vance asked.

"No."

"Do you think that maybe she was just mad?"

"Yeah."

Even after surgeons removed the slugs from Terry's face, he remained jumpy. For more than two months after the acci-dent, he said that he continued to taste the repugnant blend of blood and gunpowder. His cheekbone floated around his face, below his skin. Early one morning, a doctor working outside Terry's hospital room dropped a clipboard on the tile floor. Terry reacted with panic to the clanging noise, leaping out of bed and pulling wires from his chest and catheters from his arms.

Along with his post-traumatic stress, the loss of his wife and two children, and his daughter's incarceration, Terry also had to worry about paying his bills; the Caffeys counted themselves among the ranks of America's uninsured. Fortunately, pastors from every church in Rains County—including those with divergent viewpoints on Scripture from Terry's—volunteered to assist, asking congregants to contribute whatever they could. "Best thing living around here is everyone helps with everything," an Emory resident told the *Tyler Morning Telegraph.* "We take care of each other."

The Austin Bank in Emory set up a benefit account to help with Terry's mounting expenses. The Carter BloodCare Stewart Center arranged a replacement blood drive.

One week after the attack, Terry was released from the hospital—with a broken nose, two fractured cheekbones and minor nerve damage in his right arm. "I remember the nurse coming in and saying, 'Mr. Caffey, you can go home now,'" he told *Texas Monthly.* "All I heard was the word 'home.' I thought, 'I don't have a home. I don't have a family to go home to.' And I remember weeping, just weeping uncontrollably."

Terry camped out with his sister an hour from Alba in Leonard—an old cotton town still primarily comprised of farms and ranches—sleeping on her couch and storing his remaining possessions in one small cardboard box.

Despite the calamity, Pastor McGahee viewed his friend with admiration. "I don't even think I would have crawled out of the house," the preacher said at one church service. "But God has a purpose for Terry's life. God has a reason. God gave him the strength to get out."

It was a widely shared opinion. The very fact that Terry could walk out of the hospital after such a brutal attack, maintain his mental faculties and offer himself to law enforcement as the reliable witness—all of this was viewed as a medical miracle.

Although he could walk unassisted, a pallid Terry followed doctors' orders and conserved his strength by attending the funeral for his wife and sons in a wheelchair, his arm in a sling. Debbie Hendricks was among the mourners. "I didn't know the Caffey family," she said. "I have several good friends who were close to the family—and they did attend the church next door to my house—so I came out of respect. The day was really filled with grief and bewilderment and fear that something like this could happen in such a wonderful community."

Pastor McGahee warned the faithful that this would not to be the last time they'd find themselves exposed to an atrocity as nefarious as the murders. "We live in an evil world," he was quoted in *The Dallas Morning News*, "and it will continue to be evil until Jesus comes back."

Nonetheless, he maintained, there was nothing to fear; Penny, Bubba and Tyler were truly in a better place.

"We know where Penny and the boys are," he said.

Although Terry embraced the same belief structure, it was a battle for him to take comfort in these words, or feel exultant in his survival. On many occasions, he wished that he'd died instead of his sons, and in the months to come, he'd wonder whether it was time to do something to join them.

CHAPTER 18

Shortly after his release from the hospital, Terry walked into the Sulphur Springs office of William Howard McDowell. "It was a surprise to me," said the defense attorney. "This had just happened and now he was out of the hospital, looking to see what he could do for his daughter.

"I understood that he was in a difficult position. But at the time, he didn't know how involved she was in this."

McDowell was the son of a lawyer, the grandson of a lawyer, even the brother-in-law of a lawyer. "It was an easy avenue for me to follow," he said.

Like Charlie's attorney, Ron Ferguson, he saw his vocation as preserving the rights of even the most marginalized members of society. "Sometimes, it's kind of tough to defend somebody that you know has done something terribly wrong," he said, "but you have to make sure that all the rules are followed."

Since 1993, he'd been involved in untold murder, rape and drug cases, and generally displayed the same attitude: "I tell my folks that my job is to get them the least amount of punishment as possible, whether that's a dismissal, or ninety-nine years instead of a hundred. Basically, what I try to do is get them the best plea offer we can, and let them make the decision about whether to [accept the plea or] go forward from there."

By and large, he managed to compartmentalize his life, drawing a distinct line between the private and professional sides of his personality. "If I let these cases bother and get to me," he explained, "I don't think I would be able to effectively represent folks in these types of situations. So I have to have a thick skin."

Within hours of the Caffey murders, McDowell was watching the news with his family when the report came on. "I'm going to get one of those guys," he predicted, pointing at the television. "Sooner or later. It won't be long."

Within days, his office received a call from Bobbi Johnson's family, as they shopped for an attorney. But Terry was the first relative of a suspect to actually meet McDowell one on one. "It was an unusual situation," the attorney observed. "He was not only the victim of a crime, but the parent of a defendant."

The lawyer agreed to take on Erin as a client, believing above all else that her particular case should be dealt with through the juvenile courts.

The moment he met Erin, he knew that his instincts were correct. The girl fidgeted and looked away from the attorney. He concluded that this was not an adult, but "a little kid." Yet, because of the severity of the crime, there was already a great deal of momentum to certify her as an adult. "You still have to fight it," he said, "and make sure the courts do it right."

Because the McDowell family was so entrenched in the area, it was difficult for Erin Caffey's new attorney to go anywhere unnoticed. And people weren't shy about walking up to him and voicing their sentiments on the case. Remarkably, though, not every comment was negative.

Recalled McDowell, "I got a lot of folks saying, 'We know it's real tough on you. We're praying for you,' things like that. Which was nice."

*   *   *

After a number of days on his sister's couch, Terry was engulfed by despondency. Maybe this was all his fault, he thought. Had he been too strict with Erin? Sure, kids from other families went out and drank and drugged. But Erin was the one facing homicide charges. Was there *anything* to look forward to?

Feeling detached from his family and the place where they'd made their home, he thought about going back to the property and shooting himself. As he told *Texas Monthly*, "I wanted to die where they died."

Then, he thought about his gore-soaked corpse, and revised his plan. Enough blood had been shed, he reasoned. There was no need to subject the world to more. No, he would use the antidepressants the doctors had prescribed, gulp them down with a bottle of bourbon, run a hose from Erin's tailpipe to the inside of her pickup, roll up the windows, and say good-bye.

Erin wasn't going to be using her truck, anyway.

Terry considered this scenario for a day, then another one. On the third day, he opened up a Bible and read the Book of Job, the story of a devout man whose ten children are killed and whose possessions are destroyed. Covered in ashes, Job is inflicted with a unbearable case of boils, and scrapes them with broken pottery. He literally "curses the day he was born." Job's friends believe that he has sinned, and done something to warrant his pain. Job contends that he is a good man who has done nothing to justify his punishment. Yet he refuses to curse God. All he seeks is an explanation. In the end, Job learns that the ways of God are mysterious, but everything is done for a purpose, and the Lord rewards the man's rectitude by providing him with a new family, doubling his previous riches and allowing him to live for another 140 years.

"I'd read the story countless times before," Terry said, "but I read it again, and it was almost like I was there with Job. . . . That turned me around, and got me thinking that God might have a plan for me. He didn't bring me through all that for nothing."

Terry asked his sister to hide his medication, and only

dole it out as needed. With the help of a counselor, the aspiring minister vowed to continue his journey. "I couldn't become a bitter old man," he told the *Times* of London. "I'd seen people go through a lot less than this, hit the bottle and hate the world, and I didn't want to let that happen. That wouldn't be honoring my family. That wouldn't be honoring the God who saved my life. So I wanted to make it my life's mission to . . . be an inspiration to people who were struggling or hurting."

Terry visited Erin in jail. She spoke about the anger she felt at her parents for interfering in her relationship with Charlie, and admitted saying that she wished they were dead.

"I understand," Terry told her. "I said those very same things when I was a child."

In April, Terry testified at a pretrial hearing, requesting that Erin go home with him while the case moved forward. The two sat together at the defendant's table, but neither held hands nor exchanged eye contact. Penny's mother, Virginia Daily, sat behind them, and also spoke on the girl's behalf. "Bless her heart," commented Charlie's lawyer, Ron Ferguson. "It was almost like she was melting. It was very difficult to see that."

Despite the family's earnest sentiments, the judge refused to release Erin from juvenile custody.

When the hearing ended, Ron's wife, Stacy, suddenly hugged Virginia and her husband. "They almost seemed shocked," Stacy remembered, "and I did it without thinking, to be honest. It was probably something I should not have done. But I really felt for them. No matter who was responsible, what happened was a terrible thing."

Like Erin's surviving relatives, Pastor Todd McGahee's compassion extended to the teen, and he hoped his congregants felt the same way. "We believe that nobody's beyond forgiveness," he said in a phone interview several months later, "no matter what they've done, or been accused of, or whatever. So the church has stood behind her.

"When you are forgiven of your sins, it makes it hard to hold other people's sins against them. Because I know in this society, we kind of rank sins—we have bad sins, and not so bad sins. But we have to understand that, in God's eyes, all sin is bad. There are no degrees of sin. So the Bible makes it clear that if you will not forgive, you have probably not been forgiven—if that makes any sense."

After the hearing, when reporter Lynne Sullivant began doing man-on-the-street interviews in Emory, she was struck by the condemning tone that prevailed. "People were just coming down so hard on Erin and the other defendants," Lynne said. "Then I randomly found a woman who happened to be a substitute teacher at Rains High School, and knew all the kids. And she told me, 'As a parent, I understand unconditional love.' I got choked up during that interview, thinking that Penny and Terry loved Erin the same way, and hearing what these kids were like in and out of school.

"This woman's daughter had an art class with Charlie Wilkinson on Friday, just before everything happened that night. And the girl told her mom how Charlie was the class clown, how funny he was, and apparently how they were joking around that day. So I'm thinking of this killer, and kind of forgetting the fact that he's a teenager, and that he has friends, and that this nice woman's daughter was hanging out with him.

"You just *never* know. At one moment in the day, Charlie's just a kid making people laugh and, then, that night, he was able to go and commit such a heinous crime."

Another couple regaled Lynne with tales about their nine children, and strong faith. But they were divided on their feelings for the suspects. "The woman spoke about how God wants you to forgive. She told me it would be hard to do that in Terry's situation, but even harder to think of her daughter doing this to her. And the husband was just as adamant that this was premeditated murder, that Erin knew the difference between right and wrong, and that she should be punished to the full extent of the law.

"This couple, who'd been married fifty-two years, were at such opposite ends. The husband couldn't relate to Terry at all. He said, 'If that was one of my kids, I would not want them in my house. I'd be scared that they'd come after me again.' And, as a Christian, it made me think. I'd want to forgive, but I'd also be scared that my daughter would kill me in my sleep. And I felt such a strong respect for Terry Caffey because he really lived his faith."

Yet, Lynne could relate better to Erin, having been a rebellious teenager in the not-too-distant past: "I was very disrespectful to my parents, and not exactly dating quality guys. My parents were also heavily involved in the church—my mother taught Sunday school, my stepdad was the music minister. So I saw a lot of my parents in the Caffeys. And I remembered being sixteen years old and being stuck in high school and thinking my first boyfriend was going to be the love of my life, and just having no idea what was really out there. And I thought about Erin, and how she did all this for a guy, and now, she was sitting in a jail cell for that.

"It was just a very hard experience for me."

In court, Erin appeared nervous and vulnerable. Despite everything they knew about the case, observers couldn't shake their perception of her as the kind of person who didn't *belong* in jail. Among those exploring the possible events leading up to the incident, the tale of feeling suppressed by her parents didn't seem severe enough to validate the explosion of violence.

"I think it's a very desperate thing to kill your parents," said reporter Lauren Grover. "Despite their faults, it sounded like the Caffeys were a loving family. The parents were overbearing, but that's not so unusual. When I'd covered cases of children harming their parents and grandparents, the attacks were generally abuse-related—the kids were being abused and decided, 'No more.' There was no hint of that here."

Grover pondered whether Erin's home schooling had inadvertently contributed to the catastrophe: "She was probably oversheltered, and was sort of lashing out. First, she was homeschooled, then she was thrust into public school, which is a very different environment, and couldn't handle it."

Of course, the Rains County public school system was

packed with kids from fundamentalist homes—including Erin's two brothers—as well as teachers with similar backgrounds. Most seemed to adjust to the balance between church culture and public education. Why, then, had Erin and her friends fallen off the rails?

"I kind of wished that these kids were high and drunk, and just went crazy," Lauren said. "At least, there'd be an explanation. But it was a lot worse. These young, young kids thought this out and talked about it like criminals. Charles Waid was offered money.

"I think I was disappointed that meth *wasn't* involved."

Terry was convinced that Charlie was the culprit in the incident, controlling Erin with alcohol and sex. "I think giving herself to him like that messed her up," he told *The Dallas Morning News*. "We brought her up to believe sex was for the marital bed, and I think she figured, 'I already slept with this guy, now I'm going to have to marry him.'"

As Terry's strength increased, he left his sister's couch and returned to his property. Every day, he picked through the ashes, finding remnants of the happy life he thought that he'd still be leading—a Hot Wheels car belonging to one of the boys, a horseshoe-shaped belt buckle that the children had purchased him for Christmas. To heal himself, Terry bought a used RV, and parked it on the space once occupied by the house.

"Everybody said I was crazy for going back," he told *Texas Monthly*. "I was so stubborn, I thought, 'I'll be darned if somebody is going to run me off my property. When I leave, it'll be when I'm ready, and God is ready for me to leave.'"

Dark nights were the hardest, bringing back memories of the blackness through which Wilkinson and Waid passed, guns and swords in hand. On those days when Terry arrived home late, he'd sit in the car, hesitating before opening the door. But just as his body could summon the vigor needed to become healthy, Terry always conjured up the valor to step onto his land. Unlike before—when he stood out from many of his neighbors by being woefully underarmed—Terry now had a 9mm pistol. He claimed that he couldn't fall asleep unless he knew that the gun was loaded and next to him.

Late one Saturday afternoon, a New York–based author tried finding the property, and was surprised to see a small cloud of smoke rising above the rocky road and overhanging trees. It was a puzzling image. Was the fire still burning, all this time later? Upon pulling up in the rustic driveway, the source was discovered—a collection of branches burning in the yard. An air conditioner hummed from inside the RV.

Terry answered the door, crew-cutted and squinting slightly, wearing a white t-shirt and plaid sweatpants, looking so robust that it was unfathomable that this was the same man who'd been blasted in the face and crawled through the woods with grass and mud sticking to his wounds. Not a burn could be detected on the victim's skin.

There was no suspicion or anger, only civility, as he chatted briefly with the unexpected guest. Then, Terry excused himself.

"I'm fixing to visit my daughter at the juvenile detention facility," he explained.

Terry saw his daughter in Greenville twice a week, cherishing the opportunity to spend time with his only surviving child. At first, he couldn't bear the sight of the musical child surrounded by correction officers, her blond hair tied behind her orange jumpsuit. Water would fill Terry's eyes, and Erin would plead, "Daddy, don't cry."

Because their conversations were recorded, the two tried not to discuss anything that could be used against Erin at her trial. Father and daughter often sat on opposite sides of a plexiglass window, telephones to their respective ears, passing time by conversing about their meals, the weather and other topics neither really cared about. Despite the restrictions, there were important questions that consumed Terry and, on a few select occasions, he managed to ask Erin about them.

"Were me and your mom good parents?" he ventured one day.

Erin's eyes moistened. "Yes ... You treated us real good." She claimed that she couldn't have wished for a better mother or father.

At other times, Terry felt angry, and attempted to gather information with hand and eye gestures. He'd heard the negative commentary about Erin, and wanted to learn how much information she knew before the crime.

Forgetting the need to monitor her language, she cried, "Daddy, I tried to stop them, but I couldn't."

Terry took Erin at her word.

According to *People* magazine, Erin maintained that she didn't realize that Tyler had been stabbed, and broke down in front of Terry after learning the circumstances of her eight-year-old brother's death. During another visit, Erin suddenly blurted, "I want Mama."

"Mama's not here," her father replied.

"Take me home. I want to see Mama and the boys."

"We don't have a home anymore."

At that point, the two appeared to be united in their misery. Over time, Terry claimed, Erin accepted responsibility for her part in the murders, and understood that she deserved to be punished for it. At home, Terry would look through his Bible, finding passages that justified his support of his daughter.

Romans 12:14: "Bless those who persecute you; bless and do not curse."

"I know she loved us," Terry said, "and didn't want us dead."

Richard Almon remained dubious. The detective admired Terry, but believed he was a victim, first, of his daughter's murder plot, and then of her exploitation of his emotions. "She's just evil," he told *The Dallas Morning News*. "She's a manipulative, evil person who can basically turn on the smile and charm and the 'I love Jesus' one minute, and the next minute turn into a cold, ruthless, calculating young lady."

If it weren't for Erin, he reminded himself, none of the

suspects would be in trouble—and Penny, Bubba and Tyler would all still be alive.

And when Terry's feelings for Erin became public, he discovered that much of the public embraced Almon's attitude. In an on-line post, a *Dallas Morning News* reader expressed compassion for Terry, then quickly added that the victim's characterization of his daughter as "a good kid" is "a bit naïve. Good kids don't go around murdering their families. Just an FYI for you."

Oddly, Charlie was still not willing to denounce Erin with the intensity of her other critics. "Was Erin evil?" he repeated when asked about his ex-girlfriend's character. "No. The way it was when we were dating—no. What she wanted me to do, yes, that was evil. But I can't say that Erin was evil."

When Erin discussed the case with Israel Lewis, a mental health counselor hired by the defense to evaluate the notorious teen, she appeared to be devastated over losing her family. Lewis attempted to pull something out of the family dynamic to elucidate the girl's motives, but she would not utter one negative comment about her parents. "My only guess is that she blocked out what was going to happen," he said, in an effort to read Erin's thoughts on the night of the murder.

The Erin that Lewis grew to know was "sweet, compassionate and cared deeply for her family. Others that knew her before would say just the opposite, I am told."

His goal was never to coerce Erin into divulging details that cops and reporters hadn't discovered, nor to help invent a story that might sway a jury. From the beginning, his intention was "trying to give her a hope and a reason to live."

Lewis, whose "solution-based" method of therapy was respectful of the region's style of Christianity, had been a counselor, primarily working with juveniles, for close to two decades, but had never dealt with a person like Erin before. "Working with a sixteen-year-old who plotted and helped execute the plan to murder her family was a first for me," he said. "She would say she embraced all her parents' values, loved singing in church with her mom. But how could she embrace these Christian values when the Bible says, 'Do not murder'?"

As he struggled to solve this enigma, Lewis often left Erin's jail cell crying. "She seemed totally sincere and genuine, and I would have put my license on the line to say that she was telling me the truth," he told *Texas Monthly*. "She spoke with tears in her eyes—'God will save me. He knows I'm innocent.'"

Her contention was that Charlie had snapped after she'd broken up with him, murdered Erin's mother and brothers, then managed to dupe police into arresting her. But as Lewis learned more about the case, he concluded that she was playing him the way she might have been deceiving her father.

"I have worked with some good liars," he said, "but Erin was one of the best."

CHAPTER 19

For the three defendants already certified as adults, time moved slowly and repetitiously at the Rains County Jail, a small, nondescript, stucco and cinderblock building, with the Texas and American flags flying lazily in front, located to the immediate right of the Emory water tower. "Life never changes," Charlie told a friend. "It's the same ol', same ol'." Always, there was the uncertainty over whether the suspects would receive the death penalty. But their family members appeared to be coming to terms with the circumstances.

"My mom and dad left after visitation to go to a motorcycle rally in Austin," Waid wrote in a letter found smuggled into Bobbi's cell. "He seems to be doing better . . . He almost looked happy, and that made me feel kind of good."

But the positive outlook was fleeting. Several sentences after expressing relief over his father's reinvigorated mindset, Waid was back to focusing on the murder case, particularly his irritation at Charlie Wilkinson. Charlie was going to blame the majority of the bloodletting on his accomplice, Waid predicted, adding that he expected to receive the harshest penalty. "But whatever does happen will be God's will," he continued. He hoped God's plan included "another chance to be in the free world someday."

Since the arrests, Wilkinson had spent a great deal of time alone in his cell, worried about an encounter with the vengeful Waid. But earlier that day, Waid wrote, the two had seen each other in the jailhouse yard. "It [took] everything I had not to just walk up to him and just start beating the hell out of him," Waid said. "He was scared so bad that . . . every time he looked at me, he started stuttering and shaking. I think that's kind of funny."

During his regular Wednesday phone call to Teresa Myers, Charlie spoke about feeling threatened by Waid. He knew that, if punches were thrown, they'd both be written up—an infraction that could impact the opinions of the people considering their fates. "Just don't give in to all of that," Teresa advised. "Just be the kid that I know. Stay out of it."

In his letters to friends, there were times when Charlie could separate himself from his own problems and feel joy through the experiences of others. "Something pretty cool that has happened is my uncle and aunt got two foreign exchange students," he wrote. "I'm not sure, but I think one's from Poland, and the other one's from Russia or Ukraine. He says one of them kind of resembles me."

The story buoyed Charlie, as he pictured himself switching places with the other young man—free, living in an exotic spot, receiving an education, his whole life ahead of him. The thought of international travel was a consistent theme of Charlie's writing. In another letter, he disclosed a naïve strategy he had for getting out of jail.

"I screwed up big this time," he said. "There might be a way out, though." Charlie was considering a plan to relinquish his U.S. citizenship and join the French Foreign Legion. "Dad is looking into it for me. You can, too. Try and get a hold of the French consulate in Dallas to find out what paperwork needs to be filled out."

Still, in Charlie's letters, every burst of optimism seemed to be followed by a shift back to reality, and the ominous conditions in the Rains County jail. "It sucks being all alone in here," he wrote at one point. "All I have to look forward to is that little bit of hope that I'll get out one day. But every day, that hope is slowly slipping away." He listed his only sources of strength as his "family, friends and God."

By now, he knew that he couldn't rely on Erin.

Word had trickled into jail that, in his interview with investigators, Michael Washburn revealed that Erin had told him about her desire to murder her parents. According to the version of the story that Charlie heard, Erin had asked Michael to commit the crime himself.

"She'd asked her other boyfriend to do the same thing," Charlie said. "I'm pretty sure that, if I'd known that, this whole thing wouldn't have happened. There were so many people who tried to point out the truth to me—that Erin was trying to control me, and manipulate me away from my friends and family. I was too blind to believe them.

"I knew about Michael. I knew Erin had gone out with him. But I didn't know that she'd asked him to do this until after it already happened. It hurt because now, I knew I'd been used. She was using me for something she wanted done."

In a letter to a friend, Charlie warned, "Whatever you do, don't get caught up on any girl. . . . I should have listened to you, and got rid of [Erin] . . . She said we were going to be together forever. So much for that.

"I wish I had a time machine so I could go back in time and change it all."

Despite the twisted nature of the crime, Charlie believed that his participation suggested a special bond with Erin, a blood oath of sorts, a testimony to the intimacy of their relationship. The fact that she'd also shared the desire to eliminate her family with Washburn—a character she'd never described to Charlie as anything more than a passing crush—was humiliating. After a lifetime of being passed around, Charlie had invested his deepest emotions in Erin. Sure, he was attracted to her beauty, like the other guys in the area. But he deemed that, out of everybody else, Erin had chosen him because she was committed to the permanence of their romance. The notion that she would just as easily have picked up with Washburn if he'd accommodated her wishes brought on a sense of worthlessness. With a trial approaching, Charlie wondered if it was even worth lobbying to save his life.

"It was as if someone let go of a blown-up balloon," recalled Stacy Ferguson. "He was so crushed at that point. He said he knew that she didn't truly love him. This is when he told us that he hoped to get the death penalty."

Yet, Charlie knew that his lawyer would not assent to his wish; there was no way that Ron Ferguson would go into court and tell the judge, "Let's skip the formalities—we opt for the lethal injection." No, Ron Ferguson felt obligated to ask for life imprisonment—decades of detention in a small cell until time expired, and death came in the form of relief. So Charlie decided to do something to break free from the chains—literally and figuratively—that restrained him.

On March 25, corrections officers received an anonymous tip that Charlie had a metal shank that he hoped to use in an escape attempt. A shakedown of every cell in the male unit of the Rains County Jail was ordered, and when authorities searched Cell Number Ten—Charlie's area—they found what appeared to be a piece of wire from a chain link fence, nearly two feet long. There was also a device that consisted of a toothbrush handle with a sharp metal rod approximately eight inches long protruding from it. As officers looked further, they concluded that Charlie had used these hand-crafted tools to burrow a small hole into the north side of the jailhouse wall; sunlight peered into the cell from the opening. The mortar had also been dug out around one of the blocks in the west-side wall.

Despite the fact that Charlie had been keeping to himself, someone else in the jail had observed him enough to inform authorities. Already estranged from Waid, Charlie now went to sleep each night, knowing that another inmate—perhaps one who'd treated him as a friend—had scored a few points with the jailers by snitching on the facility's most infamous guest.

In addition to the multitude of other charges, Charlie was now also indicted for attempted escape—a felony.

"I think he took to a spoon to the wall," Erin's attorney William Howard McDowell told the Greenville *Herald Banner* with a touch of humor.

It would be one of the last statements he'd make to the press for several months. Shortly after becoming Charlie's attorney, Ron Ferguson filed an application for a gag order, barring anyone close to the case from speaking to the press. The judge had put the request on hold. But when prosecutors called for the same measure, the magistrate decided that the ban made sense. The less coverage the case received, it was reasoned, the less likely the defendants would face a tainted jury.

With that out of the way, Ferguson could concentrate on the hours of videotape and hundreds of pages of written reports from police, pursuing his task of proving that Charlie's life was worth sparing.

While the recriminations between Charlie and Erin started shortly after the arrests, the relationship between Waid and Bobbi endured the twin stresses of prison and an upcoming capital murder trial. From the beginning, the lovers managed to pass notes and letters to one another, but, eventually, they were busted. On May 6, Bobbi was in her cell when she spotted a female trustee at the jail—a nonviolent inmate assigned chores like tying up trash and mopping floors— walking to the kitchen. Bobbi thrust a letter into the woman's hand, and appealed for her to pass it to Charles Waid.

"I took the note and read it, planning on throwing it away," the trustee reported to authorities. "But due to the contents, I decided to turn it in to the jail administrator. [Bobbi's] tried to get notes passed before, and I kept putting her off."

In Bobbi's letters, she not only seems completely devoted to Waid, but willing to make excuses about an incident in which she actively participated: "Baby, I miss you so much, and I'll always be by your side through anything. My lawyer keeps . . . asking . . . how could I love someone who killed a boy, and I simply say that I know you and you wouldn't do it in cold blood." Bobbi said she knew Charles probably just, "got scared when the boy came at Charlie" and shot him "without fully thinking.

"My lawyer told me that . . . I have to start acting as if I don't love you anymore. That pissed me off. But know that I love you oh so much baby and won't say a bad thing about you. I just have to convince everyone else I don't love you." In truth, Bobbi said, "I know that every day our love grows stronger."

She signed this particular letter "Your Little Miss Whistlin Dixie."

In another communiqué, she asked Waid to draw her a tattoo; she'd get it as soon as she was released. On a shorter-term basis, she planned to work on her General Equivalency Diploma (GED) behind bars, and was excited about the fact that authorities had released her car back to her family. She was looking forward to driving the murder vehicle again.

"Sweet huh?" she asked.

At one point, it seemed as if Bobbi was mocking well-meaning relatives who'd urged the couple to turn to God with their problems: "Don't forget to pray. Okay!! LOL. . . . You're my soul mate . . . Dream of me because I dream of you."

This letter was signed "Sugar Britches." At the end of the epistle, she'd drawn a pair of lips beside the entry, "I kissed here for you." Just above her sketch, she'd scribbled, "Sexy!!"

In his replies, Waid was far less effusive. Nonetheless, he displayed genuine affection for his girlfriend, as well as regret for not only participating in the mass murder, but also the fact that—unlike a true conscientious boyfriend—he hadn't shielded Bobbi from the trouble that ensued. He said he hated himself "for letting you get in that car" on the night of the massacre, and for "doing what I did to get in here . . . If they let you go, then I wouldn't care if I got the dp [death penalty] or not because I would know that you were ok."

He claimed that he thought about Bobbi and his daughter "every single day and night," and said he had faith Bobbi would "get out real easy in the end."

* * *

Even with a gag order, and the drop in press coverage that went along with it, talk about the crime remained incessant in East Texas. As the months passed, and the prospect of a trial came into view, conversations centered not so much on the legal arguments but the punishments that would follow the proceedings. With the exception of a choice few, most citizens hoped to see at least some of the defendants put to death. And while the New Testament spoke of forgiveness, citizens pointed out, the Old Testament preached an eye for an eye.

One Biblical passage popular with the death penalty crowd was Ezekiel 18:20:

"The soul who sins shall die. . . . The righteousness of the righteous shall be upon himself, and the wickedness of the wicked shall be upon himself."

"We're in the Bible Belt, and all a lot of Texans want to do is kill," noted Stacy Ferguson. "It's a scary place to live sometimes. When Charlie said he wanted the death penalty, I encouraged him that he could have a life, only inside the walls. We talked frequently of the things he could do in prison in order to give back to society."

These included furthering his education, involvement with the various prison ministries and communicating with at-risk youth not to make the same mistakes. Yet, every time Charlie considered these options, he also imagined the vitriol of the potential jurors.

"My fate is in the hands of 12 people that I've no connection with at all," he wrote. He feared they would ignore "all the good stuff I've done" and judge him on "the one bad thing they say I've done." He wished for a "second chance."

Even in the more urbane Dallas area, where Charlie's lawyer conducted a mock trial to gauge the instincts of a possible jury, that possibility seemed a long shot. For three days, Charlie's defense team laid out the case, working on each pseudo-juror individually for thirty minutes. In the end, only two members of the test group claimed that they'd consider a sentence of life imprisonment—and not with a great degree of certainty. "Everyone else was angry," Stacy said, "telling us that they didn't want to spend their tax money on housing and feeding the defendants. The most consistent comment we heard was, 'Give them the needle.'"

Ranger John Vance also had a fairly good sense of how the public felt. As he made his rounds throughout East Texas, he heard people say that they were willing to permit the girls to live because Erin was a minor, and Bobbi hadn't actually killed anybody. The two boys, they added, deserved death, and should receive it.

With the trial still months away, Charlie tried to force himself to think about more immediate goals, like acquiring a phone card to expedite his communication with the outside world. While awaiting a pretrial hearing alone in his cell, he wrote, "The worst part is not having anyone to talk to." But he was grateful to have "a single cell [so] . . . that way . . . inmates won't start fights with me." Charlie believed there was an irony in the fact that he might have been facing "the worst charges" of anyone in the jail, while he was actually "one of the nicest guys here."

Although he'd always felt closest to his father, Charlie now needed his mother, and worked hard to maintain a friendly rapport with her. In a typical letter, he told her about his various activities, meals and health issues—as if the knowledge that his mother cared could relieve his problems from afar.

"We got to go outside yesterday. Dad said he'd bring a basketball up here for us. At least then I'll have something to do besides walking in circles." A preacher had visited him and he had asked his grandmother to tell the family to write him letters.

"They're still feeding us good." His stomach problems were better but he still had chest pains, he said. He assured his mother, "I'll be fine.

"They just turned the lights out, which sucks cause now the TV has to go off. . . . [so] I'll write you again in a few days."

In another correspondence, he aroused his mother's sympathies by stressing his seclusion while playing cards and reading by himself in contrast to other inmates who could talk to each other. "The only person I've got to talk to is God. Too bad he don't talk back to me."

At the end of the letter, Charlie wrote out his entire name, then signed "Charlie Wilkinson" below in script.

Because of the sparse population in East Texas, the magistrate in the case, Judge Robert Newsom, served four separate counties, conducting trials in Emory in Rains County, Sulphur Springs in Hopkins County, Cooper in Delta County and Mt. Vernon in Franklin County. Both prosecutors and defense attorneys barnstormed on the same circuit and, as a result, most knew one another—and the judge—relatively well. But in Ron Ferguson's case, his relationship with Newsom went beyond the professional. Newsom, after all, had been a friend who'd encouraged Ferguson to attend law school. Had it not been for the judge, Ron's life would have turned out drastically differently.

He almost certainly wouldn't have met his wife.

Nonetheless, Ferguson knew better than to expect special treatment from Newsom. As a prosecutor, Ron had worked under Newsom when the judge served as Hopkins County Attorney. "A judge is supposed to be neutral," Ron said, "but Newsom remained pretty much a prosecuting judge. If the DA wanted something in Judge Newsom's courtroom, the DA usually got it.

"We'd had words occasionally, but I always considered him a friend—a friend who didn't rule in my favor because he was so prosecutorial-minded."

For the Caffey case, the Rains County district attorney asked the Texas attorney general's office for help. They received it in the form of assistant attorney general Lisa Tanner, who, in an eighteen-year period, had helped convict four defendants sent to death row.

She was anxious to face Wilkinson and the other suspects in court. "When you took all the different factors and put them together," she told *Texas Monthly*, "how young and seemingly normal the perpetrators were, how ruthless they were, how stupid they were, how cavalier they were, how utterly undeserving this family was—it was, without a question, the most disturbing case I'd ever dealt with."

Although Erin had disclosed little about her actual role in the murders, Tanner believed that the phone records said it all. From 11:46 PM to 12:48 AM, Erin had called Charlie six times from her house. This was consistent with Charlie's allegation that Erin had urged him to come to the murder scene. After he arrived and left because of the barking dog, the records showed that Erin phoned seven more times between 1:22 AM and 1:58 AM.

Said Tanner, "This comported completely with what Charlie told us, that she kept calling and saying, 'Where are y'all? What's the holdup? Hurry up. Come back and I'll keep the dog quiet.'"

In the prosecutor's mind, the testimony of the other suspects was almost immaterial. The circumstantial evidence told everything that jurors needed to know. She was eager to see Erin certified as an adult—and, as the mastermind of the plot, convicted of capital murder.

As he'd told his client, Ron Ferguson cared little about Erin Caffey's destiny. His job was saving Charlie's life. Since he wouldn't insult a jury by claiming that his client was innocent, Ron had to come up with a defense that would at least invoke some empathy. "My whole strategy was to blame it on Charlie's parents," he said, "that they put him in a place where he did not value human life. And I'll be honest with you—of everyone I talked to about that defense, no one liked it. No one wanted to blame the parents. No one wanted to accept that the parents were to blame.

"When you look back at the childhood, what else was there? In talking to Charlie, I never found anything that was so serious it would warrant this behavior."

CHAPTER 20

A certain exhilaration crept over the prosecution team as they reviewed their evidence; the case seemed as easy as anything they'd ever tried. The confessions of Charlie Wilkinson, Charles Waid and Bobbi Gale Johnson had been more effective than the work of any confidential informant. And Erin's words and deeds made her look pretty guilty as well. The problem was that Erin was just a teenager, and a rather capricious one at that. It was a matter prosecutors were careful to take into account.

For instance, after the killings, Rains County attorney Robert Vititow contended, Erin shouted, "That was awesome." Had Erin been thirty-five years old, there'd be little question about her sentiments. But because of Erin's age, and her fickle behavior, the prosecution had to tread lightly.

"Yeah, she was rejoicing and excited about it," Vititow told *The Dallas Morning News*. "But did she really want them dead? Or was it one of those stupid things kids say? I just don't think any of them thought it was real. It was like they were living a fantasy, like a video game."

As a juvenile, Erin could receive life without parole. As an adult, though, she was as eligible for the death penalty as the other three defendants. Assistant attorney general Lisa Tanner did not intend to compromise. She was going to insist that Erin be tried as an adult, and then show as much mercy in the prosecution as Tanner believed Erin exhibited toward her parents and brothers. But, first, Tanner felt compelled to explain her evidence to the only living victim, Terry.

"It was an awful thing to have to do," Tanner told *Texas Monthly*, "to lay out to a man that his daughter wanted him dead, and was responsible for the deaths of the rest of his family. I brought all the relevant documents and pictures, and we went through everything. I showed him photos of the suitcases that Erin had packed, and the burned-out lockbox that was open to the combination that she had given Charlie. I showed him the statement that a friend of hers had given to investigators about how Erin had wanted them to be killed. I told him about her and Charlie having sex afterwards, which was by far the hardest thing to have to tell him."

His reaction was no different than it had been in the hospital when Chief Deputy Kurt Fischer informed the father than his daughter's involvement was "great." Terry cried, and asked why.

"I don't understand," he said. "We didn't see any of this coming."

On June 25, 2008, Erin was officially certified as an adult—a foregone conclusion given the gravity of the crime, and the evidence that, though the girl was a childish thinker, she had an adult proficiency at manipulation. Erin was now facing three counts of capital murder in the same court where Charlie, Waid and Bobbi would be tried. Bond was set at $1.5 million dollars. Erin remained incarcerated—now in the Hopkins County Jail in Sulphur Springs, rather than the juvenile detention facility in Greenville.

Childhood was officially over. For the defendants, the best prospect for the future appeared to be decades of hard time.

Because he was the most visible inmate in the county jail, Charlie was also the biggest target—for guys who wanted to establish a reputation by attacking him, or prisoners who hoped to gain credit with the authorities by snitching on the accused mass murderer. On August 12, 2008, jailer Chris

Jackson ordered the inmates into the recreation area so their cells could be searched. As the officers swept through the building, they found clotheslines and stockpiled medicine in the various units. In Charlie's area, Jackson reported, a garrote was located.

"What's a garrote?" jail administrator Nancy Brixey asked. "I don't know what that is."

"It's a weapon used to slice someone's neck," Jackson replied. "We find them here all the time."

In Charlie's case, he'd tightly twisted a garbage bag into a noose and hung a razor blade from the middle. Jackson offered to demonstrate for the administrator, and summoned a deputy. The jailer then wrapped the object around the deputy's neck. As the deputy's face reddened, Jackson eased the pressure and explained that the razor blade—if thrust into the neck—would slice it, and likely cause death.

No one was sure whether Charlie was stashing the object for self-defense, or had come up with a plan to murder again. Either way, he was in trouble.

Eventually, the prosecution agreed not to seek the death penalty for Erin, since she'd been a minor at the time of the crimes. Lisa Tanner insisted that this was the only reason. While the plan was for the other defendants to be tried in Emory, Erin's trial was slated to take place in Sulphur Springs, where the jury pool maintained many of the same social connections—and biases—as the people in Rains County.

When plea bargains were discussed, Bobbi was offered forty years by the prosecution. Her lawyer, Eddie Northcutt, rejected the overture, convinced that Bobbi could receive a better deal. Most likely, this would involve Bobbi testifying against her co-defendants—something that would take a great deal of convincing, given her dreamy infatuation with Waid.

In his moments alone, Terry yearned for recapturing the sounds of family life, Penny practicing piano and the boys rough-housing. "What I miss is hollering upstairs to tell the boys to knock it off," he told *People* magazine. "I miss the squeaky drier that used to drive me crazy."

At pretrial hearings, Terry would quietly sit with his in-laws and Tommy and Helen Gaston, the neighbors who helped save his life. Sometimes, tears would appear on the perimeter of his eyes. At other times, he'd stare straight ahead, lost in his memories. When it was necessary, church members formed a civil but protective shield around the victim.

Erin was also quiet in court, her hair in two braided pony-tails, her hands and ankles handcuffed. Out of embarrass-ment or indifference, she often avoided eye contact with her father.

Charlie's mother generally stayed away from the court-house, but her relationship with her son seemed solid, and they continued to write one another. The inmate wrote of his excitement over receiving her letters. "Thought I had better write you back," he said. "Don't want you to get angry about it! Ha! Ha!"

Charlie reported that he missed his friends. "But most of all, I miss being needed for something. . . . I mean there was a lot of people who looked up to me as a role model, and I let them down. . . . Sad part is that part of them still does look up to me and . . . shouldn't."

Before Charlie folded and sent the letter, he scrawled "I love you" in the margin, next to his name.

Behind the scenes, there was talk of a January 2009 trial, even as the plea bargain discussions persisted. "The offer was conveyed to us that, in exchange for a guilty plea, they would not seek the death penalty," Ron said, "which meant life in prison without parole. At that point, that was the best that I could hope for anyway. There was no reason to go any further.

"Charlie was not a psychopath. He was not a gang member. Charlie was not a cold-blooded murderer. He was, in my opinion, essentially a good kid. But I didn't know how I would ever get that across to a jury. I didn't think that there would have been enough time for the jury to interact with Charlie to get them to realize he was really a nice kid."

There was one precondition, however. In order for Wilkinson and Waid to be spared the death penalty, each would have to be debriefed about what occurred in the early morning hours of March 1, 2008. Ron and his client readily agreed—Charlie, after all, had already incriminated himself in considerable detail just hours after the crime—and soon found themselves in a room with Detective Richard Almon and Ranger John Vance.

Vance had been almost as surprised as the defendants to learn about the plea offer. "The attorneys immediately jumped on that," he recalled. "We had so much. We knew we had the whole story, or pretty much the whole story. We didn't gain a while lot more knowledge the second time. But I realized that we were not going to go to trial, and we would not seek the death penalty for Wilkinson and Waid."

Ron estimated that the room "wasn't six foot square. I mean, it was a very small interview room. And it was very warm in there. And I was thinking they're offering this to Charlie because Erin never admitted to being there, and they needed someone to tie Erin to the planning and the execution of the plan.

"I was trying to take the event moment by moment. And I'll be honest with you—a lot of times, police officers don't do a very good job of that. They want to skip to the main point. They jump too much. I wanted the evidence to make clear Erin's part in this, so I was trying to do that step by step.

"What I didn't know was that everyone else—[County Attorney] Robert Vititow, Stacy, Lisa Tanner, I think the sheriff—was in another room, watching us on a television monitor. And they wanted Charlie to admit his role with the children. At one point, I believe it was Lisa Tanner who said, 'He's not doing it. Let's just call the whole deal off.'

"That was the part that was confusing to me. I thought I was in there to gather evidence for the state to be used against Erin. But they wanted Charlie to actually say that he was involved with what happened to the children. They wanted to hear him admit it. Once he did, Lisa Tanner said, 'Okay, that's enough,' and they stopped the interview."

Terry Caffey had been notified about every step of the plea bargaining process, and wanted to quietly meet with Charlie and Waid before their sentencing. In another jurisdiction, it would have been unthinkable to allow a victim to sit across from the two young men who slaughtered his wife and sons and nearly killed him. But in the homey precincts of East Texas, Terry was granted his wish.

Ranger Vance watched the exchange, captivated, from the doorway. "It was unique," he said. "You've got to admit, Terry Caffey is a strong individual. I don't know if I could have done that. I don't like the word 'closure' because you're not going to achieve closure after something like that. But he asked honest and sincere questions—questions that he wanted answered. I don't know that he got all of them answered. But the majority of them were."

Charlie recalled seeing grief in the eyes of the man he shot, and feeling grief, as well. "And I could see a lot of hate," Charlie said. "He asked us a few questions—are you saved, do you believe in God, do you feel sorry for what you did, was Erin really behind all this? I told him the truth. 'Yeah, I'm saved. I believe in God. I've asked for forgiveness, and I'm sorry for what I've done. And Erin's the one who wanted this done.' I know he didn't want to hear the part about Erin. I don't think he believed me."

Even so, Terry was able to forgive the assailants by framing the attack in Biblical terms. "As a spiritual man," he told *The Dallas Morning News*, "I don't believe it was Wilkinson or Waid. Satan was present. Demons were in my house that night."

There were no handshakes or attempts at friendly conversation. But it didn't matter. Terry had given his assailants a gift they'd never anticipated.

"My heart tells me there have been enough deaths," he wrote the county attorney. "I want them, in this lifetime, to have a chance for remorse, and to come to a place of repentance for what they have done. Killing them will not bring my family back."

Robert Vititow maintained that Terry likely saved the defendants' lives: "Had it not been for him, I would have sought the death penalty on three adults."

Because of the gag order, few were expecting the plea, and so the morning of November 7, 2008, seemed deceptively routine in Emory. Because the classic Rains County Courthouse was in the midst of renovation, proceedings had been moved to an annex, a small, gray brick and aluminum-sided building that resembled a machine shop or farm supply store from the road. The parking lot in front of the building was occupied not by satellite trucks, but the standard assortment of pickups and SUVs. A small but pleasant breeze blew across the street in the direction of the carwash and Donut Supreme. A nearby billboard proclaimed, "Keep East Texas Purdy. Report Illegal Dumping." A dog lounged on a grassy incline leading to the rear of the county jail.

Inside the temporary courthouse, photos of the past three Miss Rains County beauty queens ornamented the walls, while government workers, attorneys and jury duty candidates filed past a CPR poster and a clipping of an article entitled "The ABCs of County Court." Yet, few would have guessed that this was a place where issues of life and death were decided until they entered Judge Robert Newsom's courtroom. With his dignified presence, the wiry, silver-haired man elevated his surroundings, seated on the bench below fluorescent lights and in front of a makeshift panel wall, against which the United States and Texas flags hung flatly, flanking seals for the federal government and "Great State of Texas." In the corner of the room, a gray cowboy hat drooped from a standup coat hanger, beside the juror gallery and an easel customarily used for blown-up evidence photos and charts.

Throughout the morning, defendants in orange jumpsuits rotated before Newsom, some tired, some tense, some relaxed and chatty as if they'd been through the customs of the courthouse so many times that a day in front of the judge was as natural as a trek to the convenience store. Crimes ranged from marijuana possession to forgery to stalking. Newsom addressed them quietly; this was not a showman or a loudmouth, but a man fulfilling his civic mission.

In the third row, Terry sat with Penny's family, his hands folded in front of him. Across the aisle, Charlie's mother politely waved off an author who wished to chat, maneuvering her body to watch her son enter the courtroom, shackled and shuffling in flip-flops. Charlie neither looked at his victim nor his mother, but the ground. When Wilkinson was seated, Ferguson bent and stood beside him, speaking in parental tones.

The twenty-year-old Waid gazed around the courtroom, but never at Charlie, as the details of the murders and arson were repeated one more time for the record. Then, both defendants pleaded guilty.

"Are you pleading guilty because you are guilty?" Judge Newsom asked.

"Yes, sir," Waid replied.

Ferguson was very careful with his wording when he addressed his client. "When people go to prison, they have nothing to do," he explained, "nothing but time on their hands. And they always come up thinking, 'It must be the attorney's fault that I'm here.' So one of the last questions I usually ask is, 'Have you been satisfied with my services?' I wanted to make sure that was on the record."

Both Charlie and Waid promised to provide "powerful testimony" at the trials of their girlfriends and fellow defendants.

Terry's letter urging life and not death for the defendants was entered into evidence, along with a similar letter by Penny's mother. "It was our strong recommendation to seek the death penalty," Lisa Tanner told the judge. "However, after contacting the victims' family, it was their profound desire that we offer life in prison without the possibility of parole."

From the gallery, Terry nodded in assent.

Ron Ferguson placed an arm around his eighteen-year-old client as he was led away. Stacy hugged the boy's mother. On the other side of the courtroom, loved ones rubbed Terry's back, as he dabbed his face with a tissue.

Even Charlie's closest advocates were in awe of Terry. "I don't know that I would have had the strength to sit in that courtroom and be as calm as he was," said Teresa Myers. "I don't know if I could have said, 'I don't want those boys to have the death penalty.' That took a very strong, religious man—very in touch with himself and with God."

Since the Caffey murders, Teresa had seen other stories about parricide, and urged Charlie to use his misfortune to better society. "For the longest time, he said that he would never let his story get out," she remembered, "that he didn't want anyone to write about it. And I told him many times, 'Charlie, you have the ability to show people that this can happen to everyday kids. Parents think they have these great children who would never do these things, and then something like this shocks everyone. You have the ability to stop this from happening again. But you have to talk, and you have to be honest.' "

Once the gag order was lifted, she encouraged Charlie to tell the world about how he became embroiled in the scheme. He was handsome, relatable and polite—the kind of young man who sought out neighbors to ask permission to fish on their property—and if one kid was touched by his words, another family, and another community, might be spared the same kind of heartbreak.

"This is your opportunity," she told Charlie. "There are other kids like you out there. If they don't know your story, they won't realize that what you did isn't the right answer."

Observers now set their focus on Erin's trial. This would be a media spectacular, featuring a father unwillingly testifying against his pretty daughter, a boyfriend bearing witness to his girlfriend's manipulation, and possibly the teenager herself taking the stand and shifting the blame to her older, overassertive lover. The proceedings would be full of salacious details like Erin badgering Charlie to kill, and police discovering the condom in Matthew Waid's trailer, and realizing that Erin and Charlie had had sex after the murders.

"We were getting ready for the trial, and had experts lined up," said Erin's attorney, William Howard McDowell. "We had an excellent investigator. We had a psychologist. We had counselors. We were working on all aspects of it."

Unlike Ferguson, though, McDowell did not stage a mock trial. "If you have the time and if you have the resources," McDowell said, "I could see how it could be a good deal." Even without this type of preparation, however, he knew what to expect from potential jurors. "It was going to be pretty difficult to find somebody that knew absolutely nothing about the circumstances, about the facts. They'd have to put their feelings aside to be on the jury."

Given his understanding of the East Texas mentality, he suspected that even those jurors who swore to be objective would be unable to fully wipe their minds clean of the opinions they'd already formed about the case.

As with Wilkinson and Waid, the prosecution and defense began conferring about a plea bargain. Because of his unusual status, Terry was kept conversant of the discussions. Although prosecutors intended to thwart any chance of parole for Erin, Terry fought them; he wanted Erin to have something to live for behind bars. "Even when our children break our hearts," he explained to *People* magazine, "we still love them. She isn't some stranger—she's my flesh and blood. It's my job as a parent to forgive her."

On January 2, 2009, Terry was in court, holding his daughter's hand, when she and Bobbi Gale Johnson pleaded guilty to three counts of capital murder. Erin, now seventeen, appeared frightened, as she learned that she'd received two life sentences, plus twenty-five years. Nonetheless, because of Terry's lobbying, a loophole—the sentences were to be served concurrently, rather than back to back—would allow Erin to be eligible for parole at age fifty-five.

That was, Rains County Attorney Robert Vititow emphasized, if she behaved herself in prison. "Will she ever parole out?" he said. "I can't answer that."

Afterwards, McDowell commented, "I think it was a just sentence. Everyone is pleased with it."

McDowell was cautious about discussing the case: "The problem is that when [Erin] entered her plea, she did not give testimony. Anything I say may violate attorney-client privilege."

In exchange for *her* guilty plea, nineteen-year-old Bobbi received forty years behind bars—the same sentence she was offered at the start of the plea-bargaining process. With good behavior, she stood to be paroled after twenty years.

Bobbi's former classmate Vanessa Hendricks and the other Rains High School theater kids wondered how the ambitious girl who sang "The Star Spangled Banner" got herself into such a quagmire: "I feel sorry for her. I really do. We're upset with what she did, but we all cared about her, and we just want to know why, really."

While preparing for his transfer from the county jail to the state penitentiary, Charlie also experienced remorse for Bobbi's plight. "She didn't deserve as much time as she got," he insisted. "She really didn't do anything. I feel bad about it. She just went along for Charles."

CHAPTER 21

One week after Erin and Bobbi learned their futures, Charlie Wilkinson and Charles Waid were officially sentenced. Because Texas law allowed victims to make an "impact statement" in the courtroom, Terry asked to address the defendants. By this point, everyone involved in the case knew exactly what the victim was going to say. But those less familiar with the behind-the-scenes discourse of the past several months were riveted, as Terry spoke directly to the killers.

"God has shown me what it means to forgive," he said. ". . . I want to say to you today, I forgive you, not so much for your sake, but for my own. I refuse to grow into a bitter old man. If I want to heal and move on, I must find forgiveness in my heart, and that has been the hardest thing I have ever had to do because you took so much from me."

Waid listened, but appeared emotionless. Charlie, who'd been known to zone out during prior hearings, seemed focused and sad. When he turned to the side, even people in the back of the courtroom noticed that there were tears in his eyes.

"What I didn't expect was, when he got into court, he showed a picture of his family," Charlie recalled. "I don't know how to explain it—the fact that I know that I was the one that did it, the fact that I knew they were good people for the most part, that really hit me. Everybody's got their quirks, but they didn't deserve it. I'm just a caring person."

With the gag order officially lifted, Terry began working on a book, and selectively making himself available to the media. In conjunction with a series on the crimes published in *The Dallas Morning News*, he engaged in a web chat, opening himself up to the questions and judgments of readers.

"Terry, were you angry about your daughter's part in the incident?" asked a reader named Tawny. "Did you express that anger to her? I feel that she got off too easy—not so much on the prison sentence but on being brought into the fold of your . . . family. I don't know if she deserves that so soon after the tragedy."

Replied Terry, "Yes, there have been times that I was very angry and, even though I don't believe that she was the main mastermind in the crime . . . I do believe that she had knowledge and could have helped stop it. So now, she will have to face the consequences of her actions."

The *Morning News* articles were picked up by a variety of publications, as were stories from the Associated Press and other sources on the guilty pleas and sentences. In every city, whenever a recap of the Caffey case appeared online, readers were quick to e-mail their commentary.

"This is the hippie free love and spare the rod mentality," said one reader, comparing Terry and Penny's parenting to that of couples weaned on Janis Joplin and Pete Seeger. "I was spanked and you bet I spanked my kids when they needed it. They didn't have phones, computers or TVs in their rooms either."

Others expressed equal abhorrence at the departure of corporal punishment from the American household:

"My mother whipped me with everything possible while I was growing up, even making me go 'pick' my switch from the Chinese Tallow tree. . . . I learned my lessons and NEVER felt unloved and I believe it made me a more respectful person. . . . Did I whip my boys as much as my Mom? No, but they did get pops when they stepped out of line. Kids nowadays have no idea what discipline is until they are in a 6x6 looking through bars."

Another armchair reviewer seconded the statement, offering this retroactive punishment for Erin's offenses: "Take that kid to the woodshed."

As with every high-profile capital case, the Caffey murders rekindled debates over the death penalty. Unlike professional politicians forced to cite statistics and judicial rulings, Internet observers were free to react from the heart, rather than the head—forsaking flowery eloquence for the brevity of the text message age.

"Thank you Supreme Court and all of you anti-capital punishment advocates. Teenage killers hunt and kill us just like animals. . . . Hope & Change. Hail Obama!"

Although fewer in number, adversaries of the death penalty were swift in branding their foes antediluvian savages:

"Has your beloved death penalty stopped or deterred crime? . . . Violence and hate begets more violence and hate. The sooner that you wackos learn that the sooner you can move out of the middle ages."

And so the debate was waged—back and forth:

"Get 2 short ropes and a tall tree. Lets see what kind of 'PLEA DEAL' they can work out with God."

"I don't like . . . people who claim to be good conservative Christians but cry out for the execution and blood of a 16 year old girl and suggest we torture her as if we live in nazi Germany! I'm guessing that some of my anti-violent attitude upsets some of you people and maybe you . . . suggest that I should be on mood stabilizers. . . . No wonder why this state is still 500 years behind the rest of America (and much more inbred)."

"What's going on in Texas? Fry their asses."

"The families of the other defendants deserve the same."

At least one reader argued that Erin and her cohorts were part on a generation far beyond redemption. "Kids nowadays are evil. I am not speaking about ALL kids just the evil ones. . . . Kids nowadays are taught early how to lie and get over."

Another claimed that Erin should be brutalized and un-
leashed on America's enemies: "Don't send her to prison.
Send her to an elite team that will beat her, rape her, tear her
down and brainwash her. Turn her into a killer. . . . Then drop
her little ass deep into Taliban territory and set her loose."

Regardless of how one felt about the participants, this was
a ridiculous comment, composed either to amuse or antago-
nize readers. Prior to the Internet era, the statement would
have gone no further than a barroom. Now, it went all over the
world.

Likewise, the type of people who previously railed
against the news media could shift their condemnations to
the online pundits, indicting them in the standard conspiracy theories.

"Why are there no insults toward white people and talk
about how horrible they are? Any time that there's an article
on a black or Hispanic criminal, the insults and racial stereo-
types begin to fly. Shouldn't there be at least some trailer
trash . . . jokes?"

Despite the court proceedings, psychological evaluations
and public scrutiny, though, no one could pinpoint exactly
why the murders occurred. "If Erin loved her parents so much,
why did she want them dead?" asked Israel Lewis, the teen's
mental health counselor. "If, as Terry reported, the family
was so religious, then why was there such hatred between
daughter and parents?" Even if the tragedy hadn't occurred,
he theorized, "there would have been much conflict and
chaos, since Erin did report there was strain within the relationships."

But was this strain so different than the pressures found
in every home? Even if it were, why had three people from
outside the family united to resolve it in such an iniquitous
manner? Readers had an array of theories, but one chose to
dwell on the feeling that lingered afterward:

"Well, you know what they say—love hurts!!"

In Rains County, the people who knew Bubba and Tyler
were saddened by the understanding that those dissecting

the details of the massacre would forever focus on the inter-play between Erin and Charlie and Terry and Erin. "The two little boys have been forgotten," said one woman in down-town Emory.

But members of the children's church family pledged to remember the boys with fondness and permanence. And, because of their belief system, they almost became exuber-ant when imagining Bubba and Tyler in the afterlife. "What happened to them shouldn't happen to anyone," said Jerry Carlisle, "but I truly feel that they're walking on streets of gold in heaven. To be absent in the body is to be present with Christ. That is what we believe."

There was little question that Terry would always feel the presence of his sons as he went though his daily chores—he now repaired rental houses for a real estate investor—and embarked on his path to becoming an evangelist. "I don't believe God saved my life to go to work in a factory making pencil erasers or something," he said. "I feel God saved my life because he's got a purpose for it. I want people to know you can move forward, and you can find happiness. I want my life to be a testament to that."

His CD, *Walking in the Light of the Living*, could be pur-chased from Terry Caffey Ministries for ten dollars, and included the victim's memories of the worst night of his life. "As I fell to the ground outside the window," he told listen-ers of his escape from his burning home, "I looked around, not knowing if [the killers] were still out there around the house. So I quickly crawled to the woods. . . . And again, the hardest thing was to look back and see the house on fire. . . . I crawled on my hands and knees . . . knowing I was shot, but not knowing where. . . .

"It was pitch dark. You couldn't see the hand in front of your face. It was 3 AM. I'm running into trees, tripping over logs. I fell into a creek, crawled myself out of that. And as I looked up . . . I saw a small glimmer of light. . . . It was de-cision time at this time. Return to the flame. For certain death it would have been. Or turn to the light."

Terry spread his message in churches and youth groups,

evangelizing that just as he found the light of Tommy and Helen Gaston's home on the night of the murders, Jesus, the "light of the world," could lead the faithful away from whatever darkness surrounded them. At middle schools and high schools, he laid out his story to students, beseeching them to reconsider the one destructive choice that could ruin their lives.

Jerry Carlisle felt moved by every sermon. "When you lose your wife and your only two sons to your daughter, that is a real test of faith," he marveled. "Terry talks about coming to the realization that it was God's will. God had a reason for it, and, of course, we don't know what that reason is. But Terry is a very devout person. He is a very faithful person to God."

Pastor Todd McGahee was among those who felt empowered not only by listening to Terry in church, but also by witnessing the progress of his physical and spiritual potency. "It's proof of what God can do in our lives," the minister said. "I know Terry has hard days and times he can't sleep. Of course, life's hard after this. But he's doing so much better than anyone could have ever imagined in such a short period of time. He's out preaching and traveling and spreading the gospel. He's a reminder of what God wants to do for us, and sometimes it takes going through something hard to get to that place, you know?

"Terry will be the first to tell you that it's not him that has the strength, but Christ *in* him. And that's basically what it's all about."

The pity that some felt when they'd spotted Terry in public now gave way to veneration. How many Bible-wavers had they seen before who folded when a real challenge presented itself? But Terry leaned on his savior and allowed his love to come rushing in. Now, Terry wasn't stumbling anymore. Maybe he needed Jesus Christ to get out of bed in the morning. Yet, once he was out the door, it was Terry who was saving new souls.

Stacy Ferguson, the wife of the attorney who'd defended Charlie Wilkinson, became first Terry's admirer, then his friend, chatting with him on the phone about the challenges of raising a family and adhering to principle.

And when he stepped up to the pulpit, never once did Terry ask for a collection to be taken. If the congregants decided to gather money themselves, he wouldn't turn the donation down. Why should he, given the rising price of gas and expenses? And yes, a special fund had been set up with the First National Bank of Emory to help with the cost of Terry's Bible education and other fees supporting the ministry. But when Terry preached it was always about the Alpha and the Omega, not the almighty dollar.

Terry spoke about his ministry during *The Dallas Morning News* web chat, and encountered criticism from cynics worn out by all the talk about God's glory, and more righteous types who feared that he was becoming too secular. Charged one reader, "You are taking the Lord out of your testimony."

But many more contended that no one was better suited to preach The Word. "Mr. Caffey is a strong, humble man of God," wrote a stranger. "His love for his daughter is the same as God's love for all mankind."

CHAPTER 22

At the White Rose Cemetery, on the edge of the town of Wills Point, Terry would drive to the shady spot where his family's graves stood together—Penny's etched with piano keys and music notes, Bubba's with a guitar, and the baby of the family, Tyler's, with a toy cart.

There was also a memorial at the entranceway to the Caffey property. Below the sign that previously quoted Joshua 24:15, Tommy Gaston fashioned a new woodcarving: INTO THE ARMS OF JESUS . . . PENNY BUBBA TYLER.

The website memorial to the Caffeys is gone; Sean Krause, the upstate New York man who'd attempted to honor the family online—and raise money for Charles Waid's children—died in February 2009, after a three-year battle with cancer.

In Emory, though, Debbie Hendricks, Miracle Faith's next door neighbor, predicted that the lessons of the tragedy would not be forgotten. "We're taking a look at our own lives," she said, "and it's given us an opportunity to really reflect on what's important to us. I think that all of us have kind of pulled our kids a little closer.

"My daughter still can't make a lot of sense of this. As for me, before she goes anywhere, I want to know the parents. I want to meet the parents. I want to see the dynamic in the home."

Noted Pastor McGahee, "There's been a change . . . in this community. And we can't just wish it away. . . . It will be the same loss, the same hurt tomorrow."

One afternoon, Charlie's lawyer, Ron Ferguson, was striding through the Town East Mall in Mesquite, Texas, talking to an author in New York on a cell phone, when he suddenly paused.

Terry Caffey was walking past the attorney with a new wife—and a new family. He'd known Sonja Webb from the time they worked for rival medical supply companies. Divorced with two boys of her own, Sonja invited Terry to lunch in June 2008. There was no clumsy conversation. Rather, the couple found that they could talk about virtually anything.

In October, they married at Miracle Faith Baptist Church, moving into a ranch house close to White Rose Cemetery. Some of Terry's old associates were shocked, fixating on the fact that Sonja was an attractive woman, and her sons, Blake and Tanner, resembled the boys Terry lost to the killers.

He referred to the children as his "new family."

"I didn't think I'd ever get married again," Terry told the *Times* of London. "Some people may think how callous— that it was so soon. But I loved my family. Even my former mother-in-law said I fulfilled my vows, 'Til Death Do Us Part.' "

Terry openly admitted that his stepsons closed a void for him; he boasted that Tanner's outgoing personality was reminiscent of Tyler's. At times, when he watched the kids play, he pointed out, he felt as if he were "looking at ghosts." But was there really any problem with that? One afternoon, while Terry was working at home, he listened, as the boys argued, and the washing machine rumbled. He told *People* magazine that when his wife noticed him crying, he explained, "This is the most beautiful sound I've ever heard. It's the sound of home."

As before, he took the role of fatherhood seriously, hugging and laughing with the boys—they dubbed him "T-Daddy"—but also passing down his principles.

He told *The Dallas Morning News* about an incident in which he found Tanner, nine at the time, playing a violent video game. Terry asked for the disc, then destroyed it.

"He didn't understand completely why he couldn't play it," Terry said, "because other kids are playing it. I'm pretty much the same parent I've always been, in terms of my values and belief systems."

Once again, the inevitable comparisons were made to Job—except, while the Biblical figure was also rewarded with a second family, his wife lived and daughter never went to prison for murder.

Needless to say, the gossip, while hardly reaching the epidemic proportions that followed the murder, was noteworthy. Before the case was resolved, observers would watch Terry closely in the courthouse. If his new wife accompanied him, and Penny's mother chose to sit a few feet away from them, word spread that Virginia Daily had become estranged from the victim. If Erin appeared teary or upset, there was speculation that she disapproved of the marriage.

But Erin's mental health counselor, Israel Lewis, contended that this wasn't true: "She is happy for her dad, loves him dearly, and now loves her stepmom."

In fact, Erin's stepbrothers had visited her behind bars, and the revised family even took a photo together.

Naturally, as soon as Terry spoke publicly about his second marriage, online commentators deluged him with denunciations. "I cannot believe he is married again," wrote one self-professed authority on these matters "That is not normal at all."

Added another critic, "Anytime anyone tells you they're doing something because a god or gods told them to, they should be considered insane [including] jumping headlong into a quickie marriage before the ashes from your burned down homestead have cooled."

It was the people who actually knew Terry who were the first to defend him. "Terry and Penny were married for a long time," said Pastor McGahee, "and it gets to the point where that's the life you know. I've told my wife before—and I think she understands this—that I love her and all, but if something happened to her, I wouldn't stay single.

"God made us to meet that other person. And that's how I see it with Terry. God has blessed him with a beautiful wife and family. And I just see it as a blessing from God."

When Terry was asked about the timing of his second marriage during the *Dallas Morning News* web chat, he responded that neither he nor Sonja had been "looking for love. It just happened. I thank God every day for her and the boys in my life. . . . I have no regrets about moving on with my life. It's easy to judge someone unless you have walked in their shoes."

Later on during the same dialogue, he described waking up in his smoky bedroom to find Penny nearly decapitated. "I would have died for them if I could have," he said of Penny and his two late sons. "I have gone through and seen images that most people would never go through. Maybe only a combat soldier. So most people will never know what I go through on a daily basis." Those who criticized his lifestyle, he added, "should come spend one day with me."

It was a persuasive argument, but not enough to move those who not only begrudged Terry's remarriage, but belittled him as a gullible bumpkin too quick to pardon Erin for her monumental sins. "Terry Caffey needs to take responsibility for his own daughter," wrote one newspaper reader, "and accept that she was mentally unstable, and he should have gotten her help. Mr. Caffey remarried . . . at a local cowboy church, and is now driving a new [car]. This man is simply looking to earn a quick buck off of his story, and blame someone else for his psycho daughter's actions. THIS ABSOLUTELY MAKES ME SICK!!!"

Once Erin pleaded guilty, neither she nor Terry had to worry about their recorded conversations finding their way into a trial. As a result, they were finally able to talk about the night of murders in language other than code. Erin claimed that she'd been planning to run away from home that night, then changed her mind. All the phone calls to Charlie invoked by the prosecution, Erin argued, were her attempt to talk him out of the crime.

She insisted that Charlie was the one who talked repeatedly about killing the family. "I think she thought Charlie was just blowing smoke," Terry told *Texas Monthly*. "I don't think she actually thought he would go through with it. I *know* my daughter. She cried one time when we were in the truck and I ran over a squirrel. She's tenderhearted. No kid's an angel, but I know what she's capable of, and I know she's not capable of murder."

And she was doing good work behind bars, he added. Once she settled in to the prison routine, Terry maintained, Erin began preaching the Bible to fellow inmates. He cited this as an example of her intrinsic decency and ability to give to others.

"She was, and still is, a good kid," Terry said. "All people are seeing is what we're seeing in the media. They don't know how much she loved her family. You haven't seen her in our home night after night, and watched her with her brothers. All the family vacations, all the sitting up with her as a baby when she's sick, watching her grow up—I know the love she had for people."

As a mother, Teresa Myers could relate to Terry. "I truly believe that he thinks Charlie was the mastermind of it all," she said. "I think that's how he sees it, and maybe that's the way he has to."

In Gatesville, Texas, outside Dallas, Bobbi Gale Johnson rose at four AM to work in the prison laundry. Months after her sentencing, she still claimed that when she drove to the Caffey house, she believed that the group was simply picking up Erin. "It made me sick, hearing what happened to Penny and those little boys," she told the *Times* of London. "They didn't deserve that."

She ridiculed the suggestion that Erin was powerless to stop Charlie from carrying out the murders: "She had Charlie around her finger. She got anything and everything she wanted from him. She's very manipulative. She's a good liar."

But Charlie was also a dangerous presence, Bobbi

contended—and that's why she didn't speed away from the house once the boys went inside. Wilkinson, she alleged, had threatened her if she dared to defy him. "He knew where I lived," she said, "where I went to school."

At the Polunsky Unit in Livingston, Texas—home to the state's death row—the young male in the white jump suit made eye contact, and smiled warmly through the plexiglass, as he watched an author rig up an audio device to record their interview. "You don't have to rush," he said, as if joking with an old friend. "I have nothing but time."

If this was how a killer was supposed to look, Charlie Wilkinson didn't fit the profile.

The grin faded when Charlie spoke about the actual killings—he was truly sorry, he pointed out—and his relationship with Erin. He hadn't spoken to his girlfriend since the morning he'd told her to hide, just before Chief Deputy Fischer placed him under arrest. In fact, they were banned from ever communicating again. But he still cared about her. In fact, he loved her. Once you fall in love, he reasoned, even prison bars couldn't dull the feelings.

Nonetheless, he also blamed her for devising the plan that annihilated her family, as well as the lives of her accomplices.

"I don't like talking about it," he said. "There's a lot of people in here who like joking about my case—they say they would have planned it better. I don't want to hear it. It's a very serious thing to me, and it's not something I like to talk about."

Charlie's father, Bobby, avoided visiting his son in prison; he had other children, and needed to concentrate on raising them. He and Charlie wrote to one another, and Bobby was not about to disown his own blood. But he wasn't going to defend him, either. The elder Wilkinson had been particularly appalled by the way Bubba and Tyler were slain, and the people who knew him around Emory realized this about his character. By and large, Bobby's neighbors were considerate of his dilemma.

Teresa Myers was far more comfortable in the role of being Charlie's advocate. "My whole deal is to let people know that not all people who do bad things are monsters," she said. "Charlie is still the same boy that everybody knew and loved.

"We spend a lot of time on the phone. He always tells me, when the conversation ends, that he loves me. And I always say, 'I love you, too, kid.' I think he knows that I love him like I would my own child. We have a bond.

"I'm here."

At times, Teresa imagined what would have occurred if Charlie had begun his romance with Erin just a few months later. Perhaps he could have been rescued by the military before the emotions—and the murder plot—escalated. Even if he'd been sent to war, she asserted, it would have been better.

"I wish that he went off, fighting in Iraq," she said. "Then, I could have had that little bit of hope that told me, 'He's coming back. It's okay.'

"But I can't."

Charlie also contemplated the course that his life might have taken if the timing were slightly different. What if he and his buddy hadn't gone to Sonic on the night he first spotted Erin and decided, then and there, that he wanted to marry her? Could he have grown into middle age without ever seeing the inside of a holding cell?

There might have been some minor altercations with the law, he admitted, acknowledging a problem with alcohol. But he was all but certain that he never would have walked into a home in East Texas and started killing other human beings. "You know, there are people who say different because I already committed it," he said. "They say, 'If he could commit it once, he probably would have done it.' But if I never met Erin, I wouldn't be here.

"I let the wrong girl talk me into something I shouldn't have done."

One thing he knew, he claimed, was that given another chance, he'd never repeat his mistakes: "A couple of months after this happened, the same thing happened a couple of counties away. Again. And when I heard that, I thought, 'Didn't nobody learn from the papers? Why did they do that?' It bugs me when I see people who've come here before, and this is their third time back. Why didn't they learn?"

Reminded that the mantra was a common one among the prison population, Charlie emphasized that he truly could lead a productive existence beyond the barbed-wire-topped walls. "Without a doubt, I could," he said. "I try to do my best at everything I do. That's the way my dad taught me. If you're going to do something, do it right."

Still, he accepted that there was nothing that could be done to change the past. And, in some ways, it was easier to come to terms with this among a community of men who'd also committed horrific crimes. "Most of them know about it," he said, referring to the case. "They read the papers, everything. Some even looked me up in the law library. The way the people look at it is, 'It happened. We're all here for bad things we've done.' I look at their cases the same way. I know what they did, and they know what I did."

The uncertainty he'd experienced in county jail, when he wasn't sure if he'd receive the death penalty, faded in the Polunsky Unit. Physically, Charlie had aged—he was a teen on the cusp of his early twenties—but not because prison was unbearable. In fact, he seemed more self-assured than he'd been back in Rains County. This was his life now. It wasn't the life he'd wanted, but at least, he wasn't judged as cruelly as on the outside. "This place preserves people," he offered. "I met a guy when I was in county. He was fifty-eight. He looked like he was thirty. He had twenty years in the penitentiary. It's less stressful to live here. If people respect you, you ain't got no problems. If you respect people, you ain't got no problems."

Nonetheless, he still fantasized about reintegrating into society one day. "There are things that can change," he said, "specifically with the Democrats in office, no matter how much they're screwing up. I mean, the Democrats do some bad things. But the law can change. I'm a first time offender.

Maybe I can get out in thirty, thirty-five years. That would still be enough time to have a personal life."

He paused, then laughed out loud when it was pointed out how unusual it was to see a conservative country boy rooting for the Democrats.

Charlie pumped his fist in the air and laughed some more: "Go, Democrats."

The image of Charlie's young face, grinning with eyes sparkling, was so incompatible with the penitentiary setting that it was only natural to ask about the source of the evil. Did he think that it was something he carried around day to day, or had demons somehow possessed him?

"The demons weren't inside me," he answered, easily and with confidence. "They were walking around. They had blonde hair and blue eyes and talked real good."